ADVANCE PRAISE FOR
LEAD FOR THE PLANET

"You can pick up any number of books on the scientific problem of climate change and the economic or technological solutions, but what we need most right now is leadership. That is what this book is: an accessible dive into social science for the much-needed tools to guide our society, our organizations, and ourselves towards a bold and strong approach to sustainability. Pick up this book and play your role in helping 'Team Humanity' step up to save the planet."

Andrew J. Hoffman, Holcim (US) Professor of
Sustainable Enterprise, University of Michigan

"Rae André provides a practical map of what needs to be done to lead change for a sustainable future. Drawn from social science research in the fields of change management and leadership, her five practices offer a road map for individuals to lead the transition through the current climate crisis and energy revolution to save our planet for future generations."

Nancy E. Landrum, Professor, Quinlan School of Business &
Institute of Environmental Sustainability, Loyola University Chicago

"André's *Lead for the Planet* shows concerned citizens how to become leaders who can address the twin challenges of climate change and energy evolution. The author skillfully blends the psychology of leadership and influence with a wide array of facts, trends, and positions about the natural environment into five practices that anyone can adopt: crafting a compelling vision for change, rallying others around it, and developing and implementing actionable plans to confront the energy-related issues causing climate change. It's an accessible must-read for any aspiring climate leader."

Jane Schmidt-Wilk, Director of the Center for Management
Research, Maharishi International University

LEAD
FOR THE
PLANET

FIVE
PRACTICES FOR
CONFRONTING
CLIMATE CHANGE

RAE ANDRÉ

ÆVO UTP

Aevo UTP
An imprint of University of Toronto Press
utorontopress.com

© Rae André 2020

ISBN 978-1-4875-0833-3 (cloth)
ISBN 978-1-4875-3803-3 (EPUB)
ISBN 978-1-4875-3802-6 (PDF)

Library and Archives Canada Cataloguing in Publication
Title: Lead for the planet : five practices for confronting
climate change / Rae André.
Names: André, Rae, author.
Description: Includes bibliographical references and index.
Identifiers: Canadiana (print) 20200230301 | Canadiana (ebook)
20200230468 | ISBN 9781487508333 (cloth) | ISBN 9781487538033
(EPUB) | ISBN 9781487538026 (PDF)
Subjects: LCSH: Climatic changes – Prevention.
Classification: LCC QC903 .A56 2020 | DDC 363.738/746—dc23

Printed in Canada

We acknowledge the financial support of the Government of Canada, the
Canada Council for the Arts, and the Ontario Arts Council, an agency of
the Government of Ontario, for our publishing activities.

Canada Council   Conseil des Arts
for the Arts   du Canada

ONTARIO ARTS COUNCIL
CONSEIL DES ARTS DE L'ONTARIO
an Ontario government agency
un organisme du gouvernement de l'Ontario

Funded by the   Financé par le
Government   gouvernement
of Canada   du Canada

Canadä

CONTENTS

ACKNOWLEDGMENTS

First, my sincere thanks to the many students who, over the last decade, have made me think harder, experience more, and celebrate successes on the way to this book. To my co-teachers, Maureen Aylward, Ayako Huang, and Simon Pek, thank you so very much for your System 2 contributions and your System 1 support. Without the guidance of imaginative university administrators, key among them Paul Bolster, Laurie Kramer, and Jane Schmidt-Wilk, this work would not have been possible. Thanks also to Rikki Abzug, James Dendy, Jamie Ladge, Roxanne Palmatier, the late Kay Tiffany, and Pamela Weir for their insightful help at important points along the way. Finally, to the anonymous reviewers who provided formative feedback on this manuscript, and to those reviewers at the Academy of Management and the Management and Organizational Behavior Teaching Society who have vetted various related proposals, thank you. I have done my best to do justice to your expertise.

Welcome to Team Humanity

We hear a lot these days about the *what* and the *why* of climate change. Yes, it is happening, and humans are causing it by burning fossil fuels. Yes, it's melting the Arctic and causing disruptions across the globe. And, yes, it's accelerating.

We hear a lot less about the *who* and the *how* of solving the problem. Until recently, discussion about how humanity will organize to deal with disruptive climate change has taken a backseat to the essential project of convincing people that the change is real. Now most of the world accepts that reality, and people are beginning to focus on how we, the members of Team Humanity, are going to get this thing done. Concerned citizens from all walks of life want to know how they themselves can contribute: What does it take to be a leader for the planet?

Our main concerns, and the subject of this book, are the twin issues of climate change and energy evolution. The burning of fossil fuels escalated with the introduction of powered machines in the late nineteenth century. Intensified by improving living standards and a growing world population, it is accelerating worldwide. It is warming the planet, with serious consequences. To address these facts, and also because the Earth's store of fossil fuels is finite, the world's transition from fossil fuels to less polluting sources of energy is assuredly, if fitfully, underway. Across the planet, responsible people are gearing up to unleash the creativity and innovation that must fuel this transition.

Leading for the planet means protecting people and the natural systems we all depend on by sensibly managing these environmental challenges. To date, our leaders have prioritized natural science over social science, and reasonably so. Yet, to take the next step forward, humanity must now look inward. Leadership for the planet requires knowledge of both natural science and human nature.

To lead well now is to study humanity's ways of organizing and to translate that knowledge into sound decision-making and action. To help leaders understand key human factors that affect collective, systems-wide solutions, this book draws on the social sciences, from psychology to anthropology to economics. It takes a strong rather than a weak approach to sustainability; that is, it focuses on leadership for the planet rather than on leadership for individual companies alone. It assumes that the core value of "environmental sustainability" is the obligation to conduct ourselves so that we leave to future generations the option and the capacity to be as well off as we are today.

We will focus here on climate change and energy evolution, leaving for others the simultaneously critical issues of population growth and agricultural development. We address here all climate leaders (and, also, their followers) – not only those who are currently practicing but also those who are emerging, whatever your age, training, organizational position, or resources.

The fundamental question we will consider together is: Will Team Humanity step up to save the planet?

1. THE NEW CLIMATE LEADERSHIP CONVERSATION

You may be familiar with the optical illusion in which, if you squint at the drawing of two people in silhouette, a chalice appears between them. Such illusions demonstrate the interaction between *figure* (what you see now) and *ground* (what you do not see now, but which is still there). When people ponder climate and energy, they habitually experience scientific findings as figure and potential solutions as ground. This book flips that gestalt: Since we already know a lot about what natural science predicts for the future of the planet, it turns climate solutions into figure. To achieve the change we need, it prioritizes our own human psychology and systems.

What Team Humanity needs now is a wide-ranging conversation about how people can solve problems together across all levels of society. We need to embrace and develop what we will refer to here as *systemic leadership*. Systemic leaders move beyond individual psychology to weigh the design of organizations and human systems. They study not only how individuals are motivated but also who society's powerful actors are, and how key societal sectors wield influence. They figure out how to intervene in situations in which people act and influence each other, lead and follow, in a perpetual loop of action and feedback.[1] They examine how societal institutions interact and conflict.

Systemic leaders realize that the nature of a problem and the details of its context both matter. For instance, when systemic leaders ponder how they should talk to their followers about climate science, they know they must understand both how their audiences perceive truth and how society influences those perceptions. When they face the conflict between the fossil fuel and renewable energy sectors, they consider the stakes not only for each sector but also for the broader economy.

In a world that is changing quickly and perhaps drastically, it may seem self-evident that leaders should emphasize systemic analysis and action. In some ways, climate leadership *is* systemic leadership. Yet, for decades our leadership conversation, especially as practiced in business schools, has been driven by competency theory – the study of individual traits and skills. Although competency theory has been useful for developing leadership inside organizations, it is limited as a tool for promoting leadership in society. For one thing, its focus on static traits and behaviors downplays moral stewardship. Researchers

point out that it gives short shrift to the principle that moral decision-making emerges in conversations among organizational members and is subject to societal influences. Competency theory also
tends to ignore how leaders actually think and act in real time.[2] Its
focus on individual traits minimizes the importance of the emotional
connections and relationship-building that help human beings work
together in systems.[3] Climate leaders, systemic leaders, must embrace
a more comprehensive theory of change.

Systemic leadership is based on three principles. The first is that
individuals are embedded within social systems. Much like Russian
nesting dolls, we humans exist within our families and our work organizations and our national and international institutions, and all of
these systems are embedded in the natural world. Climate change
and energy evolution are system-wide issues that need system-wide
solutions. Our leaders must undertake not only individual change
and organizational change but also institutional change.

The second principle of systemic leadership is that working within
social systems requires understanding and practicing power. Leading for the planet must be a collective, cooperative effort while, at
the same time, it must unleash competition and innovation. Effective
systems leaders seek the moral compass and interests shared by these
different approaches. For example, it is well known that the fossil
fuel and green energy sectors compete and conflict. Balancing cooperation and competition, effective systems leaders must find ways to
manage these power struggles for the collective good.

Finally, systemic leadership assumes that effective decisions are
based on moral principle. A shared morality is the social glue that
binds a civilized society. It is a core reason why we humans are sensitive to the ethical practices of our companies and our societies, and
why we care about climate change even when it is not affecting us
personally.

Maintaining our dignity as human beings depends on our common
instinct to share a moral universe. No matter how hard we – including

the "we" who work in business organizations that assert moral "neutrality" – pretend to the contrary, most human beings do not exist amorally. Our personal experience confirms the importance of the moral dimension: We know intuitively that, when we are deciding whether to follow a particular leader, what he or she believes matters to us a great deal. It follows that, as leaders make hard choices about climate and energy, they will integrate moral reflection and they will lead with moral intent.

2. WHAT MOTIVATES CLIMATE LEADERS?

One popular definition of leadership is that it is *any* act of influence on a matter of interpersonal or organizational relevance. This broad definition signals that to take meaningful action, you do not have to fit a stereotypical notion of what a leader is (tall, extroverted), and you do not have to fill a particular role in an organization (owner or manager) or in society (an elected official). By this definition, whatever one's roles in life, whatever one's starting point, one can learn enough, and one can find the personal motivation and the practical means, to be a leader for the planet. This definition has merit because it is inclusive and inherently optimistic.

At the same time, leadership is magnified by resources. Individuals with limited resources find that their power only goes so far. They soon learn that their personal intent and talent can only accomplish so much. The power to save the planet lies in significant measure with those who direct organizations, build society's institutions, wield expertise, and spend money.

Leaders are essentially motivators, and motivation has three basic dimensions. Motivated individuals first develop a direction. They then pursue that direction with intensity. Finally, they persist toward that goal even in the face of obstacles.[4] Effective leaders know how to motivate both themselves and others.

Establishing a direction means choosing achievable goals that are worth working for. Like all effective leaders, climate leaders will define the challenges they face, choose the best solutions, and plan responsible, common-sense steps to implement those solutions. To attract followers, they will act responsibly by pursuing humane purpose as determined in conversation with others. When choosing their goals, they will keep in mind not only their own community and the world community but also future generations. Above all, when choosing their goals, climate leaders will continually weigh all the evidence available to them, and, as new evidence is found, they will be open to changing direction. (If evidence of global cooling appears, rumor has it that they are planning a big party!)

Climate leaders also find a personal passion for the issues – the intensity that comes from knowing deeply that making time for people and the planet is the right thing to do. Personal passion is not just about being conventionally virtuous, and virtue itself is not only about loving the planet and each other. It is also about establishing ethical systems in which the normal human propensities for cooperation and competition can thrive. Of course, intensity can also be found in intellectual and practical pursuits, such as developing innovative green technology or applying one's skills to installing solar equipment.

Above all, motivation requires persistence. In environmental circles, "persistence" is often referred to as "resilience," although behaviorally the terms mean much the same thing: to continue pursuing one's goals despite setbacks. Climate leaders who persist are likely to have found a network of like-minded individuals who support their goals and reinforce even their small steps toward them. They are able to enjoy life. They learn to avoid burnout. For example, these days people who are paying attention to climate and energy are bombarded with scientific results and real-time impacts. Yes, it's all happening – warming, melting, storms, droughts, extinctions. Without a clear path to change, absorbing so many details can foster an overload of the feeling of dread. Leaders who are resilient in the face of climate change learn to turn off, for a time, the onslaught of new findings.

3. THE FIVE PRACTICES

The narrative of this book is straightforward: To make effective decisions on climate and energy, leaders must first get the truth about the state of the planet and then use this scientific information to evaluate essential risks; next, they must identify the interests and power of key stakeholders and societal sectors; finally, they must implement change within and between organizations and sectors on a global scale.

This narrative is grounded in five practices. To "practice" means to learn a set of facts, theories, and strategies and then apply these to drive policies, plans, and actions toward a major goal. The practices described here are based on social science research and informed reasoning about human decision-making. The overarching goal of the practices is to help us all avoid the worst of global warming and create a clean energy future through democratic processes.

A complementary view of this set of five practices is that they comprise a model of effective climate leadership. Building on my experience as an organizational psychologist, I have developed the components of this model inductively over a decade in conversations with hundreds of students and colleagues in such university disciplines as business administration, natural resources, engineering, and philosophy. Academic researchers might explore this model deductively.

Each practice advances knowledge of current realities and conflicts along with psychological and other social science that can help leaders interpret those phenomena. Further, each practice is developed with facts, themes, and research that are written to spark discussion and further thinking. Many of these topics can be approached as short cases. For example, in the first practice, I describe the cooperation between politically right- and left-oriented researchers as they explore whether the temperature of the Earth is going up. This case invites a discussion: How can leaders continue to promote that sort of cooperation?

I offer this book as a framework of essential issues that readers can consider together with others. Conversational learning – learning together through dialogue – is fundamental to ethically engaged social science.[5] No one individual is going to have the information and the answers we need. As the author of this book, in these pages I am sometimes "I." However, most often I am simply one part of the "we" that is Team Humanity. "We" must work on climate and energy together.

Here is a brief introduction to the five practices.

The first practice (1. Get the Truth) is to understand and promote the truth about climate and energy. Knowing what one believes about such planetary issues as global warming and such local issues as the efficacy of solar power is fundamental to being an effective climate leader. Climate leaders must understand the truth not merely as consumers of facts but as psychologically complex and morally engaged human beings.

The chapter on this practice explores the dual origins of humans' sense of truth and shows why leaders and decision-makers cannot afford to ignore either aspect. It explores the nature of modern scientific truth and how humans' belief in the truth of climate change is influenced by scientific reports and media accounts. It weighs such issues as why leaders should both trust and distrust science, whether they can trust scientific interpreters, and how they can work with science that they do not fully understand. One goal of this chapter is to motivate leaders to explore basic climate science at a level that will help them build their influence, while not attempting to be experts themselves.

The second practice (2. Assess the Risks) is to understand the psychology of risk and how leaders and organizations make decisions about managing risks. This practice includes understanding the fundamentals of risk prediction, risk modeling, and risk management as they apply to climate and energy, and how organizations and societies plan to face risk based on knowledge and probabilities. What are models and scenarios predicting for the future of the planet? Is there a downside to pursuing risk management as traditionally practiced?

The third practice (3. Weigh the Stakes) is to identify societal sectors and systems and their effects on planetary sustainability. In this practice, we review the most powerful societal sectors and explore their stakes and conflicts. To interpret these dynamics, we go a step beyond the classic "tragedy of the commons" scenario to consider the more complex scenario of the stag hunt dilemma. Analysis of a group stag hunt reveals the roots and limitations of altruism in inter-group conflict. Finally, we weigh business's predominant impact on the environment against government's responsibility to protect individuals and communities from environmental degradation.

The fourth practice (4. Define the Business of Business) is to manage profit-making organizations sustainably while taking into consideration that they exist within the larger context of society and the natural world. We go inside of organizations to see how some leaders maximize sustainability in the context of increasing profits and reducing costs. We suggest practical steps that organizational leaders can take to better manage the adoption of strong, systemic sustainability initiatives aimed at protecting the planet. Organizational leaders drive change in part by assessing their organization's culture and understanding their own emotional investment in that culture.

The fifth practice (5. Engage Global Leadership) is to assess the realistic prospects for global change. What types of leaders and practices are most likely to be effective globally? What does economic theory contribute to our understanding of the future? How do global cooperation and competition work today, and how might climate leaders apply both philosophies to foster change?

In the final section, "What's the Plan?" we reflect on that specific question and review the choices that Team Humanity has made so far. What grade should we humans give ourselves as leaders and decision-makers? How can we minimize our weaknesses and build upon our strengths? In what should we place our hope?

PRACTICE 1

Get the Truth

The first practice of leading for the planet is to tell people the truth. This is more complicated than it may seem.

To lead authentically and convincingly, leaders must come to terms with the truth about the climate as they see it. They must then tell other people the truth in ways they will understand and accept. Climate leaders often teach others how to discover the truth for themselves, and, when the truth gets complicated, they learn how to find trustworthy experts who can help.

Thus, the creation of truth is both a personal and a social process. Leaders and decision-makers cannot afford to ignore either aspect.

1. TRUTH IS BOTH PERSONAL AND SOCIAL

A truth is a belief that a person accepts as reflecting reality, one that he or she believes to be in accordance with the facts of existence. Much of what individuals accept as truth is based on their observations of the external world, while some of their truth is based on personal observations made by people they trust. Along with observational truth, people also think in terms of experiential truth (what they experience when they act), emotional truth (what they feel), and spiritual truth (what they believe about matters they cannot observe).

Our cumulative sense of the truth, our *personal truth*, is what drives us and inspires us. It gives us integrity. It leads to conviction and action.

In 2002, psychologist Daniel Kahneman received the Nobel Prize in Economic Sciences for demonstrating in numerous experiments that human beings make decisions both emotionally and rationally. In his best-selling book *Thinking, Fast and Slow,* he observes that two decision-making processes – what he terms System 1 and System 2 – function simultaneously in our brains. Each contributes to one's personal sense of truth, and each contributes something important to a person's ability to analyze complex issues like climate change and energy evolution.

System 1 thinks fast. It establishes perceived truth by reacting to facts emotionally. It is what you experience when you first learn that much of the Great Barrier Reef is dying. It is instinctual. It "operates automatically and quickly, with little or no effort and no sense of voluntary control," and it cannot be turned off.[1]

System 2 thinks slowly. It uses analysis to determine truth – what we often refer to as "thinking scientifically." It's how we understand that pumping CO_2 into the atmosphere increases ocean warming, which in turn causes coral bleaching, which in turn causes the death of the reef. It is intellectual. It "allocates attention to the effortful mental activities that demand it, including complex computations," and is associated with choosing, concentrating, and accomplishing.[2] It feels hard.

When we imagine our *selves*, we most often identify with our conscious self and its beliefs, reasoning, and choices – our System 2. We tend to admire people with strong abilities in this system, and we strive for those abilities ourselves. People with high cognitive control – people whose System 2 exercises strong executive control over cognitive tasks – are more likely to do well on intelligence tests and can switch quickly from one task to another. They are more intellectually engaged, and they are more skeptical of superficial answers.[3] We are likely to see such people as leaders.

Yet, however much we identify with System 2, we also love our System 1. It *feels* real. With its moods and emotions, it colors our day. System 1 includes many capabilities that we share with other animals. As Kahneman puts it, "We are born prepared to perceive the world around us, recognize objects, orient attention, avoid losses, and fear spiders."[4]

Through interpersonal sensitivity and intuition, System 1 helps people develop the emotional bonds that characterize family, community, and society. Today we even have a special word for it: "Truthiness" is something that a person knows intuitively without examining it rationally using evidence and logic. After falling into disuse under its old meaning of "truthfulness," the term was reintroduced by comedian Stephen Colbert to mean truth that derives from emotion and instinct. "In the gut is where truth comes from," Colbert joked on his mock news show. "Anyone can read the news to you. I promise to feel the news at you."[5]

Sometimes we prefer System 1 to System 2. After all, it is easy. It is also reinforced by purveyors of distracting entertainment and social media. When we respond to the smiling faces on Facebook without investigating the tensions lurking behind them, we are responding to each other's truthiness – and we, being human, are tempted to substitute reaction to this truthiness for analysis of established facts.

System 1 and System 2 are partners. System 1 makes constant suggestions to System 2, feeding it impressions, feelings, and intentions. It helps us observe subtle things like hostility in someone's voice, and it brings into play our innate sensitivity to others. One reason leaders fail to convince people to act on climate change is that they overemphasize System 2 analysis to the detriment of System 1 sensitivity and intuition. They forget that System 1 helps create the interpersonal bonds that motivate people to act. Among these bonds, perhaps the most important is trust.

Trust is a mental shortcut, an essential heuristic that allows our brains to work in the moment and in a hurry. Trusting others allows us to act quickly, without taking the time to check out the credentials of every single person we interact with. It also helps build reciprocal social ties: I trust you, and you trust me, and, therefore, we automatically support each other in thought and action.

A fundamental question thus becomes: Beyond what we can personally observe, who can we trust to tell us the truth? When it comes to climate and energy issues, how we answer this question is fundamental to promoting action based on the truth.

For example, do we trust scientists? Many of us rely on scientists to give us facts, to help us make sense of conflicting facts, and to help us develop fact-based goals. We even trust scientists to help us shape our future. One study found that more than 75 per cent of Americans trust scientists (and the military) to act in the public interest, far more than trust the news media, business leaders, or elected officials.[6]

It is commonly believed that the more educated we are, the more likely we are to trust science. However, research in the United States suggests that reality is more complicated.[7] Less educated individuals actually do trust scientific methods; however, they do not trust scientific institutions. The main reason for this gap is that less educated individuals are less likely to be economically successful and are therefore more likely to be alienated by modern life. They are more likely than more successful people to agree with statements like, "These days a person does not really know whom he or she can count on," and "Nowadays, a person has to live pretty much for today and let tomorrow take care of itself."[8] In contrast, more educated individuals find more stability in modern life and so are more likely to trust existing institutions.

Individuals also develop trust in science in the contexts of their family and community. Thus, it is not surprising that people who have learned to value extreme individualism are unlikely to accept truth that is socially constructed. In an America that is "the land of the free and the home of the brave," strong individualists may see cooperation as downright unpatriotic. Research suggests that individualists who support a strongly hierarchical society are not particularly likely to believe that global warming is happening or caused by humans. In contrast, people who have faith in collective action and who are more egalitarian in their outlook are more likely to accept those beliefs.[9]

Belief in scientific truth also depends on one's power to access that truth. Those who accept science are individuals who can afford access to science and are able either to interpret that science themselves or to identify experts who can help.

Use of conservative media reduces people's trust in scientists and reduces the belief that global warming is happening, while use of non-conservative media increases trust in scientists and increases the belief that global warming is happening.[10] In recent years, trust in scientists has been in decline among political conservatives in the United States,[11] while among Democrats and liberals it has been higher and more stable.[12]

Individual personality is also a factor in trust, and while personality is 50 per cent inherited, it is also 50 per cent nurtured. An individual being open to new experiences, conscientious, or introverted each predicts a higher level of interest in science. Also, a person's "need to structure relevant situations in meaningful, integrated ways, to understand and make reasonable the experiential world" predicts interest in and a positive attitude toward science. Not surprisingly, having this "need for cognition" predicts that a person also prefers System 2 thinking.[13]

The takeaway for leaders is that both System 1 and System 2 matter in human decision-making and communication, and that assessing oneself and one's followers on both aspects is important. In the next section, we consider how these principles work in practice.

2. LEADING WITH THE TRUTH

The strengths of System 1 are also its weaknesses. Although System 1 thinking is fast and intuitive, it can also be too fast and based on too few data points. Because it is relatively easy and routine, it is likely to continue without much conscious management. This lack of awareness can lead to decisions that lack detail, structure, and, ultimately, effectiveness.

Furthermore, emotion unexamined and untempered by System 2 can run amok. With its social and emotional processes, System 1 connects one person to another. Yet, those connections are counterproductive if they are dominated by emotion – if, for example, citizens develop an emotional bond and uncritically follow a charismatic but damaging leader.

Another concern is that people can get stuck in System 1. For example, individuals who attempt to control their feelings of distress, rather than actively trying to reduce their risks, experience what is called "defensive processing."[14] The person thinks, "Yes, I understand that climate change is a threat, and I find it frightening. But since I can't figure out what to do about the danger, I will just manage the fear itself. In fact, why don't I just find a way to ignore it?" Research suggests that if people experience the threat of climate change without learning about solutions, they are likely to practice what is called "message avoidance." When learning more about climate change and discussing its dangers only increase their anxiety, they avoid both that learning and those conversations.

One of the great debates among climate communicators concerns which emotions are most likely to motivate climate actions. Some believe that people are motivated primarily by hope. These leaders prefer to downplay the difficult truths about climate change and focus instead on optimistic signs for change. Others deride this approach as "hopium." Although there is research supporting both sides of this debate, mainstream psychological research strongly suggests that fear is an excellent motivator. The drawback is that fear in the absence of coping mechanisms becomes a demotivator that leads to withdrawal. However, fear coupled with possibilities for action is extremely motivating.[15]

It follows that climate leaders who want their followers to both listen and act should assiduously avoid frightening people without giving them an out. A leader who wants to promote control of climate risks and motivate political action to mitigate climate change should provide information about the threats (engaging System 1) and *also* about how individuals can respond to these threats (engaging System 2).[16]

The strength of System 2 is the ability to make sound analytic decisions using reliable data. This skill is the basis of the scientific thought on which modern technological society is founded. It is a strength that will only become more obvious and important as society demands and produces more data on which to base decisions.

Today we live in the Age of Organizations, in part because organizations are uniquely capable of System 2 decision-making. Because they are designed to reason more slowly than individuals and to impose order on decision-making processes, organizations are better than individuals at avoiding errors made by System 1 thinking.[17] While individual human beings tend to be overconfident and optimistic, organizations are good at taming that overconfidence.[18]

In fact, well-run organizations are the best decision-makers in history. They can create and enforce the use of standardized procedures and scientifically grounded data analytics and forecasting. They not only utilize System 2 thinking, they improve upon it. As Kahneman writes, "An organization is a factory that manufactures judgments and decisions. Every factory must have ways to ensure the quality of its products in the initial design, in fabrication, and in final inspections. The corresponding stages in the production of decisions are the framing of the problem that is to be solved, the collection of relevant information leading to a decision, and reflection and review. An organization that seeks to improve its decision product should routinely look for efficiency improvements at each of these stages. The operative concept is routine."[19] Also, by conducting postmortems on decisions, smart organizations help their members learn from their mistakes.

Organizations also foster humankind's love of a cognitive challenge and ingenuity in every sphere, and this characteristic has been
highly valued by society. Of course, operationalizing ingenuity, for
example by creating cool products, draws down on the natural environment just like creating more prosaic products does. Nevertheless,
those cool products keep coming in part because we love creating
them. What is good for the individual and the organization is not
necessarily good for the planet.

In addition, it is well known that organizations are not good at
weighing moral issues. Even though ethics specialists exhort business
managers to routinely include the moral dimension in their decision-
making, they seldom do.

The strengths and weaknesses of System 2 have many implications
for climate leadership. One is that, given the recognized decision-
making efficacy of organizations, climate leaders should be thinking not merely in terms of making an individual contribution but
in terms of fostering organizational contributions (see, for instance,
Practice 4: Define the Business of Business). Effective leaders will pay
attention to how organizations optimize System 2 thinking, and how
to grow organizations that apply those principles specifically to climate and energy issues. To this end, it may be useful to consider
whether existing organizations, created originally for other purposes,
can do a good job of addressing the climate crisis, or whether the best
decisions for the planet might be made by organizations designed
explicitly to manage climate and energy issues.

Further, effective climate leaders weigh the consequences of innovation on all systems, including natural systems. Innovators should
be encouraged to work within the limits of the natural world. Part of
this effort is to encourage innovation that takes psychology into consideration. What can we substitute for technological innovation that
would still satisfy human curiosity? Perhaps the clever among us can
be convinced to engineer simplicity itself (already a trend), or to have
fun improving other aspects of human decision-making.

From the individual's perspective, solving problems rationally using System 2 is often satisfying, but it is also hard work that eats up time and requires an investment of one's limited cognitive energy. System 2 often requires special skills and knowledge that are hard to acquire and use. System 2 also requires attention, which can be disrupted if one is distracted. Leaders can make sure System 2 decision-makers get enough time for analysis and that they work in physical spaces that foster concentration.

A particular problem is that sometimes individuals get stuck in System 2 analytic mode and become isolated from human contact that includes moral and social support. By taking into consideration the important contributions of System 1, leaders can create opportunities for relaxation and human connection, intuitive creativity, and moral reflection. Professor Nate Hagens of the University of Minnesota is a resilience expert. He points out that humans enjoy novelty and that humanity needs to develop new ways to meet that need. For instance, he personally makes a point of appreciating the geology in his own region rather than create carbon emissions by travelling to faraway places seeking the same pleasure.[20] Innovative thinking like this combines moral conviction with psychological principles to address the limitations of a stressed natural world.

In sum, effective climate leaders create a blend of System 1 and System 2 approaches to communicate about climate and energy with a variety of audiences. Leaders not only alert people to problems and convince them of the truth, they also motivate them to act on what they have learned.

Understanding the contribution of System 1 helps climate leaders translate science for non-expert audiences and for all audiences that rely heavily on System 1. For example, for some audiences, a leader might describe the oceans as the heart of a circulatory system that moves heat and moisture through all parts of the climate system. "Heart" is a concept that anyone can understand, and this metaphor also embodies the System 1 sensibilities of acting responsibly and protecting people and places.[21]

System 1 also helps individual decision-makers evaluate the cultural context of the problem, including its social and moral aspects. It helps them sense which information comes from a suspicious source and decide which individuals and sectors to trust. It enables the talented among us to approach the issues from a variety of perspectives – not only as logical analysts, but as creative writers, visual artists, and musicians. It promotes ethical thinking and practice.

System 2 contributes logic and analysis. Normally operating in a comfortable low-effort mode, when stimulated by System 1 – for example when System 1 is surprised – System 2 surges into analytic action. System 2 figures out what causes climate change and analyzes what to do about it. It helps leaders understand scientific methodologies like how to measure ocean expansion.

Yet, relying on scientific reports alone is unlikely to motivate a broad public, nor is it likely to motivate their political representatives. Research by The Frameworks Institute, a nonprofit that studies communication strategies for social issues, suggests that "without a value, people struggle to see the point of engaging with an issue and frequently fall back on individualistic solutions to social issues."[22] Leaders of diverse populations develop trust with their followers by building upon their common values.

At the same time, as discussed earlier, leaders who want to educate alienated citizens about the facts of global warming must work with the issue of their rejection from mainstream society. If they do not, it is unlikely that those constituents will identify with and support the institutions that would address the problem.

3. WHAT IS SCIENTIFIC TRUTH, REALLY?

Even those leaders who are familiar with System 1 and System 2 thinking may not have thought very much about their own grasp of scientific truth. What is it, really?

Scientific truth consists of theories that correctly predict patterns in new observations. When Henry David Thoreau wrote, "Rather than love, than money, than fame, give me truth,"[23] he couldn't imagine the kinds of broad-ranging truths that humans have at their disposal today. Yet, because his observations of the natural world around Walden Pond were systematic, they enlighten science even now, providing a rare baseline for measuring the natural systems of the twenty-first century against those of 1854.

Recall the Chinese proverb that if you give a man a fish, he will eat for a day, but if you teach him to fish, he will eat for a lifetime. Informing people about the state of the planet is giving them the fish. Teaching them to fish is showing them how to get good information whenever they need it, and how to apply that information to drive decisions and action.

Learning to fish the scientific waters using System 2 thinking is an important adaptation for the times of exceptionally rapid change we face in the twenty-first century. Climate leadership today requires applying logical methods to systematically gather information and then analyzing that information to set directions and develop plans for action. For such purposes, it is useful to think about the scientific method as operating on different levels of complexity – as investigating what we will call simple truths, complex truths, and highly complex truths. The simpler the truth, the easier it is for people to understand and accept. The more complex the truth, the less people understand it and the more skeptical they are about it.

A simple scientific truth is one that is based on obvious numbers, easy-to-understand measurements, and straightforward math. You, yourself, could go out with a ruler and, over time, measure how much the sea level is rising. Or, using a thermometer (and a lot of funding), you could observe the Earth's temperatures at different places across its surface and show that the Arctic is warming twice as fast as other regions. Using a carbon dioxide meter, you could enjoy an annual visit to Hawai'i to measure the amount of CO_2 on Mauna Loa.

In practical terms, it is not all that easy to implement even such simple measurements. For many years, to measure the temperature of the oceans, scientists incorporated readings made by untrained ship personnel, a cheap method that was less than optimally systemic or accurate. Yet, to deploy highly accurate and non-breakable thermometers across the globe is expensive in terms of technology and personnel. Scientists are always trying to improve upon even such seemingly simple methodologies.

Furthermore, even a straightforward measurement procedure can be impeded by extraneous factors. For example, to predict the future of fossil fuel energy, many people would like to know how many barrels of oil are still in the ground worldwide. On the face of it, since oil is found in predictable places, this should be a simple observation problem. However, locating oil in the ground is a technical specialty that involves great expertise and great expense, and is undertaken primarily by oil geologists working for powerful, secretive companies. Furthermore, oil explorers do not have full access to all locales where oil might be discovered. The largest depository of light sweet crude, the cleanest and cheapest sort of oil, is in Saudi Arabia, yet for nearly a century just how much oil exists in Saudi Arabia has been one of the world's most tantalizing secrets.

Stepping up to more complex scientific problems, leaders take on such challenges as understanding cause and effect in common natural processes. For example, scientists accept that human injection of CO_2 into the atmosphere is causing global warming, and they consider the demonstration of this process to be absolutely reliable and straightforward. Laypersons, not being experts in chemistry and physics, may be skeptical of this belief. They simply don't know, experientially, whether to believe it. Enter System 1: People have to trust the experts.

A wise clergyman from another era once penned this interesting thought: "A lie can travel halfway around the world while the truth is putting on its shoes."[24] Today he might say that a lie can tweet around the globe while the truth is still a gleam in a scientist's eye. The point is that it takes time to imagine, develop, declare, and defend the truth. The more complex the truth, the harder it is to develop, the harder it is to explain, and the harder it is for people to accept. The truth about rapid climate change certainly qualifies on all counts.

When it comes to pursuing highly complex truths, such as how the melting Arctic is affecting the meridional overturning circulation (part of which is the Gulf Stream), or how the ocean functions as a heatsink for the warming planet, laypersons are even more dependent on experts. Many of these more complex truths rely on the manipulation of factors in statistical models to predict outcomes. Understanding them requires understanding higher mathematics that will elude most of us both today and tomorrow.

Thus, when nonscientists must grapple with science – and grapple we must when it comes to understanding the realities of climate change – we need to ask ourselves whether we trust the scientific methodology – the observations that are made and the logic that systematizes and explains them. We must also factor in whether we trust the scientists themselves.

So far, we have been reviewing the psychology and social systems that frame humans' sense of truth about climate change. We have highlighted the importance of trust and suggested that scientific complexity can make trusting science a challenge. We now arrive at the crucial question of how much trust to place in scientific research. Climate leaders need some facility with this conversation when they must convince others to pay attention to scientific results.

The hallmark of modern scientific research is that much of it is produced collectively and publicly within a system of checks and balances, and this is significantly reassuring. Most scientific findings are published within a scientific community that relies on peer evaluation to review methods and results. Scientists submit their work to peer-reviewed journals and conferences. (This process excludes most corporate research, which for competitive reasons is kept company-private.) Work that is not peer-reviewed has virtually no legitimacy in the scientific community.

Ideally, the vetting system works as follows. The authors' peers in the same field at other research institutions examine a submitted paper for its logical and methodological rigor and provide feedback to the authors and the journal's editors. Most often peer review is anonymous, or "blind." Reviewers serve without compensation, although by providing thorough reviews they can build their reputation among the editors in their research community. The more rigorous the review process, the more reviewers are used, the more knowledgeable are the scientists who are asked to review, and the more rounds of reviews and revisions undertaken. Sometimes reviewers require the authors to collect more data, and the review process can stretch out for a year or more.

To decide whether to trust a research finding, decision-makers should consider not only whether a journal is peer-reviewed but also whether it is peer-reviewed at the highest level. Scholars rank certain journals more highly than others, and higher rankings usually indicate a more rigorous review process. Another signal of high quality is a journal's acceptance rate: The rule of thumb is that the lower the acceptance rate, the higher the quality of the research.

Readers can also estimate the quality of research by finding a journal's "impact factor," which suggests how much the scientific community respects it. This number is the average number of citations from other scientists that the articles in the journal have had over some recent time period, usually a year or two. Understanding how the impact factor is important to scientists gives nonscientists an inside look at the currency of academic success. Many people agree that this measurement is imperfect, especially when it is used to evaluate scientists' career contributions.[25] However, measures like a journal's acceptance rate and its impact factor generally do point the lay reader toward the more solid journals.

A further check on research is that scientists network with peers in their specialty. For instance, they build their professional credibility by working with other scientists, who in turn provide ongoing critiques of their methods. They take sabbaticals to visit other universities and share their research in local presentations. Such peer evaluation goes a long way toward crosschecking what any one scientist asserts as the truth.

Naturally, leaders need to be aware of concerns about how science is produced and distributed. Sometimes reviewers are neglectful, and occasionally researchers do manufacture data. Also, today new journals abound, and many have low standards. Finally, from a psychological perspective, all cohesive cultures are subject to groupthink and the community of academic publishing is no exception. On balance, the proof is in the results: The scientific method of constructing the truth works. It works worldwide and it works over time.

Despite the robust system of scientific peer review, not all facts are created equal. In addition to the findings of a piece of research, the integrity of the funding and publishing system that produced it also matters. Politics and money influence which kinds of studies are pursued and published. The source of research funding for a project or a laboratory may bias its results, and particularly their interpretation. To assess these influences, leaders must apply common sense and a dash of System 1. Do the findings pass the sniff test? Is the research self-serving? Where a funding source seems to have influenced the results, replication of the study by other scientists from other networks becomes that much more important.

Consider the back story of the BEST project, named after the Berkeley Earth Surface Temperature group that directed it. This research re-examined the most widely watched measurement of climate change – the temperature of the Earth over land and water. Even though in the second decade of this century planetary warming was accepted by the vast majority of scientists, this measurement was occasionally disputed. The BEST project brought together a diverse set of scientists and funders, some from the political left and some from the political right, to see if they could develop a set of facts that all could accept.

As described in *The Economist* in 2011, the pedigree of the study was demonstrably eclectic.[26] The study was funded in part by the conservative, free-market ("Prices should be free to guide economic action") Koch Foundation. The Kochs own one of the largest private businesses in the United States, a set of companies invested primarily in oil and gas, and Koch Industries had been highly skeptical of claims of global warming. The study also examined data produced by a diverse set of researchers – the Berkeley Earth Surface Temperature group, the National Aeronautics and Space Administration (NASA), the National Oceanic and Atmospheric Administration (NOAA), and the British Hadley Climatic Research Unit (CRU). It was led by a particularly skeptical scientist, and the team included a recent Nobel Prize winner for physics.

For a period of up to 150 years, temperature collection programs worldwide had been running at weather stations and on ships. These sources were not originally designed to measure global warming, and data from them were not collected systematically. Measurements were taken at different times of the day using different thermometers. Sometimes data were collected near local heat sources such as urban environments, which tend to be heat islands. There were gaps in the data, as well. The BEST study did not collect new data but, rather, it re-analyzed existing data using a common statistical methodology that smooths the effects of missing and outlying observations. Using this technique, analysts statistically weight unusual data points to reduce distortions, giving an automatic weighting to every data point according to its consistency with comparable readings. This approach makes it possible to include outliers, such as older data, without the results being heavily distorted by them.

The BEST researchers concluded that, in the fifty years covered by the study, the land surface of the Earth warmed by 0.911° Celsius.

This was only 2 per cent less than the comparable estimate by the NOAA. *The Economist* concluded that, "at a time of exaggerated doubts about the instrumental temperature record, this should help promulgate its main conclusion: that the existing mean estimates are in the right ballpark. That means the world is warming fast."[27]

The decision-making process that produced these results had both face validity and integrity. We are likely to trust these results in part because politically opposed sides came together to produce them. The BEST study was so carefully crafted, from both the political and the scientific perspectives, that, had it disproved global warming, it would have been a sensation. What it did was to confirm important truths about the state of the planet, and to show how cooperation in science can improve leaders' understanding of the truth going forward. What it did not do, however, was to prevent the Koch brothers from continuing to fight "tirelessly" against the regulation of greenhouse gases.[28]

4. READING SCIENCE AS A NONSCIENTIST

Once climate leaders identify sound science, they must be able to use it to motivate others. Being able to read scientific reports, at least at some level, is an important competence. Conversely, not being able to do so is a weakness that must be acknowledged and managed. (If you are a scientist, you may want to skip this section. Or, you might find it mildly amusing.)

For openers, a major challenge for lay readers is the use of technical vocabulary. For example, consider that most proclamations on global warming state that if we are to fend off dramatic climate changes, we must hold global warming worldwide to "between 1.5°C and 2°C." Do you usually skip such descriptions, or do you stop to figure them out? For example, do you know how much that is, really? (Spoiler alert: The calculation is coming next.)

To understand this global warming fact as an American (a member of a primitive society that still clings to the Fahrenheit era), you must first be able to translate Celsius into Fahrenheit. Let's see now, what was that formula? The one we all remember (of course) is: $F = 9/5\ C + 32°$. Yes, but that is the formula for translating between two temperature *scales*, right? What you need now is the formula for translating one degree to the other, and that is only the 9/5 factor. Since 9/5 = 1.8, 2°C is 2 × 1.8 or 3.6° Fahrenheit. So 1.5° Celsius is 2.7° Fahrenheit. (Does the world seem warmer now?)

Right. But then, so what? To make such calculations useful, leaders must be able to put them into historical context, so you should also know that since 1880 the average global temperature has increased by about 0.8° Celsius (1.4° Fahrenheit). Also, two-thirds of that warming has occurred since 1975.[29] Also, according to the European Environmental Agency, "the global average annual near-surface temperature in the decade 2006–2015 was 0.83 to 0.89 °C higher than the pre-industrial average (mid- to the end of the 19th century)."[30] NASA scientists offer an even longer-term context: "When global warming has happened at various times in the past two million years, it has taken the planet about 5,000 years to warm 5 degrees [Celsius]. The predicted rate of warming for the next century is at least 20 times faster."[31]

In addition, when it comes to interpreting such world temperature changes, you don't want to fall for the fallacy of applying the world average to every problem. For instance, it is useful to know that the Arctic is warming twice as fast as the world average,[32] and that, therefore, many northern latitude locales, such as the tundra, are also warming quickly.

Glen Peters, a researcher in the Center for International Climate and Environmental Research in Oslo, Norway, describes the implications of these global temperature changes: "To keep below 1.5C with a 'likely' chance [implies] a very, very small remaining carbon budget. If you use the IPCC's [Intergovernmental Panel on

Climate Change] cumulative emission budget that they published in their synthesis report, we have about 400bn tonnes of CO_2 to emit [before we] go over 1.5C – and that's starting in 2011. At current emission rates, that budget will go by about 2020 ... If you want to emit for longer, then you'll have to use large amounts of negative emissions."[33] "Negative emissions" refers to the idea of removing carbon from the atmosphere and, generally, burying it deep in the ground. It is important to realize that this is a technical capability that we do not currently have at scale. Nor, at the time of this writing, is the practical application of this technology on the horizon.

So, based on existing science, to control global warming the world must balance carbon emissions and the capture of emitted carbon, achieving a net outcome of zero emissions, by sometime between 2045 and 2060. Between 2030 and 2050 we need to see significant reductions in carbon emissions. "The window for achieving this goal is small and rapidly closing."[34] How exactly does global warming damage the planet? You can find an excellent description of the carbon cycle on the NASA website, as of this writing.[35]

Imagine you are the vice president for information technology in a large company, and you have been assigned to draft a white paper recommendation on where to site your company's new computer servers. You are not a scientist, but you do know that servers require a lot of water, and your company is in San Diego, where water is in short supply. To make the recommendation, you need to understand such factors as the amount of water currently available locally and the likely impact of climate change on its future availability. In your organization, you are lucky enough to have some scientists who can help you research these factors, but you also need to understand their recommendations well enough to be able to field management's questions about practical applications.

As part of your research, you decide to investigate how desalination might enhance your local water supply. You know that, in the face of a major California drought, Santa Barbara, a city up the coast, took a desalination plant out of mothballs. In an emergency, might your community do something similar? What other solutions might be viable?

To find out what research scientists can tell you about changes in drought patterns and water availability, and about adaptations like desalination, you search in your library for the most relevant online databases and articles. You soon realize that you are trying to answer an extremely complicated question.

You want to know about desalination availability and costs, its environmental and social impacts, and any promising technological advances. So you develop a set of keywords and pull up peer-reviewed articles on these topics. You find many articles on the basic science of desalination, like one on desalination chemistry entitled, "Sustainable Desalination Using a Microbial Capacitive Desalination Cell," and a data-based article on the environmental impacts of desalination entitled, "Towards a Meaningful Assessment of Marine Ecological Impacts in Life Cycle Assessment (LCA)." You are lucky to discover a review article entitled "Desalination and Sustainability: An Appraisal and Current Perspective."[36]

Having found these articles, can you understand them? When it comes to reading an academic article, professionals have two main advantages over laypeople – their familiarity with scientific terms and disciplinary jargon, and their training in specialized statistics. As in any professional field, jargon is the shorthand that allows scientists to communicate succinctly. Academic articles tend to be narrowly focused and filled with it, so inexperienced laypeople must research every term.

Just for fun, try to interpret the following – actually very important – statement in a technical article on sea level rise: "Meltwater tends to stabilize the ocean column, inducing amplifying feedbacks that increase subsurface ocean warming and ice shelf melting."[37] Before reading on, you might want to jot down what you think this means ...

To understand this statement, you must first define "meltwater," "ocean column," and "amplifying feedbacks." Once you have done this, you would know that "water formed by the melting of snow and ice" stabilizes the "conceptual column of water from the surface of the sea to the bottom sediments" and creates a "process in which changing one quantity changes a second quantity, and the change in the second quantity in turn changes the first." (How did you do?)

In addition to the jargon, in technical articles you soon run into challenging statistical analyses. Of course, research is often designed to test models, which in turn support or fail to support broader theories. Certain types of statistical analysis have been shown to be the most useful in describing the relationships between independent ("causal" or "predictor") variables and dependent, effect variables. Even after taking a basic stats course, most laypeople need at least one statistics course on multivariate analysis to begin to understand these techniques. PhD training takes students even further into the statistical niceties of their fields.

Fortunately, the typical data-based article has several standard parts, and, as it turns out, these provide a handy framework for skimming. The abstract describes the purpose of the study and its major findings, and may suggest the implications of the findings for managerial and other applications. The body of the article includes an introduction, which often describes how the study contributes to the field. This is followed by a discussion of the theoretical background of the research, which reviews what has already been discovered by other researchers and asserts how the current study advances knowledge.

The methodology section covers which research method (laboratory study, field research, or questionnaire study) was used for collecting the data, and what sample was used to test the hypothesis. Often a layperson can evaluate whether the sample is relevant to and will reasonably generalize to the population in which they themselves are interested. Finally, the results section presents the conclusions drawn from statistical analysis of the data, and it is followed by a discussion section that describes the study's weaknesses and the implications for future research. If the lay reader is lucky – and some journals today require authors to include this – the last section has a subheading called something like "Practical Implications."

Furthermore, peer-reviewed research articles include both original research articles and research reviews. If a field of research is sufficiently developed, you may find a recent review article that summarizes the results of many data-based articles, so you yourself do not have to do all that work. As a bonus, review articles tend to follow common, obvious logic that makes them accessible to many readers.

Is knowing how to read science a good thing? Preliminary research suggests that, whether in their companies or communities, laypeople who grasp published science at a basic level at least have the advantage of being able to pose good questions to experts.[38] Leaders who are at least somewhat knowledgeable can lead where others who are less informed can only follow. For instance, in a study of policymaking for wind turbine installation, researchers found that motivated laypersons who invest enough time can acquire enough knowledge to engage in meaningful dialogue with subject matter experts. Because they have done their homework, such leaders can have some influence over the process. Less informed laypeople have less influence, in part because policymakers are likely to turn away from trying to develop consensus with them and turn instead to expert opinion.[39]

On the other hand, as the saying goes, a little knowledge can be a dangerous thing. A thorough vetting of the facts is always necessary. How you do that will depend not only on your own scientific abilities but also on your organization's resources for acquiring professional help.

Reading science can be a complicated task. This raises the question of whether leaders should study the science themselves, or delegate that learning to others. When the scientific problem a leader is trying to solve is so complex that it is beyond their own abilities or the abilities of their team, they must turn to a consultant. PhD-level and other research professionals approach essential research to understand it as thoroughly as possible. As specialists in the area researched, they will read not only an article but also most of its references. Their training in research methodology and statistical analysis allows them to see the holes in the research as well as its contributions.

Whether a leader chooses to make or buy necessary science will depend on such factors as the availability of internal and external resources, and how they will manage costs in the short- and long-term. In the end, the fundamental question is, Who can you trust to give you the truth? – and the practical question is, How much is that worth to you?

Whether your decision is to read the science in-house or to hire consultants to help you, you generally expect that at the least you will be able to obtain it. Americans, in particular, take for granted that they have access to basic science. Every year vast troves of US government science are developed and made available to the public. Every time Americans check the weather they are tapping into the satellites and scientists of the NOAA and the National Weather Service. Either they go directly to https://www.weather.gov, or they listen to media reports that are likely to use that same free information. Likewise, they rely on Food and Drug Administration scientists to monitor the safety of what they consume, and to educate them about everything from using cosmetics safely to keeping pets healthy. They rely on the Environmental Protection Agency to measure and assure clean water and unpolluted air. They count on the US Geological Survey to inform them about natural hazards related to water, energy, and other natural resources. Not incidentally, that organization's mission includes studying the impacts of climate change and educating the public about them.

Much of this science is available free online. In addition, the results of any independent research funded by the government must be published for free. Americans' ability to access all this government and government-sponsored research is enhanced by an excellent free library system.

Nevertheless, public access to science can be restricted in significant ways.

First, it can be restricted by politics. In the climate arena, an early attempt to squelch research on climate change was the well-documented case of NASA climatologist James Hansen versus the George W. Bush administration and the fossil fuel industry.[40] Hansen is credited as the first scientist to warn the world about human-induced global warming. It was his testimony before the United States Senate Committee on Energy and Natural Resources in 1988 that initiated the national discussion of climate change. One commentator has called that testimony "the official beginning of the global warming policy debate."[41]

Motivated perhaps by the Bush family's oil interests, officials of the Bush administration had tried to censor Hansen's early public pronouncements alerting the public to climate change. In part to reduce NASA's earth science group budget, they appointed political loyalists in positions formerly held by NASA professionals. They also edited government research documents on climate change to make scientists' conclusions appear much more tentative than they actually were.[42]

Today, government scientists realize the need to preserve continuity of climate data in the face of any administration that might want to eliminate such research. As one scientist puts it, "If you can just get rid of the data, you're in a stronger position to argue we should do nothing about climate change."[43]

In 2017, the incoming Trump administration began to remove climate and energy data from government websites, sparking nationwide events by scientists and their supporters to archive valuable data sets. Although it is illegal to destroy government data, it is not illegal to make it hard to access by revising a website so that certain pages are impossible to find. "At the moment, more people than ever are aware of the risk of relying solely on the government to preserve its own information," wrote two government document librarians, James A. Jacobs of the University of California, San Diego, and James R. Jacobs of Stanford University, in February 2017. "This was not true even six months ago."[44]

Another restriction on access is cost. Much of published science is not free. If one is interested in, say, "Enhanced Desalination Performance of Carboxyl Functionalized Graphene Oxide Nanofiltration Membranes," as a layperson you can purchase the original research article directly from its publisher for $37.95.[45] Typically, researchers do not get a royalty for these downloads, but their publishers do. In fact, the profit margins of academic publishing companies are among the highest in the world.[46] These days, some academics are finding research articles to be so expensive that they share papers free online, and paper-sharing Internet sites are being developed for scientists.

Alternatively, if you are a professor or a student, or an employee of a business organization that relies heavily on research, you may have access to academic science through your institution. Universities, businesses, and libraries often purchase individual journals and sets of journals and provide access to their readers for free. For example, to find this article on desalination, you might download it from your university library online. Alternatively, you might discover that your own university does not subscribe to the database in which it can be found, but that you can order the article through an interlibrary loan system.

Independent researchers are on their own nickel. For them, the price is still $37.95, which can add up to a huge amount for any sort of serious investigation. Thus, the expense of researching in peer-reviewed articles excludes some interested and no doubt very interesting people and projects. There does exist a cadre of consultants who trade in their access to databases by providing nonaffiliated organizations with the scientific information that they need, but this information also comes at a price.

Users searching outside of the databases, using a free resource like Google Scholar, are probably searching too broadly. They may waste time sifting through some less than excellent research, and, in the end, may find that the resource is neither as comprehensive nor as focused as they need. Even if they find citations that interest them there, they may still be up against a paywall.

Obviously, expensive access to research can stifle its production and application. Also, powerful owners might influence the content of their databases. Suffice it to say that the situation has prompted a movement in which some researchers prefer to publish in open-access journals, and there are now over 10,000 such journals.[47] These journals often require authors to pay a fee that defers their costs. In some disciplines, these journals are not the most prestigious, in part because they are newcomers. In other disciplines, government regulations require authors to make their work public in this way.

In response to these threats from politics and the profit motive, the Union of Concerned Scientists advocates for democratic access to all science data. Their view is that "scientific integrity includes the open, reliable conduct, supervision, and communication of science as well as the appropriate use of science and policy creation ... Regardless of decision makers' political affiliation, good decisions require the best available independent information we can gather."[48] In a related effort to protect access to climate science, the Climate Science Legal Defense Fund offers legal assistance to researchers facing lawsuits over their work on climate change. Its general guidelines can be found in the publication *Handling Political Harassment and Legal Intimidation: A Pocket Guide for Scientists.*[49]

5. TRUTH INTERPRETERS

Given their busy lives, modest scientific training, and limited access to scientific data, many climate leaders will rely on science interpreters to help them obtain and understand scientific truth. Most nonscientists, most of the time, rely on the Internet, television, radio, newspapers, and magazines for their scientific information. Today more than ever, we need to be rational consumers of such information. Leaders, whose influence is magnified, have a special responsibility to ferret out the truth.

Journalists' professional norms influence how they present climate and energy issues and, therefore, what the public takes away from their coverage.[50] The norm of balanced reporting, for instance, in which the views of experts on both sides of a conflict are presented, is assumed to be a hallmark of good journalism. Yet, when practiced simplistically, this principle may give a voice to fringe minorities that are clearly wrong.[51] By giving both sides of an argument equal time, a journalist magnifies minority influence and distorts the truth as heard by the public. For example, although most of thousands of scientists believe in anthropogenic climate change, a few do not. Always presenting both sides of the story leaves the false impression that there is a lack of consensus among mainstream scientists, or that both sides are in some sense right. Less engaged readers and viewers may not read and view broadly enough to know the "whole truth" – that is, the truth.

Responsible news organizations combat this problem by construing the norm of balanced reporting in the context of their entire news organization and its product, not just in terms of one article. For example, this policy of National Public Radio distinguishes between daily reporting and longer-term investigative reporting:

> When we say our [daily] reporting is complete, it means we understand the bigger picture of a story – which facts are most important and how they relate to one another. It's unrealistic to expect that every story should represent every perspective on an issue. But in our reporting, we must do our best to be *aware* of all perspectives, the facts supporting

or opposing each, and the different groups of stakeholders affected by the issue. Only then can we determine what's best to include in the time and space we have.[52]

In other words, each story exists within a larger system of stories, and it is that system that embodies legitimacy and truth.

Another common journalistic norm is to rely on authorities. Authorities can be especially helpful to journalists when they address complex issues like climate change and energy evolution. However, journalists are sometimes tempted to reduce the complexities of a story that has many voices and many angles to a simple conflict between two authority figures. For example, in a segment called "The Climate Feud," Fox News host Bill O'Reilly once pitted Vice-President Al Gore against former Alaska Governor Sarah Palin. Gore had shared the Nobel Peace Prize with the Intergovernmental Panel for Climate Change for their combined efforts to disseminate knowledge about human-made climate change, while Palin, in a contemporary editorial, had been so uninformed that she conflated climate and weather.[53] Inviting confrontation between such so-called experts can undermine the authority of actual experts and does little to offer listeners the truth about climate change.

To bring their listeners broader truths rather than just single-minded opinions, National Public Radio's decision about what to include in a daily report is, again, contextualized within an ongoing investigation:

> As journalists, we strive to master broad domains of information. We often seek the expertise of specialists who might have a greater grasp of facts within their specialty. Our challenge is not to be dependent on what any particular source tells us, but to have enough mastery of our subject that we can accurately situate each source's knowledge and perspective within a broader context. This means we strive to

know enough about a subject that we can tell when a source is advocating a disputed position, advancing a vested interest or making a faulty claim.[54]

Following this logic, their reporters attempt to substantiate a given fact using a variety of sources. Also, while their daily reporting may be less in-depth than their investigative journalism, reporters strive to know enough about the big picture, about the wider system, to be able to ask critical questions of any and every source.

Other journalistic norms include personalizing news stories with anecdotes, emphasizing crisis and conflict, and focusing on the present. These norms make stories more appealing to audiences. Writers particularly favor interpersonal conflict. As an op-ed editor at the *New York Times* once said, "Let's face it, newspaper editors prefer bullies."[55] Unfortunately, this approach engages System 1 and avoids more complex, systemic, System 2 theories and solutions. It also downplays issues of power and action that are not breaking news, but only play out over time.

When reading climate journalism, leaders should pay attention to how journalists describe impending threats and the actions that can address them. Given how leaders motivate people to engage with climate issues, it is important that they cover both.

In television news, broadcasters typically discuss either climate change threats or climate change actions. Seldom do they discuss in the same broadcast both the threat of climate change and actions to reduce that threat.[56] Of course, this news pattern appeals to System 1 fears but fails to encourage System 2 solutions. It gives people little sense of efficacy about managing their fears, and it encourages an attitude of passivity toward change.

A related problem is that when they do discuss prospects for effective action, news programs tend to split the difference. They might say, "Yes, we might be able to manage climate change, but on the other hand maybe we won't be able to," or "Yes, we have an environmental problem, but we also have a political conflict about it." Deeper, more hopeful analysis is rare.

Most newspapers also separate threats and impacts from actions to resolve them. Research suggests that among leading newspapers, the *Wall Street Journal* is the least likely to discuss in the same article both the threats posed by climate change and the potential impacts from taking action. It is also the most likely to emphasize how difficult change can be and that change will involve conflict that will negatively affect the economy.[57]

Energy journalism illustrates many related challenges.[58] To begin with, much of energy journalism is a context desert. Energy journalists often fail to provide data that help the average reader to interpret their reporting realistically. One might read, for example, that a certain new oilfield holds 3 billion barrels of oil. If that sounds like a lot to you, consider this: If world usage is 96 million barrels of oil per day (MBD) – call it 100 million barrels for estimation purposes – 1 billion barrels lasts about ten days, and that 3 billion barrels of oil will last the world roughly one month. The International Energy Agency publishes frequent data and forecasts about worldwide average demand.[59] Meanwhile, decontextualized energy journalism gives readers the false impression that 1 billion barrels is a huge amount of oil.

Another concern is that many energy journalists ignore the fact that the "oil" of today is not the "oil" of yesterday. Light sweet crude oil is not shale oil, which is not tar sands oil, which is not natural gas. While in common usage the word "oil" at one point in history referred only to light sweet crude oil – the least expensive type of oil to extract and refine and the least polluting to burn – today it refers to a variety of different types of oil. Sometimes, too, reporters revert to the term "oil" when they really mean oil and other liquid fuels like gas. Interestingly, these kinds of semantic changes by the fossil fuel industry itself have kept the supply of "oil" strong and growing in recent decades.

Sometimes, too, energy journalists fail to do their math properly. For example, an energy blogger for the *New York Times* points to a source that argues that "if [a] power plant [that] supplies the electricity starts with 100 units of energy, it will lose two-thirds of that in making the current and another 10 percent in transmission and distribution. The motor will be only 90 percent efficient; so pumps, motors, drive trains and throttling valves along the way will lose more, leaving the plant with 93 units of energy."[60] Right?

Like other journalists, energy journalists rely on authority, but, in their exceptionally complex field, they are rather more likely to accept an authority's view without criticism. For example, they often quote Daniel Yergin, Pulitzer Prize–winning author of *The Prize* and an oil industry economics consultant. Yergin is invariably optimistic on the future of the oil supply and the benefits of low prices. In all 721 pages of *The Prize* there is no numerical estimate of the amount of oil left in the ground. The result, as energy futurist and media critic Chris Nelder points out, is that "in the eyes of most editors, an optimistic take on future [oil] supply is just good energy journalism. And a balanced, nuanced article with indeterminate conclusions doesn't sell papers. But a pessimistic take (no matter how true, or buttressed by facts) is *editorializing*, which is bad" (emphasis in original).[61]

In all human communication, power affects point of view. Therefore, in addition to understanding journalistic norms and foibles, climate leaders will want to know who owns a media outlet.[62] As of this writing, the conservative Murdoch family, alternatively represented as climate skeptics and climate deniers, owns Fox News, the *Wall Street Journal*, *Barron's*, and *National Geographic Magazine*. The liberal *New York Times*, which regularly reports on climate change, is owned by The New York Times Company and has been controlled by the Ochs-Sulzberger family since 1896. *The Economist* had been purchased by publishing and education giant Pearson PLC, but in 2015 was bought by Cadbury, Rothschild, Schroder, Agnelli, some related family interests, and some staff and former staff shareholders. The *Financial Times* had also been owned by Pearson and was sold in 2015 to the Japanese company Nikkei. These two British publications routinely report on climate change, and the *Financial Times* is especially strong on energy reporting. Likewise, the online magazine *Slate* has a heritage of liberal owners and reports regularly on climate change, and the independent newspaper *The Guardian*, owned by a trust that safeguards its journalistic and liberal values, reports frequently on climate and energy.

We don't have enough space here to tease out the numerous influences that ownership might have on the content of these publications. (Certainly, disclaimers that owners have no influence should be ignored.) A related concern is that the business models of the traditional media are under severe attack, with print editions losing money and online editions failing to make up the difference. Suffice it to offer a warning, and, also, the advice to make clear and deliberate decisions about which media to trust.

We are what we learn, and the further we get away from our formal education the more our information sources determine what we believe. Online posts disconnected from journalistic norms become popular because of their direct appeal to System 1. On the other hand, some bloggers consistently contribute to sound System 2 analysis. Consumers of climate and energy news must be vigilant. They should skim less and investigate more, even if this means limiting the subjects they can cover. They should examine the ownership systems in which a piece of media is embedded to ferret out news bias. To know something about the context of a given fact, they should look around in other media for both conforming and alternative views. We all need to do the math.

Along with all this, news consumption as we know it is being upended by technologies like smartphones and social media, a crucial topic that is beyond the scope of this book. "The traditional media ecosystem is changing and disintegrating," asserts *The Guardian*.[63]

Their research on how smartphones intermingle entertainment and news further illustrates how System 1 gets to go first.

• • •

In sum, to address the climate problem, Team Humanity must first face itself. We human beings use System 1 to motivate ourselves to seek the truth and System 2 to tell ourselves what the truth is. Only when leaders know the truth can they act with conviction and attract followers. Climate leaders can help by guiding their communities to develop trust in sound science. Responsible media consumers need to scrutinize climate and energy journalism, and monitor their own media habits.

On the way to discovering the truth, leaders need to both trust and distrust. They need to work with others in the community – in scientific communities, business organizations, and governments – to develop, test, and retest the facts that people can agree on to drive change.

PRACTICE 2

Assess the Risks

Calling this chapter "Assess the Risks" is a typical writer's tactic to entice your System 1 to pay attention. Every media outlet, including this one, wants to capture you for its own purposes. Some want to engage your System 1 so you will continue to read and pay attention to their ads (think Facebook). Others target your System 2 so you will continue to read and pay attention to their ads (think the *New York Times*).

This writer wants you to think, "What risk? Risk to me? Really, that bad?" so you will be motivated to engage in the more challenging, time-consuming work of System 2 risk analysis. When we think about climate and energy evolution, "OMG it's happening!" competes in our thoughts with "How fast is the planet heating up?" and "What is the probability that global warming will affect my life and the lives of other living beings?" A climate leader's challenge is to hold System 1 emotions and quick-fix decision-making in perspective and apply System 2 capabilities to analyze climate and energy risks systematically.

Thus, the second practice of leading for the planet is to understand the nature and psychology of risk and learn how decision-makers today are addressing the risks to the planet.

1. THE PSYCHOLOGY OF RISK

Risk specialist Paul Slovic notes that a person's perception of risk has two psychological dimensions. The first dimension is dread, or "dread risk." People who experience high dread are likely to believe that a risk they face will bring catastrophic, fatal, and global consequences, and that the risk is not easily reduced and is increasing. They are likely to feel out of control, fearful, and apprehensive. In contrast, people who experience low dread perceive a risk as controllable, easily reduced, and decreasing, and they feel relatively calm and in control.[1]

The other dimension of risk is familiarity, referred to as "unknown risk." People facing an unfamiliar risk are likely to believe that it is new, unknown to science, and unknown to those exposed to it. They believe the risk will have delayed effects. In contrast, people facing a familiar risk are likely to believe that the risk is observable, that it is known to those exposed to it and to scientists, and that it has immediate effects.

These two dimensions of risk parallel Kahneman's theory of humans' dual systems of thinking.[2] Dread operates within our automatic System 1. It works by using emotion and direct experience to identify similarity and make associations. Familiarity operates within our analytic System 2, which works by developing algorithms and rules and following normative models of decision-making to process the likely effects of risk.

Much of how humanity operates in the world comes down to how people perceive risk. How individuals understand a risk affects both how negatively they rate it and how they try to reduce it. Different opinions on what strategies to pursue are often based on different perceptions about the risks at hand.

For example, some envision an imminent collapse of the fossil fuel energy system and have taken up homesteading off the grid. Others believe the demise of that system is decades if not hundreds of years in the future, and in their lives today they are ignoring even the possibility. Risk experts point out that risk analysis always contains elements of subjectivity, including factors like values, process, power, and trust.[3] They note that subjectivity is a cognitive and rational phenomenon, but is also experiential and emotional.

When assessing a risk, Systems 1 and 2 work, as always, in complementary fashion. Unfortunately, sometimes they produce conflicting answers to the same problem.[4] For example, if we are in the middle of a wicked cold snap, it is hard for our System 1, which works in the present, to warn us that the climate is warming. Meanwhile, in order to make sense of the climate risks associated with said cold snap, System 2 has to have learned that in a warming world the Arctic is the fastest warming region, that Arctic warming alters the path of the jet stream and may influence polar vortices to descend upon us more intensely and haphazardly than in the past, and that, therefore, even this cold snap may be a sign that the planet is warming. Clearly, leaders who want to manage risk must take both systems into account.

Risk analysts have found that we humans are likely to turn away from a risk that causes high dread (System 1) and, at the same time, is also relatively unknown to us (System 2). In an attempt to reduce our anxiety we may ignore such a risk altogether, and so we do not act. This psychological inability to grapple with a high dread/low knowledge problem is explained by the theory of cognitive dissonance,[5] the mental discomfort (usually confusion or tension) we often feel when we hold ideas or values that contradict each other. When we experience the discomfort of being inconsistent in our own thinking, we are likely to change our ideas or attitudes even if they are based on fact. When "I believe we are experiencing a decades-long drought" competes in a person's mind with "I don't believe in climate change," dissonance theory predicts that they will drop one or the other belief.

Cognitive dissonance is actually physiologically annoying, which is one reason we try to reduce the discomfort by changing one side of the equation or the other. We either ignore the problem as best we can, or we delve into it to make it more observable and familiar, and more amenable to change through action. Either way, we are determined to make ourselves feel better.

Cognitive dissonance occurs not only when we hold conflicting attitudes but also when our attitudes are inconsistent with our behaviors. Citizens might regret that their region is experiencing water shortages, but if they make no effort to conserve water, they may feel vaguely uncomfortable. Either their ideas about the risk or their behavior in response to it must change, so to make peace with themselves they will either deny the shortages or start to conserve. Leaders who understand these processes can focus appropriately on influencing either ideas or behaviors. For instance, they can see that there are long-term benefits to encouraging people to take even baby steps toward conservation.

Novices in risk management are likely to be proponents of formal risk analysis (System 2) and to view the emotional side of risk (System 1) as irrational. Yet, as we have seen, the systems operate simultaneously, and often cooperatively. Your fear of sea level rise might cause you to delay your dream of buying a home in the low-lying Florida Keys. However, it might also prompt your analytic side to bypass dread-filled media accounts to carefully estimate the actual probabilities of sea level rise over the lifetime of the property. You might decide to buy after all. Of course, knowing that Hurricane Irma devastated the Keys in 2017 would add an important factor to your risk analysis.

The System 1 approach to risk creates several roadblocks to change. The first is that its focus on the immediate encourages "psychophysical numbing," which includes the inability to attach feeling to extreme losses of life.[6] Although System 1 makes it easy for us to feel empathy for one individual, it does not help us to experience empathy for millions of people. As the saying goes, one death is a tragedy, but a million deaths is a statistic. Climate and energy issues will affect the entire world population eventually, but when they don't affect us as individuals in the here and now, or they don't affect people we know personally, we tend to ignore them.

Also, when individuals are caught up in System 1, they tend to over-weight the importance of rare events. Unfortunately, rare events often evoke strong emotions that preclude more analytic processing. Some of the leaders of the city of Rotterdam in the Netherlands remember a devastating flood from decades ago, but if they rely too much on their emotionally colored memories they are likely to shy away from modern flood solutions. For example, they might lean toward build-ing more dikes rather than adopting the newer, data-supported idea that some floodwaters should be allowed to flow over the land and escape.

Yet another roadblock to change is that by acting to reduce a risk, people may satisfy their immediate emotional needs and then simply walk away from any larger problem. Psychologically speaking, having taken that one action reduces their anxiety and dread and thereaf-ter quells their motivation to do more. Sophisticated risk managers know they must plan to reduce this "single action bias."[7] For example, rather than sponsor one big climate-related event annually, a leader might plan a series of small actions over months.

A related phenomenon is "psychological distancing." It is common for individuals to think of climate change in the abstract – as a set of uncertain events that may or may not occur far in the future, that will impact faraway places, and that will mainly affect people who are not like themselves. Psychological distancing is one more factor that reduces the probability that people will act, and studies of people's perceptions of global warming suggest they may be reacting in this way. An ongoing survey by Yale University found that, in 2019, 67 per cent of Americans believed that global warming will harm future genera-tions, yet only 48 per cent believed it is harming people in the United States now or will within ten years.[8] It is likely that, as global warming escalates and more people experience its effects personally and share their experiences with others, psychological distancing will diminish.

Leaders can identify the ways in which their followers are distancing themselves psychologically and act to counter this tendency. For one thing, they can recognize that people ask themselves whether a phenomenon is socially relevant to them. Individuals are more likely to want to take on mitigation efforts when they can imagine that climate impacts will be experienced by "people like me."

People weigh their own sense of uncertainty about a phenomenon, and they are more likely to act when they can believe that "climate change is really happening." Individuals also weigh geographical distance. They are more likely to act when they consider how climate change will "impact my country." Finally, they weigh distance in terms of time. They are more likely to act when they believe that climate change is "harming people right now all over the world" and that "we must tackle the issue now."[9]

By reducing psychological distance, climate leaders can strengthen people's motivation to act. Based on what the research is telling us so far, it appears that leaders should continuously provide information that shows that climate change is really happening and that it is caused by human actions. They should craft messages that emphasize (1) local risks, such as impacts on one's community; (2) immediate risks, such as those that will occur in one person's lifetime; and (3) relevance to the audience's social groups, whoever the audience believes are "people like me."

Like the COVID-19 pandemic, the climate change crisis is a "wicked problem" – a society-wide disruption in which many problems are interconnected and about which knowledge is unclear and incomplete. Such problems have no obvious solutions. They involve a large number of diverse decision-makers and often have significant economic consequences. Obviously, an important difference between risk perception in the COVID-19 pandemic and the climate change crisis is that the latter feels remote in place and time. Meanwhile, experiencing a pandemic is all too immediate. Nevertheless, there are many parallels between these two wicked problems, and what we learn from our experience of the pandemic should help us to address climate risk.

One way to gain perspective on the psychology of risk and its effect on behavioral change is to imagine future events in terms of a straightforward theory of punishment and reward. If I (or we) do X, will I (or we) be punished or rewarded by impending climate or energy changes? What is the probability that buying an electric vehicle or installing solar panels will "pay off" for me? For my family? For my company? For the planet? Conversely, what is the probability that such actions will harm me?

Framed this way, climate and energy issues become challenges of psychological motivation, the principles of which are well known. The purpose of reward and punishment is to change behavior, including climate-related behavior.

Psychologists know that for a reward or punishment to be effective, it must be delivered soon after the target behavior occurs. Yet, with climate and energy initiatives, such timely links between behaviors and outcomes are often broken. If you drive an electric car, you have some satisfaction in knowing you are reducing pollution right now, but your imagined, ultimate goal may be saving the planet from catastrophic destruction centuries from now (a long time to wait for your reward). Likewise, when we burn oil to heat our houses today, we may have a hard time imagining how our behavior will cause severe climate events and economic disruptions in the future. If people think about future rewards and punishments at all, they experience the link between their behaviors now and their impact later not viscerally, but intellectually and remotely – not as easy System 1 but as difficult System 2.

A related problem is that when we imagine future rewards and punishments, we are attempting to consider many different time frames and stakeholders all at once. We wonder about punishment and reward to ourselves right now (on a monthly basis, what is the cost-benefit analysis of installing solar panels?), and also in the short term (how soon will the panels be obsolete?) and the long term (would geothermal heating be a better option?). We also think about effects on ourselves and our children now and in the short and long term. In the very long term, we think about our descendants. None of these calculations is simple, and wondering about all of them simultaneously complicates decision-making considerably. As when a person tries to change several behaviors all at the same time, confusion fosters inaction.

If your neighbor installs solar panels (or better yet, your town builds a solar array) while everyone on the block advises her she's an idiot for doing so, her main reward may well be her hope for the future. In the face of a community punishing our behavior, not all of us have that kind of personal conviction and perseverance. Our inability to be lone cowboys is one reason why many activists seek out supportive communities in which to live and work. They hope to develop a community of people who can reward them in the here and now for behaviors that have mainly long-term consequences. Their attempts at incremental change may be noticed and rewarded immediately by friends who hold similar convictions, and may ultimately add up to major change.

In many circumstances, humans focus on impending punishments – on risks – rather than on potential rewards. Having rescued us in hostile environments across the millennia, our brains continue to prioritize fending off the mastodon over hunting for berries. Behavioral economists find that investors are more sensitive to losing money than to making money, and that during market downturns they tend to focus on avoiding loss rather than achieving gains. Similarly, communities build floating barriers to hold back floods (as in London, England) and require buildings in flood zones to be built on stilts (as in Florida), but do little to reward people who reduce their emissions. System 1 gets to go first.

Because we don't focus first on gains, we are also unlikely to consider that the potential rewards to humanity from mastering climate and energy concerns could be tremendous. Imagine: Using renewable energy sources, we could build renewable communities and create economic stability worldwide. We might create a whole new, positive world order. Even today, if we act quickly and effectively, we may yet be able to slow climate change and save many of the species of the world, including our fabulous giraffes and magnificent old-growth forests. We can still preserve for our children's enjoyment a stable, healthy, gorgeous planet. These would be incredible rewards.

How much of this positive future have we really imagined together? Surely not enough. Certainly, some of the specific defensive actions we are taking now, like using the Clean Air Act to reduce the health impacts of burning fossil fuels (pre-Trump), may enhance the probability of world peace and prosperity. The connection to that rewarding future is, however, subtle and unheralded.

Meanwhile, we keep looking over our shoulders for those shaggy beasts.

2. CARBON RISK

Generally, "risk" is defined as "the possibility of loss or injury."[10] More precisely, and from a psychological perspective, a risk is an anticipated punishment to which one can assign a probability. It can be measured and priced. Humans attempt to manage risk by accurately assessing the probability of its occurrence and adequately planning for its effects, a practice that is termed "risk assessment." Since it is evidence-based and ostensibly value free, risk assessment is widely seen as a science. Risk "management" is defined as the making of policy decisions by applying values to decide among multiple goals as analyzed by risk assessors.[11]

"Carbon risk" is the term policymakers use to describe particular bad things that can happen to the planet if we pump too much carbon into the atmosphere. Most importantly, over time climate scientists have observed the increase in carbon dioxide (CO_2) in the atmosphere, and, by evaluating the trend line in the data, have decided that the increase is likely to continue. Scientists have also established that there is a significant relationship between the amount of CO_2 in the atmosphere and a warming planet.

What is their assessment of current carbon risks for the planet? Data from the observatory on Mauna Loa in Hawai'i reveal that the atmospheric concentration of CO_2 has reached more than 410 parts per million (ppm).[12] The last time atmospheric CO_2 concentrations were this high was before humans existed – 3 to 5 million years ago in the Pliocene era. At that time the world was warmer on average by 3 to 4° Celsius, while the poles were as much as 10° Celsius warmer than now.[13] Scientists reason that to maintain a moderate climate we should keep CO_2 within the range found in the Holocene period, which is the recent 12,000-year period in which civilization originated.[14] That range is between 260 and 285 ppm. Ice core samples suggest that during the 200,000 years that Homo sapiens has existed on the planet, CO_2 concentrations have typically been below 300 ppm.[15]

Looking forward, using models that predict how CO_2 concentration increases planetary warming, scientists now estimate that an atmospheric carbon concentration beyond 350 ppm is likely to put the planet at some risk. At any concentration above 450 ppm, most of them throw up their laptops and say they don't know what will happen. At such a point risks are often described euphemistically as "uncertainties."

In recent years, the CO_2 concentration has climbed annually by between 1.89 and 3 ppm.[16] The annual increase has tripled from about 0.7 ppm per year in the late 1950s.[17] As one commentator described these changes, "in the 1980s and 1990s, the CO_2 level increased at about 1.5 parts per million each year. The last two years [2015–16], it's been rising at nearly twice that rate – 2.9 ppm – as emissions overwhelm the oceans' and forests' ability to take CO_2 out of the air."[18]

In response, writer and climate activist Bill McKibben founded the worldwide 350.org movement that promotes actions to reduce concentrations back to preindustrial levels. The International Energy Agency calculates that if we are to maintain the temperature of the planet below 2° Celsius of warming, world societies must leave two-thirds of existing fossil fuel reserves in the ground.[19] Co-founder of Microsoft Corporation and global philanthropist Bill Gates points out that to forestall dramatic climate shifts, by 2050 wealthy nations like China and the United States, which produce the most greenhouse gases, should be adding no carbon whatsoever to the atmosphere.[20]

Planetary changes create both investment risks and investment opportunities. As one major investment research firm observes, "Whether or not you believe in climate change, an unstoppable shift away from coal and oil towards lower-carbon fuels is under way, which will ultimately bring about an end to the oil age."[21] There will be risks investing in green energy but also risks in sticking with fossil fuels. Al Gore and David Blood of Generation Investment Management, which promotes green energy investments, point out that most investors are treating carbon risk as an uncertainty, and, therefore, are not incorporating it into their investment decisions.[22] They argue that to actually minimize investment risk investors should begin to drive their portfolios toward assets with low carbon emissions.

To help such decision-makers assess risk, science says ... model it. MIT professor Neil Gershenfeld, listed among *Scientific American*'s 50 Leaders in Science and Technology, observes that "the most common misunderstanding about science is that scientists seek and find truth. They don't – they make and test models ... Making sense of anything means making models that can predict outcomes and accommodate observations. Truth is a model."[23]

Basically, a model is a set of ideas about relationships. Most models include three components: an information input, a logical way of processing that information, and an output of expected results. For practical purposes, a model is an example to follow or imitate that helps people understand real-world systems and their risks.

A model is the missing step between two variables that are correlated; it is a rational attempt to explain why. Astrology predicts human behavior from the positions of the planets, yet without describing a mechanism that connects the two it cannot claim to be scientific. In fact, humans use many conceptual systems that have various kinds of validity – religious validity comes to mind – yet are not scientific.

The distinguishing characteristic of scientific models is that they must be falsifiable; there must be plausible ways that data can be collected to disprove them. Scientists evaluate a model by its consistency with empirical data, using quantifiable observations that are made precisely and consistently. All scientific models are tentative in that they can always be disproven by contradictory evidence provided by new scientific studies. Scientific thinking moves forward not because of factors like a scientist's authority or prestige but because his or her models are effective predictors.

Scientific models explain how the amount of CO_2 in the atmosphere is related to the temperature of the planet. When scientists get new information, such as the latest ice core data on the amount of carbon in the atmosphere and global temperatures thousands of years ago, their existing models should be able to explain that relationship. If the models cannot do that well, they will be replaced by newer models that will in turn be tested against existing facts.

Although scientists understand that all models are imperfect, the public does not always get this point. Because what scientists do is to test "hypotheses" to substantiate "theories," even well-proven science is often misunderstood by the public as "hypothetical" or "theoretical." This misunderstanding is exacerbated because, when publishing their results, scientists usually include an estimate of the magnitude of their uncertainty about their findings. Often the "right" answer to a problem falls within a range of plausible values. That "confidence interval" and the values above and below the most likely answer are referred to as the "margin of error." Publishing the margin of error can easily be misconstrued as suggesting the scientists are uncertain, or, worse, that all scientific knowledge is uncertain.

Yes, all scientific knowledge is uncertain in the sense that it is always open to question. Yet in modern times, we have an incredible body of useful science that has been, for practical purposes, proven. Scientific models tested in the real world have revolutionized society on every front, from healthcare to rocket technology, and we are constantly improving such System 2 analyses with better research methods. In professional mode, scientists would never say that a theory is "proven," even when, for use in practical applications, it is.

Models are useful for predicting risks and rewards. Suppose a farmer decides to grow a forest. What is the reward he seeks? He may want to make money, sequester carbon, enjoy the beauty of the trees, or perhaps all of the above. Well before planting, he sets his goals and studies how to grow strong trees. He learns all he can about fertilizer and soil and rainfall. He considers the known risks. He must protect new seedlings from overheating and drying, and from predatory deer, mice, and weeds. He hopes to avoid bankruptcy. In time, he will measure the growth of his forest, analyze his results, and use the results to decide how best to manage his forest in the future. To be an effective farmer and forest manager is to avoid punishment and seek reward through applied science.

Although he most likely calls them plans, the farmer is using models. Compared with a manager who depends on his instinctual System 1, his analytical System 2 approach is more likely to be successful. Using a model is even more likely to be successful when farmers face complex and novel long-term growing situations, like those created by rapid climate change.

Suppose our farmer-entrepreneur takes a course in management and begins to wonder whether using a particular style of leadership might improve his crop of trees. Unfortunately for him, models in the social sciences are much less likely to be successful predictors than

models in the natural sciences. Why so? The modeling process itself
is the same: Any model of human behavior provides a set of variables
and an explanation of why those variables lead to certain outcomes.
The problem is that in the social sciences the variables themselves
contain a considerable amount of ambiguity and uncertainty. What
is "leadership," anyhow? What, indeed, is "behavior"? The social sciences of psychology, political science, human geography, and economics are perhaps best known to the public. Yet, because of the
often ambiguous nature of their constructs, social science models are
not as robust and predictive as those of the hard sciences. For this
reason, the science of human behavior sometimes gives a bad name
to the science of natural systems.

Nevertheless, our intrepid forest manager perseveres. He splits
his forest in half and gives one half to an authoritarian leader, who
spends much of his time telling his employees what to do, and the
other half to a participative leader, who spends most of her time lis-
tening to her employees' ideas. Later, the forest manager measures
the growth of the trees in the two different plots, but to his dismay,
he realizes that his process has raised all kinds of measurement issues.
What did his authoritarian leader actually do differently than his participative leader? Also, did he, the manager, observe and measure
those behaviors directly himself, or did he infer them from what people reported? His process also raises modeling issues. How can he
know whether some other unidentified human factor, such as level of
motivation or skill in decision-making, was not the real cause of the
different outcomes? If the forest manager were a doctoral student,
he would discuss such ambiguities, publish his results, and move
on. However, as a practical manager, he suspects that he has made
inroads in getting at the truth, but he still harbors some uncertainty
about cause and effect.

Social science aims to mimic natural science because the latter has
models that can be replicated, and, when replicated, these models
can be understood to essentially prove things. Arguably, some social

science today is based on well-specified variables (witness the impact of neuropsychology). Nevertheless, it is also true that management studies, in particular, are seldom replicated.[24] Economics is known as the "dismal science" in part because its findings often lack controls and are therefore debatable. Furthermore, all social science research is subject to ethical constraints. For example, social scientists do not do controlled studies – for instance, meting out help to some but not to others – on people who are suffering.

It follows that when climate leaders apply science to risk management, they should anticipate the understandable confusion of lay audiences who face technical terminology. They should also be able to clearly communicate the basic philosophy of models and research, including their methodological limitations.

The carbon model is fundamental to climate change science. Our understanding of climate change is based on knowledge of how CO_2, along with other greenhouse gases like methane, is distributed on the planet, and how that distribution affects natural systems.

Carbon is an element that is found on Earth in what scientists refer to as "reservoirs." It is found mainly in rocks, but also in plants, soil, fossil fuels, the ocean, and the atmosphere. Over the years, scientists have modeled how the Earth's finite amount of carbon moves from one reservoir to another across the planet. Oil, for instance, was created over a period of millions of years during which the carbon in living plants was turned into fossil fuel deposits in the earth. When we burn it, we cause much of its carbon to move into the atmosphere in the form of CO_2. The understanding of this "carbon cycle" is based on many years of scientific research.[25]

For millions of years, the carbon cycle was stable, meaning that carbon moved very slowly from one reservoir to another. We know this in part because paleoclimatologists have studied ancient air samples from bubbles trapped in the ice in Antarctica. Very recently, under human influences that include the burning of fossil fuels in great quantities, the carbon cycle has begun to change rapidly (so have the cycles of nitrogen and phosphorus). Today, scientists can also demonstrate that the carbon cycle is related to sea level rise, the movement of species, and accelerated extinctions.[26]

The models that best describe climate change include as a major factor that humans inject CO_2 into the atmosphere by burning fossil fuels. It is well accepted that burning fossil fuels sends CO_2 into the atmosphere, which is causing the atmosphere to trap some of the heat that ordinarily would escape the Earth. We also know that these days the atmosphere contains more CO_2 than at any time in millions of years: "In the entire history of civilization CO_2 levels have not been this high,"[27] and "CO_2 levels have not been as high as they are now for at least the past 10 to 15 million years."[28] The effect of human influence on the planet is now so evident and consequential that scientists have declared a new era on Earth and named it the Anthropocene ("anthro" is derived from a Greek word for "human").

Scientists continue to have many questions about the carbon cycle. For instance, forests are a reservoir of carbon, which they give off into the atmosphere when they are cut down and burned or otherwise decay. Scientists are studying how quickly reforestation, which reabsorbs CO_2, can reduce the amount of CO_2 in the atmosphere. They also want to understand what happens when the tundra that encircles the northern latitudes of the planet melts and releases large amounts of CO_2, and the even more potent gas methane, into the atmosphere. And they are examining how changes in the carbon cycle affect warming, desertification, and extreme weather events.

Finding answers to such questions requires developing and testing models, of course. In addition to effectively modeling the carbon cycle, scientists have had many other successes modeling climate processes. One of the clearest has been their prediction that as the Arctic melts, the albedo effect would kick in and accelerate that melting. Albedo is a measure of the reflectivity of the Earth's surface – its whiteness. Ice reflects solar energy more than brown soil or dark water does, and so it has a higher albedo. Scientists predicted fifty years ago that as the planet warms and more dark water appears, the melting of ice in the Arctic would accelerate. They were correct, although their models predicted less melting than has occurred.[29]

Given humankind's incessant curiosity, we can expect that scientists will continue to improve their models of the natural world. While Team Humanity cannot predict where the next great idea will originate, it is fair to say that it is unlikely to come from people who are thinking fast and easy in System 1 and more likely to come from those performing the slow and difficult work of System 2 analysis. When it comes to solving complex problems like climate change, individuals and organizations that rely on instinct and emotion alone are less likely than more analytic folk to prevail. Of course, marrying the two is ideal.

In the pursuit of such complex truths, we would do well to remember that relying on the judgment of individual experts – even the judgment of seasoned, respected leaders – may lead to less than optimal decisions. Indeed, research in recent decades suggests that relying on data-based models created by groups is more likely to be successful. Atul Gawande, an American surgeon, author, and public health researcher, is among those who champion the use of group wisdom when making decisions in the face of uncertainty. Based on his experience and research in medical settings, he notes that "in the face of the unknown – the always nagging uncertainty about whether, under complex circumstances, things will really be okay – [we should trust] in the wisdom of the group, the wisdom of making sure that multiple pairs of eyes [are] on a problem and then letting the watchers decide what to do ... Man is fallible, but maybe men are less so."[30]

In fact, scientists are effective System 2 analysts who often do work collectively, and their best models have proven to be excellent predictors of many natural phenomena. Decision-makers rely on their models to anticipate rewards and punishments, opportunities and risks. For practical purposes, climate leaders often turn scientific models into scenarios.

Scenarios are models of the future that integrate assumptions with current knowledge. Since scientists cannot get data from the future, they predict the future by extrapolating trends from existing data. For example, since they know how much fossil fuel is being burned each year, they extrapolate from these data to make an educated guess about how much will be burned in the future. This estimate can be used to predict future amounts of CO_2 in the atmosphere, which in turn can predict impacts on planetary systems like atmospheric and ocean currents. By varying assumptions, such as how much fossil fuel will be burned given future regulations and demand, decision-makers develop a set of scenarios that can foster debate and improve planning.

The Intergovernmental Panel on Climate Change (IPCC) is the foremost international group of scientists dedicated to advancing discussion about the future impacts of climate change. Sponsored by the United Nations, the IPCC scientists do not themselves make policy. Instead, they offer scenarios that inform policymakers. At the time they are created, IPCC scenarios are humanity's collective best guess about climate risks.

In addition to making global predictions, the IPCC's work is often applied at the country level. For example, the National Climate Assessment for the United States, which is an interagency project of the federal government, pairs IPCC scenarios with regional climate models to provide local projections for climate change. It also suggests how federal, regional, and local organizations can network together, share information, and collaborate on projects for climate adaptation.[31]

The IPCC is an ongoing collective that includes thousands of scientists from dozens of countries. Its decision-making processes have been designed to help it avoid System 1 superficiality. For one thing, the sheer number of participating scientists, who hail from a variety of disciplines, suggests that its results will be widely debated. Likewise, the scientists come from a variety of political perspectives – from countries with different political systems, from countries that are energy-rich and energy-poor, from countries that have contributed a great deal to·climate change and from those that have contributed little.

The IPCC reports are summaries of peer-reviewed science, and the IPCC reports are themselves peer-reviewed. Delegates meet collectively, in often hard-fought, in-person meetings, to debate their findings and hammer out public statements that are at once scientifically valid and interpretable to a lay audience. IPCC reports are published periodically and are free to the public. Synthesis reports, called Assessment Reports (AR), appeared in 2007 (AR4) and 2014 (AR5), and another will be published in the 2020s (AR6). More focused reports are published periodically between the synthesis reports.

Of course, people are justifiably skeptical about any process that attempts to predict the future, and scenarios are projections that contain uncertainties. Furthermore, as MIT atmospheric scientist Kerry Emanuel suggests, when people look at climate models, "we operate under the expectation that the real climate will fall among the projections made with the various models – that the truth, in other words, will lie somewhere between the higher and lower estimates generated by the models. It is not inconceivable, though, that the actual solution will fall outside these limits."[32] In other words, it is conceivable that climate change will be less damaging than the models predict, and it is also conceivable that climate change will be more damaging than the models predict.

An additional reality is that not all natural systems can be modeled. Climate models typically include millions of lines of computer code that simulate "an enormous range of physical phenomena" such as "the flow of the atmosphere and oceans; condensation and precipitation of water inside clouds; the transport of heat, water, and atmospheric constituents by turbulent convection currents," and many others, writes Emanuel. It is "computationally impossible to keep track of every molecule of air and ocean," so some processes, particularly those that happen on small scales, cannot be modeled. Emanuel, who is known among his students as "Dr. Doom," points out that "computer modeling of global climate is perhaps the most complex endeavor ever undertaken by mankind."[33]

Are the IPCC scenarios correct? Emanuel writes: "While it is easy to stand on the sidelines and take shots at these models [of the future], they represent science's best effort to project the Earth's climate over the next century or so. At the same time, the large range of possible outcomes is an objective quantification of the uncertainty that remains in this enterprise. Still, those who proclaim that the models are wrong or useless usually are taking advantage of science's imperfections to promote their own prejudices."[34]

Put another way, without scientific models our assessment of climate change might vary all the way from, "We are going to burn out Earth's atmosphere just as happened on Mars," to "Who cares, the Apocalypse is coming soon." Instead, decision-makers can rely on a reasoned IPCC statement that "continued emission of greenhouse gases will cause further warming and long-lasting changes in all components of the climate system, increasing the likelihood of severe, pervasive and irreversible impacts for people and ecosystems. Limiting climate change would require substantial and sustained reductions in greenhouse gas emissions which, together with adaptation, can limit climate change risks."[35]

The IPCC reports its findings in a set of scenarios it calls RCPs, in which "RCP" stands for "representative concentration pathway."[36] As scientists are wont to do when they express themselves in words, they have already lost some of us readers – so herewith, an explanation. First, the IPCC's focus, the thing it most wants to tell policymakers about, is what we think of when we loosely imagine "the amount of greenhouse gases in the atmosphere." They focus on this because, as is widely accepted, more greenhouse gases lead to more global warming because of the "greenhouse," or "hothouse," effect.

What their models specifically measure is radiative forcing, which is the difference between incoming and outgoing radiation. That is, radiative forcing is the difference between the sun's energy that arrives at, and is absorbed by, the Earth and the energy that is radiated back into space. Changes in forcing cause temperatures to rise or fall: The more energy that is radiated back into space, the cooler the planet. Forcing is affected by such factors as greenhouse gases, air pollutants (aerosols and other substances that create ozone), and land use. Less energy escapes when the atmosphere, altered by these factors, prevents it from doing so.

Each RCP is identified by a number that refers to the amount of radiative forcing it allows, such as RCP 2.6, RCP 4.5, RCP 6, and RCP 8.5. For instance, RCP 2.6 is a scenario in which greenhouse gases increase by 2.6 W/m^2 (watts per meter squared). Unfortunately, these numbers are also often referred to informally as the "quantity" of greenhouse gases in a given scenario, which is inaccurate. What is more accurate to say is that the more energy that escapes through the atmosphere, the less the global warming, and the lower the RCP. An RCP with a low number assumes society will get emissions under control to some extent, while a high number assumes emissions will grow.

By "representative" concentration path scenario, the IPCC means, "Here is one scenario that is a summary of a set of scenarios in this range." Each scenario is created from a review of the existing scientific research, including peer-reviewed models developed independently by various modeling groups, and each represents all major scenarios known in that range.[37] A range could include low or medium or high values, for example.

To make things easy for policymakers, the IPCC typically publishes four scenarios, but they might have chosen three or eight or some other number (and simply crunched the numbers differently). The RCP projections are used to help lay audiences predict and plan for future events like changes in Earth's surface temperature, sea ice extent, and ocean acidity. They mainly predict out to 2100, with some extensions to 2300, and they use comparative data back to 1850.

To further aid policymakers, the IPCC scenarios also express how confident scientists are in their predictions. They do this in two ways. One process is entirely quantitative. It considers the amount, type, quality, and consistency of the evidence and assesses risk quantitatively based on that evidence. Its results are expressed as probabilities, which are further summarized in a five-point range from "exceptionally unlikely" (0) to "virtually certain" (5).

In a parallel process, the scientist-authors of the scenarios get together to discuss their accumulated results and debate how confident they are as a group that their recommendations are correct. This evaluation is subjective, because it is based not strictly on the data but rather on the scientist-authors' discussions. It is expressed as a "level of confidence" in a five-point range from "very low confidence" to "very high confidence."

Of course, humans' subjective assessment of rare events like high RCPs is influenced by their distinctive decision-making capabilities. Research suggests that when people have not actually experienced a rare event such as an earthquake, or a long-term environmental threat like climate change, they are likely to downplay the probability of it happening in the future. In fact, they are likely to assign to it a lower probability of happening than objective facts would indicate. This human tendency may influence scientists' assessments of climate risks. As Kahneman observes, "When it comes to rare probabilities, our mind is not designed to get things quite right. For the residents of a planet that may be exposed to events no one has yet experienced, this is not good news."[38]

3. WHAT EXACTLY IS AT RISK?

Based on these scenarios, the IPCC examines the state of the planet today as compared to the state of the planet historically, and then offers predictions of the future. A typical report like this summary from the IPCC in 2013 describes both its specific findings and general trends:

> Warming of the climate system is unequivocal, and since the 1950s, many of the observed changes are unprecedented over decades to millennia. The atmosphere and ocean have warmed, the amounts of snow and ice have diminished, sea level has risen, and the concentrations of greenhouse gases have increased.
>
> Each of the last three decades has been successively warmer at the Earth's surface than any preceding decade since 1850. In the Northern Hemisphere, 1983–2012 was *likely* the warmest 30-year period of the last 1400 years (medium confidence).
>
> The rate of sea level rise since the mid-19th century has been larger than the mean rate during the previous two millennia (high confidence).
>
> The atmospheric concentrations of carbon dioxide, methane, and nitrous oxide have increased to levels unprecedented in at least the last 800,000 years (very high confidence). Carbon dioxide concentrations have increased by 40% since pre-industrial times, primarily from fossil fuel emissions and secondarily from net land-use change emissions. The ocean has absorbed about 30% of the emitted anthropogenic carbon dioxide, causing ocean acidification.[39]

After assessing the current state of the planet, the IPCC researchers then offer scenarios that describe probable changes in the carbon cycle and the Earth if humanity continues to burn greenhouse gases. For instance, in 2013 they had decided that:

> Continued emissions of greenhouse gases will cause further warming and changes in all components of the climate system.
>
> Global surface temperature change for the end of the 21st century is *likely* to exceed 1.5°C relative to 1850 to 1900 for all RCP scenarios except RCP2.6 [in which emissions are reduced].

The global ocean will continue to warm during the 21st century. Heat will penetrate from the surface to the deep ocean and affect ocean circulation. It is *very likely* that the Atlantic Meridional Overturning Circulation (AMOC) will weaken over the 21st century.

It is *very likely* that the Arctic sea ice cover will continue to shrink and thin and that Northern Hemisphere spring snow cover will decrease ... Global glacier volume will further decrease.

Climate change will affect carbon cycle processes in a way that will [accelerate] the increase of CO_2 in the atmosphere. Further uptake of carbon by the ocean will increase ocean acidification.

Most aspects of climate change will persist for many centuries even if emissions of CO_2 are stopped.[40]

These atmospheric changes influence key global systems including the water cycle, the air, and the oceans. The IPCC concluded, for example, that these changes will exacerbate current trends in precipitation, bringing more drought to some regions and more rain to others. They will increase local air pollution. They will slow the AMOC, which is the ocean current that flows between the Gulf of Mexico and the North Atlantic, and which warms Europe, but they will not drive the AMOC to collapse in the twenty-first century. (That's important: Were the AMOC to collapse, surface temperatures in Europe might decrease by a dozen degrees Fahrenheit.)[41]

The IPCC predictions are not without their scientist critics, some of whom see them as too conservative in identifying risks. This concern makes sense. Taking their information from peer-reviewed journals that are subject to publication time lags, and utilizing a time-consuming group processing of that data, IPCC information must always be seen as a screen capture that does not account for more recent research and which may be affected by compromises and various psychological phenomena.

For instance, the AMOC is such an important phenomenon that it is continually being studied by numerous scientific organizations, including the US CLIVAR (Climate Variability and Predictability) Program, which is a joint effort of NASA, the NOAA, the National Science Foundation (NSF), and the US Department of Energy. One recent study by this team suggests that the AMOC may be slowing down faster than the IPCC summary reports of 2013 suggested.[42]

Other recent scientific opinions emphasize that the loss of ice mass and the impact of various climate feedbacks worldwide may be exponential rather than linear. Because the melting will grow not at a steady rate but rather more and more rapidly, it will cause much faster sea level rise than has been predicted.[43] A group of scientists led by James Hansen points out that while the Earth has warmed 1° Celsius since 1850, and 75 per cent of that warming has occurred since 1975, we have yet to see the systems impact of that recent warming.

Further, some independent scientists suggest that if greenhouse gas emissions continue to grow, multi-meter sea level rise will be "practically unavoidable, probably within 50–150 years."[44] Also, they argue, the AMOC would most likely shut down fully within the next several decades. They warn that setting a target of limiting global warming to 2° Celsius "does not provide safety."[45]

Understanding the psychology of risk is important and developing human systems to deal with risk is crucial. Two practical questions are: Where are climate and energy risks playing out now? and How are people dealing with them? Next, we examine some of the implications of climate and energy risk that leaders must weigh in real time, on the ground in their local communities, businesses, and nations.

Among policymakers, it is a truism that the most important impacts of climate change and the actions to deal with them are being experienced at the local level. It is the city or county, the state or province, that must bear the brunt of climate risks. Local governments manage the nitty-gritty details of predicting extreme climate events and planning how to mop up afterward. They are the people who work to stay current on scientific and engineering developments. They are the

policymakers who prepare for a challenging energy future by diversifying energy sources now.

Rotterdam and New York are major coastal cities that have already
experienced significant climate-related impacts. How they are managing risk today demonstrates a diversity of approaches that can be
instructive to other municipalities.

Rotterdam is the second-largest city in the Netherlands, a country
reclaimed from the ocean that today is 24 per cent below sea level.[46]
The city itself rests 80 per cent at or below sea level. It is built on peat,
which is partly decomposed vegetable matter that settles and com-
pacts over time and further lowers the ground. One of the world's
most vulnerable cities, Rotterdam is at risk from sea level rise and the
impacts of extreme precipitation like flash floods and droughts.

Rotterdam has a population of over 600,000, and it is Europe's largest port. As one of the world's earliest adopters of climate resilience
planning, the city emphasizes climate policies that embrace both
opportunities and risks. The international Institution of Civil Engineers (ICE) publishes case studies on how communities assess and
adapt to risk, and it offers the following analysis of how the city is
coping.[47]

In 1953, a flood in the Rotterdam region killed 1,800 people and
led to the construction of many of the protective features that exist
there now. These include protective dikes, dams, and surge barriers.
Nevertheless, today much of the city's infrastructure, including power
stations, railways, and water purification plants, is located outside of
the dikes. In fact, about 40,000 of Rotterdam's residents live outside
the dikes. Moreover, as the city's peat foundation settles, it destabi-
lizes the dikes.

Officials in the Netherlands believe that climate change cannot
be prevented "even with all the good intentions of the world," that
the country must adapt, and that decentralizing decision-making to
provinces and municipalities is the best option.[48] To some extent,
Rotterdam pursues climate mitigation by attempting to reduce CO_2

emissions using energy efficiency, sustainable energy, and carbon capture and storage. However, it focuses even more on adaptation. Its target is to be climate-proof, to "ensure not only residents' safety but also their perceived safety from extremes of precipitation, water level fluctuations, droughts and heat, and groundwater salinization."[49] Rotterdam also sees an opportunity to present itself as a world leader in the development of strategy and technology for climate adaptation.

The ICE analysts make a point of critiquing all the community interventions they report on. In this case, they note that mitigation as a local concept has had little real effect on the broader picture of carbon emissions in the Netherlands. They also point out that the city's adaptation plans were created by organizational stakeholders and adopted by the city without much public involvement.

Indeed, they note, in part because flood prevention measures are so widely visible in the city, Rotterdam's citizens have become complacent. More than half of them don't even know whether they are living outside or inside the dikes. We know that people are more likely to act after they have themselves experienced such climate impacts as flooding, yet recent generations living in Rotterdam have not had any such experience. ICE analysts believe that making Rotterdam climate-proof is an inspirational goal that could be motivating to the local citizenry. They also note approvingly that the city's mitigation goals are specific and can be independently verified. Unfortunately, that few of Rotterdam's citizens know about these policies continues to be a major challenge for the city and the country.

New York City residents may be more motivated. Hit hard by Hurricane Sandy in 2012, the city suffered a blow to its citizens, its infrastructure, and its classic hubris.[50] At the time, the hurricane was the second most costly in American history.[51] Damage in the United States alone was estimated at over $70 billion and hundreds were killed along the storm's path, including seventy-one who died in New York State.

New York City has more waterfront than Miami, Boston, Los Angeles, and San Francisco combined.[52] According to the Federal Emergency Management Agency (FEMA), because of anticipated sea level rise, by the 2050s, 24 per cent of New York City will be in danger of flooding in a 100-year storm.[53] The definition of a 100-year storm is not, as one might imagine, a storm that might occur once every 100 years. It is, rather, a storm that has a 1 per cent chance of occurring in any given year. When one considers the potential effects on millions of people and thousands of businesses, including some of the most important company headquarters in the world, these odds are short.

The insurance firm Swiss Re predicts that, in New York City, climate change will double its anticipated annual losses due to claims by 2050, and catastrophic events that happen on average every seventy years will quadruple its costs. The New York City transportation system has had a hard time finding traditional flood insurance for the subway system. It relies instead on a debt instrument called a catastrophe bond, which pays high interest to investors betting against the occurrence of such a disaster.[54]

Soon after Hurricane Sandy, Mayor Michael R. Bloomberg committed the city to a resilience plan that would cost nearly $20 billion, second only to the resilience budget for the Gulf Coast of Louisiana, which in 2012, after Hurricane Katrina, was set at $50 billion. Among other things, the New York plan supports raising homes, buildings, and vital infrastructure to avoid rising sea water. It enhances existing natural barriers, such as dunes, wetlands, and beaches that dampen waves. It plans levees and flood walls. It offers loans and grants to help people retrofit their homes. The plan does not include retreating from the Manhattan waterfront or buying out owners.[55] New York City citizens can see how their tax dollars are being spent on a detailed website initiated by the Mayor's Office of Recovery and Resiliency.[56]

Steve Cohen, executive director of the Earth Institute and Professor in the Practice of Public Affairs in the School of International and Public Affairs at Columbia University, says it isn't realistic to view the risks to New York as "solvable" problems. Rather, he says, we need to view them as problems we can "make less bad."[57] Vicki Arroyo, director of the Georgetown Climate Center at Georgetown University Law Center, a clearinghouse for climate adaptation programs, observes that citizens now view climate planning as inevitable: "People realize this is the new normal and the next normal. It's going to be a future that doesn't look like the past, and it's going to be a future that is dynamic."[58]

Rotterdam and New York have a lot in common. They are cities constructed in risky venues, and the climate clock is ticking. Meanwhile, rather than focusing on mitigating risk by reducing their greenhouse gas emissions, their policies emphasize local risk and possible adaptations. The two cities also illustrate the important role of subnational governments in acting on climate change. As noted by David Miller, former mayor of Toronto, cities matter because in the twenty-first century, "for the first time in the history of human civilization, urban populations surpassed rural ... And the trend to urbanization is only growing more pronounced."[59]

Governments at this level are today coming together for systemic change. For instance, in 2016, the State of California hosted the first international Subnational Clean Energy Ministerial for cities, states, and regions that have endorsed the goals of the Paris agreement. Encouraged by Governor Jerry Brown, the goal of this organization is to bring together subnational governments to share information and resources. The coalition represents 17 per cent of the global population and nearly 40 per cent of the global economy.[60]

Businesses today face a wide range of climate risks, from the physical to the legal. The obvious risks are physical, including the associated costs from damage by storms, wildfires, drought, and sea level rise. Among other things, physical damage incurs replacement costs and leads to production disruption.

Many companies are insured against these risks. One might think that the insurance industry itself would bear the brunt of their costs.

Warren Buffett, of insurance giant Berkshire Hathaway, clearly expresses concern for communities: "As a citizen, you may understandably find climate change keeping you up nights. As a homeowner in a low-lying area, you may wish to consider moving."[61] But he reminds us that many such expenses are pass-throughs. Given that insurance premiums are rewritten each year and repriced to reflect changing risks, much of the cost of insuring physical risks is passed on to the consumer, including businesses and their customers. As Buffett observes,

> When you are thinking only as a shareholder of a major insurer, climate change should not be on your list of worries ... *Up to now*, climate change has not produced more frequent nor more costly hurricanes nor other weather-related events covered by insurance. As a consequence, U.S. super-cat [category storm] rates have fallen steadily in recent years, which is why we have backed away from that business. If super-cats become costlier and more frequent, the likely – though far from certain – effect on Berkshire's insurance business would be to make it larger and more profitable. (Emphasis added)[62]

However, costs are now rising. Buffett was writing in 2016, just one year before the 2017 Atlantic hurricane season that brought Harvey, Irma, and Maria and constituted the most expensive hurricane season in history.[63] The 2018 season had fifteen named storms (the average is twelve), including the major destructive hurricanes Florence and Michael. The 2019 Atlantic season was the fourth consecutive year of above-average storm activity, during which Category Five Hurricane Dorian devastated portions of the Bahamas. In January 2019, after major fires and financial setbacks in California, the large utility PG&E was forced into bankruptcy.

Business risk also includes lawsuits and litigation. For instance, major economies, including the United States, have required businesses to disclose climate-related risks in their periodic financial reports, but the level of disclosure has varied widely. Companies that have faced lawsuits due to alleged lack of disclosure to shareholders include oil and gas giant ExxonMobil and the world's largest coal company, Peabody Energy.[64]

Additional risks to business include regulatory changes that disrupt business as usual. For example, the Clean Air Act reduces the viability of industries that pollute, and it improves opportunities for those that do not. Also, all government-subsidized energy industries, whether fossil fuels or renewables, face the vagaries of politics. Finally, all businesses face the risk that their competitors will outcompete them in managing climate risks.

Even now, climate change certainly presents risk to governments and societies. In Syria, the 2006–10 drought turned 60 per cent of that country into a desert and killed 80 per cent of its cattle. It forced farmers into cities and was a factor in the devastating civil war that emerged.[65] In the Sahel agricultural regions south of the Sahara, climate refugees are travelling north over treacherous desert to escape desertification and more frequent droughts. Islands already vulnerable to sea level rise include the Marshall Islands, Kiribati, Tuvalu, Tonga, the Federated States of Micronesia, and the Cook Islands (all in the Pacific Ocean); Antigua and Nevis (in the Caribbean Sea); and the Maldives (in the Indian Ocean).[66] In North America, areas under near-term threat from sea level rise include Tangier Island in Virginia and Prince Edward Island in Canada, as well as communities in Alaska on the Bering Sea coast and in the Arctic.

Since the carbon from burning fossil fuels remains in the atmosphere for tens of thousands of years, in the longer term even more sea level rise will occur. If humanity burns all of the planet's fossil fuels, scientists suggest that seas will rise on average tens of meters.[67] As one eclectic group of high-level scientists warns, "That order of sea level rise would result in the loss of hundreds of historical coastal cities worldwide with incalculable economic consequences, create hundreds of millions of global warming refugees from highly-populated low-lying areas, and thus likely cause major international conflicts."[68]

In his book *Collapse: How Societies Choose to Fail or Succeed,* geographer Jared Diamond examines how societies disintegrate. After an exhaustive review, he concludes that they collapse mainly because of environmental problems and resource shortages. Clearly, whole societies can fail to make the right decisions, for, as Diamond puts it, a "whole sequence of reasons: failure to anticipate a problem, failure to perceive it once it has arisen, failure to attempt to solve it after it has been perceived, and failure to succeed in attempts to solve it."[69]

Diamond points to Easter Island as one example of how a group of people can destroy themselves by overexploiting their natural resources. Easter Islanders deforested their small island over a period of about 800 years, with the consequence that they had fewer and fewer raw materials, wild-caught foods, and even crops. Eventually, the society went extinct. "How on earth could a society make such an obviously disastrous decision as to cut down all the trees on which it depended?" Diamond's students have asked. How often have people intentionally created ecological damage? How often have they done so by accident? How did the guy feel who cut down the last tree?[70]

It should be noted that Diamond is not without his critics, who argue that on Easter Island factors like the introduction of diseases and predatory species played a more important role than resource depletion in that society's demise.[71] Yet, Diamond argues that it is not just one but many societies that have collapsed because they overran their resources. He warns that the world is moving that way today. He notes that the environmental problems facing societies then and now fall into four categories: destruction or loss of natural resources, ceilings on natural resources, harmful things that people produce or move around, and population issues. In all the societal collapses Diamond studied, deforestation was the major factor.

Today we are rapidly destroying the natural environment, including, yes, the forests, but also wild foods, wild species, and soils. Like other threatened societies, we face ceilings on existing amounts of energy and freshwater. Even our photosynthetic capacity is threatened: About half of our available sunlight is diverted away from practical uses like growing crops and falls instead onto concrete roads and buildings. At the same time, we are producing and distributing toxic chemicals, alien species, and atmospheric gases. Finally, our population is growing, and as living standards improve worldwide, low-impact people are becoming high-impact people. Low-impact people are also moving to high-impact countries and adopting their standards.

On the one hand, brave leaders and peoples can see these problems and work to fix them, and on that score Diamond is optimistic. On the other hand, will we know when to really start worrying? Diamond thinks probably not. One of the main lessons of his research is that after a society reaches its peak in terms of population numbers, wealth, and power, a steep decline is likely to begin within decades. Societies have been powerless – one might say leaderless – to stop it.

4. PROFESSIONAL RISK ANALYSIS

Risk analysis is a well-accepted and rapidly advancing set of techniques for analyzing how environmental (and other) threats may impact business and community assets. In many organizations, risk management is a job description, and it is also an umbrella term that includes a wide range of risk analysis and uncertainty analysis. In business, risk management professionals are found in finance departments, insurance brokerages and underwriting, human resources departments, and safety units. Increasingly, they are found in divisions that work on business strategy, including the legal department and the corporate board of directors. In government, they work on loss prediction, prevention, and services for communities.

Not surprisingly, risk management professionals typically study management science that includes predictive modeling. Specializing in risk management requires strong quantitative skills and is often the purview of majors in finance or operations. Experience in law, accounting, compliance, insurance, or operations is also considered useful.

Trained risk managers periodically reassess ongoing risks to their organization. They know how to find the best available information, notably scientific information, and how to take human factors into account. They create value for their companies and communities when the resources they expend to identify and mitigate risk are less than the consequences of inaction.

An important aspect of their work is to routinely introduce risk concepts into organizational processes and decision-making. They begin by identifying threats and estimating how strong the risk is that the identified threats will impact important assets. Risk managers then help their organizations prioritize which risks will have the greatest probability of occurring and the greatest impact. For instance, if an investment will exist in the year 2100, it will, according to most models, exist under significantly different climate conditions. How should owners prepare? Risk professionals identify interventions to reduce the risks and help their companies or communities prioritize for action.

As a global institution that assesses risk, the World Bank advises businesses and governments worldwide on how to make optimal decisions about climate risk.[72] The Bank helps decision-makers identify the best ways to incorporate climate change over a project's lifetime, including assessment of a project's vulnerability and costs. The Bank points out that while some climate change decisions have relatively short-term impacts and can be reliably quantified, others are more challenging.

Short-term decisions include figuring out how much insurance to buy and what financial investments to make. However, other decisions will have impacts over 50 to 200 years and cannot be so easily quantified. Where to site a building, how to design buildings that must survive a variety of climate conditions, and how to develop infrastructure for water management and transportation are all decisions that must be made under conditions of uncertainty. The Bank recognizes risk and uncertainty as different levels of ignorance that planners have about the future.

Of course, when climate was more stable, risk could be more easily estimated. Earlier generations of planners could rely on historical weather and climate data to make reasonable predictions about the future. Engineers could use such predictions to design buildings, and farmers could use them to plan their crops. Planners could predict extreme flood levels and design infrastructure to cope within relatively predictable safety margins. Rapid climate change has altered all of this. Because climate warming has accelerated in more recent years, drawing straight-line extrapolations over long periods tells leaders little.

Having studied such technical strategies as cost-benefit analysis under uncertainty, the World Bank concludes that considering a blend of methodologies and carefully matching a methodology to the situation can improve decisions under climate uncertainty. It recommends that decision-makers work with the uncertainty using probabilities. It cautions that, rather than being definitive, such analytic methods are mainly tools that help to organize and drive participation and analysis. Basing decisions on probabilistic models requires stakeholders themselves to weigh those models.

For instance, under climate change, Ghana, in West Africa, faces significant changes in precipitation rates. Planners there have developed models that predict a very large potential range of precipitation, from a 20 per cent increase to a 30 per cent decrease, and Ghanaian engineers face the challenging task of designing for more than one scenario. Only by integrating actual options and weighing them with probability analysis can they plan creatively. For example, planners concerned with drought may decide to build one small dam that can be expanded rather than a larger dam that will never be needed.

Unfortunately, applying professional risk management can make problems seem more manageable than they really are. Australian business professors Christopher Wright and Daniel Nyberg, in their book *Climate Change, Capitalism, and Corporations*, point out that

> By making our climate uncertainties seemingly manageable and rendering them a basis for opportunity and profit, corporate constructions of climate risk emphasise once again a vision of human mastery over nature. Like latter-day wizardry, the calculus of risk management demonstrates the ability of markets and capital to not only control the natural world but somehow anticipate it ...
>
> However, the truth is that this approach closes off the possibility of the dramatic emissions reductions that scientists have shown are necessary to avoid calamitous climate change. Tragically – some might even say scandalously – corporate risk framings remain wedded to "business as usual" scenarios and singularly fail to acknowledge the desperate exigencies of a carbon-constrained world. Precisely the kind of devastating environmental change that is supposedly being anticipated and avoided is thus locked in to an even more terrifying degree.[73]

In this way of thinking, when it comes to contributing to Team Humanity's great climate project, risk managers and their organizations must face squarely the limitations of their predilections.

5. NO EXCUSES

Given our advanced science and technology, humanity today cannot plead ignorance about climate and energy risks. Leaders have responded by stepping up to point this out and to act on the immediate challenges.

On the climate change front, early on, the former mayor of New York, Michael Bloomberg, the former US Secretary of the Treasury (for George W. Bush) Hank Paulson, and businessman and philanthropist Tom Steyer created the Risky Business Project to focus on the economic risks and opportunities for the United States under climate change. In an op-ed in the *Washington Post*, the three founders stress the importance of taking climate risks seriously: "As businessmen and public servants, we are intimately familiar with the systems used to manage risk. They are central to informed decision-making. But today, the world faces one of the greatest humanitarian and economic challenges of our time: the threat of global climate change. And in this arena, our risk-assessment systems have broken down. This ignorance cannot be allowed to continue ... How much economic risk do we face from unmitigated climate change?"[74]

The Risky Business Project examines impacts of climate change by region and sector in the United States to help decision-makers address local climate risk. Its founders point out that "the U.S. economy faces significant risks from unabated climate change. Every year of inaction serves to broaden and deepen these risks."[75] Their initiatives include promoting clean energy as "the next big business opportunity" and electrifying the US economy.

In a related initiative, Bloomberg has chaired a task force on climate-related financial disclosures for the international monitoring group Financial Stability Board.[76] The goal of this initiative is to develop voluntary, consistent disclosures for investors and other stakeholders. Steyer's organization Next Generation, working mainly in California, has supported, among other legislation, a proposition that successfully allocated 50 per cent of a projected $1.1 billion in annual savings to energy efficiency and clean energy projects in public buildings.[77]

In a special report reviewing world dependence on fossil fuels, *The Economist* writes,

> The world needs to face the prospect of an end to the oil era, even if
> for the moment it still seems relatively remote ... Will the industry as a
> whole deal with climate change by researching and investing in alter-
> natives to fossil fuels, or will it fight with gritted teeth for an oil-based
> future? Will the vast array of investors in the oil industry be prepared
> to take climate change on board? And will consumers in both rich and
> poor countries be willing to forsake the roar of a petrol engine for the
> hum of a battery?[78]

Their questions succinctly summarize the world's global energy risks and point to businesses themselves as potential change agents.

Are our proposed interventions going to be enough? The short answer is "Probably not." Jared Diamond asserts that societies must "courageously" embrace long-term thinking and make "anticipatory decisions at a time when problems have become perceptible but before they have reached crisis proportions." There is not one prob-lem to be solved, but rather thousands and even millions of them, and because these problems are interactive with each other, human-ity must solve many of them.

Diamond argues that to do this, people must make "painful" deci-sions about core values. When earlier civilizations refused to abandon parts of their identities, the consequence was that they died out. For humanity today, Diamond puts the choice this way: "A lower-impact society is the most impossible scenario for our future – except for all other conceivable scenarios."[79]

• • •

In this practice we have examined the psychology of risk and how complex climate and energy risks are modeled for lay audiences and policymakers. We have considered practical risk management issues and strategies in communities, businesses, and society. We have noted that critics of risk management programs believe they contribute to the dangerously complacent belief that humans are in control of the natural world.

In the end, understanding risk, from perceiving it to modeling it, is essential for climate managers, policymakers, communicators, and, need we add, for citizens. Climate and energy risks are real, if sometimes remote. They are complex, if little understood. The challenge they present must be addressed by leaders now, not 100 years from now or even decades from now. Sophisticated risk analysis can help, and leaders in all sectors of society are beginning to pay attention.

PRACTICE 3

Weigh the Stakes

Just as the temperate Holocene fostered humans' development as a species, so the fossil fuel era has allowed us to thrive as a civilization. But that was then. Now we face epic changes in the natural systems on which we depend, changes we have brought upon ourselves by burning those very same fossil fuels. So powerful are we that in an historical nanosecond we have melted great glaciers, altered the acidity of the oceans, and raised the temperature of the entire planet. As fossil fuel supplies dwindle and their effects mount, that power is running out. The challenge that remains is to unravel and rework this tapestry of mad genius.

If humanity rises to the climate and energy moment, it will do so because of its leaders – individuals who observe business as usual and strive to do better. Typically, leaders work within organizations, and we will always need leaders in these kinds of roles. Yet, we also need leaders who can step up to work across sectors and for society as a whole. We need leaders who aspire to understand and improve global systems. And they, in turn, need followers who are wise enough to support them.

Change will not be easy. To cite just one obstacle, adopting this kind of global view flies in the face of a worldwide populism that today aspires to retreat to home and country. Yet, the stakes are high. Two compelling realities are driving societies toward global action. The first is the documented, ongoing damage to the planet. If sea levels hadn't already risen to engulf island nations and great storms hadn't already damaged major cities, there would be much less international concern about our warming planet.

The second compelling reality is evolution in the energy sector. After a century and a half of dominance by conventional oil, at this point a much more complex energy sector is in play. The trend line is that access to fossil fuels is diminishing, while the use of renewable energy is increasing. Yet, without a powerful source of energy like oil, there is no modern civilization. If forced to depend on alternative energy that, at this point, is intermittent (solar and wind), or environmentally risky (nuclear), civilization as we know it must change drastically. As put by Jonathan Ford of the *Financial Times*, "While talk of a fully, or largely, renewable society may not be empty, it cannot with the tools at our disposal come without impact on our lives. The variables are to have fewer people, or to reduce the scope of our activities. Otherwise we must redouble our search for other technologies that can do the job at lower cost."[1] Leaders must work with the scientific status quo while keeping an eye on potential technical solutions to our energy problems.[2]

Thus, the third practice of climate leaders is to understand the relationships among stakeholders and sectors, with emphasis on the energy sector. In this chapter, we examine a variety of energy and community stakeholders and reflect on what it takes to lead at the sector level. We explore the psychology of inter-sector cooperation and competition. Under what circumstances do humans trust each other enough to work together? Do we trust each other enough to overcome our differences?

We begin with an overview of the energy sector.

1. THE ENERGY SECTOR

Millions of years ago, decayed plant and animal matter was buried hundreds to thousands of feet underground. Over time, the energy

from that fossil matter, which originated in photosynthesis, was sub-
jected to heat and pressure, and when fossil fuels are burned today
they release that energy. Because it took millions of years and particular conditions to produce, fossil fuel energy is, for all practical
purposes, nonrenewable. Of all the energy used today in the United
States, about 80 per cent derives from fossil fuels, with the remain-
der coming from renewable energy, including nuclear power. Among
the fossil fuels, oil is burned the most frequently, followed by natural
gas and coal. In 2017 fossil fuel usage was at its lowest percentage of
overall consumption since 1902, having decreased for three consecutive years.[3] However, most observers predict that fossil fuel usage will
continue to contribute significantly to energy usage decades from
now. One prominent energy consultant predicts that in 2040 coal, oil,
and gas will still contribute about 85 per cent of the world's primary
energy supplies.[4]

Today, 94 per cent of oil is consumed in the transportation and
industrial sectors, with usage in the transportation sector 2.4 times
greater than usage in the industrial sector. The most consumed petroleum product is gasoline.[5] Oil is also used to make plastic, lubricants,
chemicals, and asphalt, among other things. (If you use a moisturizer,
you are probably wearing oil right now.) Natural gas is used almost
equally in electrical power and industrial applications, with residential and commercial applications not far behind. Only about 3 per
cent of natural gas production is used for transportation.[6] In the coal
sector, roughly 93 per cent is burned to produce electrical power.[7]

These usage statistics point to the major inter-sector relationships
that exist currently. Certain stakes are clear. The oil sector is closely
linked to transportation interests. Natural gas producers have stakes
in a variety of sectors, including electricity production and transportation. The coal sector depends on electrical power companies.

The usage statistics also show that to reduce carbon emissions
significantly, leaders must look well beyond the familiar territory of
residential and commercial uses to work with large stakeholders in

electrical power, transportation, and manufacturing. In other words, they cannot merely work close to home; they must engage in the political arena of entrenched, complex industrial systems.

The increasing competition among energy sources raises the stakes for all these stakeholders. Companies in the pharmaceutical, agricultural, and other industries that rely on fossil fuels must plan for an uncertain future in which oil prices fluctuate and, over time, rise. They must consider if and when they can transition to renewables. Countries in favorable resource positions are trying to figure out whether, as a matter of national defense, they might become energy independent. Other not-so-fortunate countries work to maintain good relationships with their suppliers. Worldwide, such global institutions as exist – mainly philanthropic organizations and a few global bodies like the United Nations, the World Trade Organization, and the European Union – are attempting to estimate future trade-offs among energy sources and local needs.

In the next sections, we explore this system of energy stakeholders and their stakes. We open with a discussion of fossil fuel and renewable energy companies, and then move to applications in communities.

2. OIL

The big three fossil fuels have always competed for the consumer's dollar, and until now oil has been the big winner. In the late eighteenth century, oil displaced coal because it was relatively easy to mine and transport, did not suffer from the disruptive (and justified) labor conflicts that afflicted coal mining, and was the fuel of choice in the new internal combustion engine. When burned, coal is also much dirtier than oil; our Victorian and Edwardian foremothers dusted their coal-fired homes endlessly and, according to my grandmother, were thrilled to switch to gas and oil.

Today, oil and gas often compete against each other. Gas is cheaper, but oil packs more energy punch. When a skyscraper needs heat, a building manager may turn first to cheaper gas, but when the temperature gets very low, he switches to a backup system powered by oil. Oil is also less volatile. While being stored or transported, it is much less likely than gas to explode. Natural gas pipelines have a limit of about 2,500 miles, whereas oil flows readily over long distances, including under oceans.

Unfortunately, oil is becoming harder to find. Early in the fossil fuel era, American companies relied on American oil alone, exploiting fields in Texas, Oklahoma, and Louisiana, and later in California and Alaska. Their main plays in those days were in light sweet crude, the kind of oil that you can see gushing out of the ground in old movies. As these resources were tapping out and light sweet crude was discovered in Saudi Arabia, Americans began to buy Middle Eastern oil.

Meanwhile, the light sweet crude of yesteryear has been increasingly replaced by more adulterated, hard-to-mine petroleum products. World oil reserves today consist of roughly one-fourth conventional oil (light sweet crude) and three-fourths nonconventional oil. The latter is made up of heavy oil, extra heavy oil, and tar sands oil (also called bitumen), each more polluting than the last.

While light crude is a relatively pure product, nonconventional oil is mixed with other substances like rock, sand, and relatively high concentrations of sulfur and heavy metals. When burned, the associated pollutants foul the air. Also, to extract nonconventional oil, it must sometimes be, essentially, cooked. Retrieving oil from gushing wells requires little energy, while cooking it out of rock requires a great deal of energy. The result is a reduced energy return on energy invested (referred to as EROEI or EROI). In 1930, one unit of energy put into producing oil created 100 units of energy: The EROEI of oil was 100. Today, according to *Forbes,* the EROEI of oil, which includes substantially more unconventional oil, is closer to 15.[8]

It follows that when trying to predict how long oil supplies will last, policymakers cannot consider only how many barrels of oil we have in the ground. They must also consider how much energy it takes to extract that energy.[9]

While the easiest oil was exploited globally, the race was on to improve technologies that could extract more oil, and more different types of oil, from more difficult places. Oil companies, at times applying federal government research, developed alternative extraction techniques like undersea drilling and hydraulic fracturing ("fracking"). Undersea drilling can now be undertaken miles beneath the ocean. Fracking releases oil embedded in rock deep underground by injecting water and chemicals under pressure, permitting the exploitation of the nonconventional oil that is often referred to as "dirty oil."

By exploiting such innovations, in 2015 the United States was the world's top producer of petroleum and natural gas,[10] and was exporting nearly five million barrels per day (MBD) of petroleum. (At the same time, it was importing nine MBD of petroleum.)[11] In 2017, imports of petroleum had risen to 10.14 MBD, while exports, including refined oil (82 per cent) and crude oil (18 per cent), were 6.38 MBD.[12] US daily consumption is about 20 MBD.[13] The United States uses about 20 per cent of all world oil production.[14]

According to petroleum geologist Art Berman, writing in *Forbes* in 2015, such numbers should not reassure Americans. Yes, production is higher, but consumption remains high. "We are far more economically vulnerable and dependent on foreign oil today than we were when crude oil export was banned 40 years ago."[15] Berman refers to the 1973 Arab–Israeli War, when Arab members of the Organization of Petroleum Exporting Countries (OPEC) placed an embargo on their oil to the United States and its allies. At the time of the Arab Oil Embargo, US consumption was only 12 MBD.[16] The experience of standing in line to get gasoline raised Americans' awareness of their dependence on foreign oil. Henceforth, discoveries of oil in friendly places like Norway and Canada, and America's own Bakken, Permian, and Eagle Ford fields (in which oil is available through fracking), have been greeted with some relief.

But Berman also reminds Americans that the world is facing the challenge of oil depletion, heralded by peak oil. He observes that "energy and oil in particular underlie everything in our global economic lives. Oil prices reflect our collective emotional response to the circumstances of the world ... It is a curious paradox that peak oil should manifest in the midst of over-supply and low oil prices. That is certainly not how I thought things would happen. Perceptions will change and oil-market balance will be restored in ways that few of us thought likely. Peak oil will be part of that change."[17] (Peak oil is the point at which the world has used up 50 per cent of global reserves.)

A 2010 peer-reviewed report on the status of conventional world oil reserves notes that "while there is [sic] certainly vast amounts of fossil fuel resources left in the ground, the volume of oil that can be commercially exploited at prices the global economy has become accustomed to is limited and will soon decline. The result is that oil may soon shift from a demand-led market to a supply constrained market."[18] Despite denials from such industry consultants as Daniel Yergin, many observers in business, academia, and government agree that oil has either peaked, or will soon.

Anecdotal evidence to this point is common enough. For example, even though it is the largest remaining reservoir of light sweet crude, Saudi Arabia is planning significant investments in solar farms and petrochemicals.[19] It has also attempted to shift some oil depletion risk to the market by creating the public company Saudi Aramco. Consider, too, the modern parable attributed to the original developer of Dubai: "My grandfather rode a camel, my father rode a camel, I drive a Mercedes, my son drives a Land Rover, his son will drive a Land Rover, but his son will ride a camel." His goal has been to modernize Dubai so that it will survive as a trading hub after the end of oil production.[20]

Recently, I happened into a casual conversation with a young man from one of the Stans countries (Afghanistan, Kazakhstan, and others). We got to talking about what his father does – he runs a very large business providing services to oil and gas companies – and I asked him when he would go into his family's business. His response? "Oh no," he said. "My father won't let me go into the business. He says that in fifty years the business will be gone."

In the same vein, Crown Prince Mohammed bin Salman of the Kingdom of Saudi Arabia has observed that his country has a "dangerous addiction to oil." Furthermore, as reported by the *Financial Times*, by diversifying its businesses, Saudi Arabia appears to be preparing for a much different energy future.[21] For example, the Kingdom is investing in petrochemicals, a non-combustible use of oil that is likely to remain viable even as the world switches to renewable energy. It is not clear whether that strategy is driven by oil depletion or by world energy evolution in reaction to climate change, or both. In either case, the Saudis must promote their oil reserves now to fund investment in that future.

The twin factors of dependence on foreign oil and ongoing oil depletion suggest the importance of energy for America's strategic planning. Periodically, the US military's Joint Forces Command publishes an assessment of what threats may exist for the United States in the next twenty-five years, with particular interest in "the future security environment at the operational level of war."[22] Its document is entitled the *Joint Operating Environment* (informally, *JOE*). In 2010, *JOE* reported:

> Petroleum must continue to satisfy most of the demand for energy out to 2030. Assuming the most optimistic scenario for improved petroleum production through enhanced recovery means, the development of nonconventional oils (such as oil shales or tar sands) and new discoveries, petroleum production will be hard-pressed to meet the expected future demand of 118 million barrels per day.[23]

OPEC nations will remain a focal point of Great Power interests. These nations may have a vested interest in inhibiting production increases, both to conserve finite supplies and to keep prices high. Should one of the consumer nations choose to intervene forcefully, the "arc of instability" running from North Africa through to Southeast Asia easily could become an "arc of chaos," and involving the military forces of several nations.[24]

The 2010 report suggested that American surplus oil production capacity might disappear as early as 2015, a projection that turned out to be wrong. It also observed that "the central problem for the coming decades will not be a lack of petroleum reserves, but rather a shortage of drilling platforms, engineers and refining capacity. Even were a concerted effort begun today to repair that shortage, it would be 10 years before production could catch up with expected demand."[25] In response, *JOE* set challenging targets for adopting renewable energy, particularly in military transportation systems. At this writing, it is not apparent, at least to the public, what has happened to those goals.

At about the same time, a parallel report on energy for the Federal Republic of Germany was leaked to their press. It came to remarkably similar conclusions. A product of a think tank that guides the German military, the report stated there is "some probability that peak oil will occur around the year 2010 and that the impact on security is expected to be felt 15 to 30 years later." The authors pointed out that oil is used directly or indirectly in the production of 95 per cent of all industrial goods. Since the transportation of goods depends heavily on oil, in the future, international trade might become subject to extreme tax hikes. "Shortages in the supply of vital goods [such as food] could arise." Price shocks would occur in most industries across the industrial supply chain. The report warned of the "total collapse of the markets," shifts in the global balance of power, the formation of new global relationships based on interdependency, and a decline in importance of the western industrial nations. "In the medium term the global economic system and every market-oriented national economy would collapse."[26]

In the United States, the oil industry touts fracking as the solution to oil depletion. It cites the billions of barrels of oil to be obtained by fracking in the Bakken field alone, for instance. Exactly how many billions exist there is, however, a matter of dispute, with the oil industry coming in on much the higher end and other knowledgeable experts on the lower end.

Also, recall as discussed earlier, that a billion barrels lasts the world only about ten days. Environmentalists and oil industry critics say that even if we use up all the fracked oil, it would not be enough to meet our supply needs, and, even if it were to supply our immediate needs, fracking is so polluting a process that it will speed global warming alarmingly. In particular, they point to the importance of keeping the dirty oil of the Canadian tar sands in the ground.

The *JOE* for 2035 hardly mentions oil. Neither does it do much with energy issues in general. In the absence of a discussion of these, it appears to advance the view that technological innovation will solve our energy problems. It asserts, "Many energy development efforts focus on making current systems and processes more efficient, often producing significant but incremental improvements. However, research into groundbreaking technologies has the potential to radically impact the future of energy. Innovative fusion, solar, and biofuel technologies might lead to the development of highly mobile, lighter weight, and more efficient power sources."[27]

Perhaps they know something the public doesn't know.

In response to competitive pressures and the depletion of oil reserves, oil companies have changed their business models to diversify away from making most of their profits from oil extraction. Many no longer strategize merely as oil companies, or even as fossil fuel companies, but rather as energy companies. The stakes for fossil fuel companies are high, and they are doing what businesses typically do to strategically adapt – diversifying, investing in research, and managing public relations.

ExxonMobil, one of the largest companies in the world, is today not just an oil company but an oil and gas company. Even though these two products differ significantly in terms of availability, refining costs, applications, and profit margins, in its annual report the company reports on oil and gas in combination, counting them in what it terms "oil-equivalent barrels." This practice has become the industry standard.

A major factor that stock watchers use to evaluate energy companies is their reserves – the amount of oil in the ground that they own. Put simply, if one is in the business of finding energy, without reserves there can be no growth. This may be one reason why, in its public-facing publications, the industry now refers not to "oil" but to "oil and liquid fuels" together. Including various types of natural gas along with oil masks the numbers on oil reserves and keeps the overall reserve figure apparently high.

Just as important in terms of diversification is that Exxon's upstream business of procuring the raw materials of gas and oil is, in terms of profits, giving way to its downstream business of refining. Hence, the company seeks to open pipelines to their Louisiana refineries. Also, they backed the groundbreaking 2016 law that allows energy companies to export refined oil for the first time in forty years.

Fossil fuel companies have also experimented with renewable energy as a potential product line. In the 1980s, Exxon invested in the solar photovoltaic business, only to abandon that investment when their internal research suggested it would not pay out until solar energy became affordable, in about twenty-five years. That prediction turned out to be accurate when the cost of solar silicon declined drastically in 2009.[28]

While considering diversification into green energy, Exxon configured and then reconfigured its public relations approach to climate change. When it was going green it publicly supported the belief in

anthropogenic climate change, and when it was refocusing on petroleum it began to deny climate change. This backpedaling eventually
drew a lawsuit from the Rockefeller Family Fund. The Rockefeller
Family Fund argues that, "for business reasons, a company as sophisticated and successful as Exxon would have needed to know the difference between its own propaganda and scientific reality. If it turned
out that Exxon and other oil companies had recognized the validity
of climate science even while they were funding the climate denial
movement, that would, we thought, help the public understand how
artificially manufactured and disingenuous the 'debate' over climate change has always been. In turn, we hoped this understanding
would build support for strong policies addressing the crisis of global
warming."[29]

The attorney general of New York State has investigated Exxon-
Mobil for being less than forthright about its own basic research into
the anthropogenic causes of climate change and its future impacts
on energy markets. For some time now, publicly traded companies
have been required to disclose material business risks to investors in
routine filings with the Securities and Exchange Commission. Beginning in 2010, that requirement was interpreted to require disclosure
related to climate change.

Today, fossil fuel companies continue to flirt with green energy
product lines. Exxon supports research on biofuels, CO_2 capture,
and photovoltaics, for instance. As Jeremy Leggett, a petroleum geologist turned solar investor, puts it, "The oil and gas majors are in a
fascinating place. They're starting to use clean-energy investments to
hedge their bets that markets for oil and gas will exist decades from
now."[30]

After a period of outright denial, large fossil fuel companies now are
on board with the idea that climate change is happening, although
they differ as to what, if anything, to do about it. Typically, companies
argue that they must prioritize profit and organizational survival over
contributing to climate change solutions. As a Shell executive puts it,

Shell has some small-scale investments in solar, wind, and biofuels, and it has a responsibility to help tackle the energy challenge, but it will "only go green 'when it makes business sense.'"[31] Amid carefully worded public relations statements, one hears many comments like this one from Ken Cohen, former head of public affairs for ExxonMobil: "Should we be on a path to do something about anthropogenic emissions? The answer is yes."[32]

From a public relations standpoint, pursuing the climate change issue may help the industry distract the public from the energy reality that fossil fuel supplies will not last forever, and, indeed, may run out in the lifetime of today's young adults. Of course, if the public comes to understand this unhappy prediction, their motivation to transition the energy sector to renewables will be that much more fervent. Americans one day may look with envy on countries that have made greater strides with renewables. In 2018, for example, the energy mix in the United Kingdom, the sixth largest economy in the world, included about 51 per cent from renewables and nuclear, and 41 per cent from gas-fired power stations.[33]

Energy companies are rich, motivated, sophisticated System 2 thinkers. What might they themselves imagine to be the biggest threat to their sector? Obviously, each company faces competition from other energy companies. A particular problem is that they must compete with state-owned, tax- and investment-advantaged companies like Saudi Arabia's Aramco and Russia's Gazprom. At any time now, too, they may be overrun by the thousands of energetic Lilliputians in the renewable energy crowd.

Threats from the government sector are portentous. Certainly, government regulation is a significant constraint. In some countries, fossil fuel companies must concern themselves with regulations that cover everything from environmental pollution to safe material handling standards. As the theory of fair competition suggests, to the extent that such regulations create a level playing field and stability, companies often welcome them. An Indian coal mogul once argued to me that he could compete anywhere in the world that all companies are treated equitably, and that when expanding a company a fair and stable policy environment is what he looks for. Of course, a level playing field is only possible when working within a functional legal system.

Within stable countries, fossil fuel companies have considerable, and increasing, power to influence regulation. Witness their 2016 success in overturning the forty-year US ban on exporting crude oil, thus reducing the amount of petroleum available to the nation in the future, including in times of emergency. The Citizens United Supreme Court decision in the United States, which allows corporations to be treated as persons, has multiplied companies' influence.

All of these factors are major industry concerns. But if ever there were a dirty word among oil barons, it would be "nationalization." Government takeover of essential energy is a possibility that fossil fuel companies fear much more than mere regulation. Interestingly, they talk about it even less, at least in public.

Nationalization of the oil industry – its takeover by government in some form of legal ownership – has occurred in many countries. In the Western Hemisphere, Venezuela, Mexico, and Brazil have each found unique paths to nationalization.[34] Canada's Petro-Canada is a state-owned oil company that has competed against the private sector since 1975, despite opposition from private companies in oil-rich Alberta. From a citizen's point of view, much of the state ownership of the oil industry has not been particularly successful; but then, neither has it been attempted in a country as well governed as the United States.

While politically nationalization seems like a remote possibility, in the future, as resources are stretched thin, prices go up, and homes grow cold, it will be more probable. Certainly, for large companies that lay out their strategies over a period of decades and even centuries, the possibility must be entertained. Just as the Great Recession of 2008 led to the nationalization of General Motors, so energy depletion may lead to the nationalization of the ExxonMobils of this world.

Nationalization of the fossil fuel industry, or of any company within the industry, would nullify everything a large company stands for – profits, excellence, pride, lifestyles, family fortunes, and personal ambitions. In this sense, avoiding nationalization is a fossil fuel company's greatest stake.

The industry's goal is to prevent the public from believing that their domestic energy supplies are owned by the people (they are), or that they are, like water, a necessity that they *should* own. To accomplish this, the industry emphasizes the importance of free markets, and excoriates any type of collective action by calling it "socialism." It attacks any regulation whatsoever, in part because a government that is more experienced and successful at regulation is a government that is more capable of nationalizing an industry. Likewise, a government that is seen to be failing could not be trusted to run an industry.

3. NATURAL GAS

We have been thinking so far about the oil sector, which, as we have seen, is for business reasons often the oil and gas sector. However, the gas sector certainly has its own interests that are worth considering independent of those of oil.

Natural gas is more volatile than oil. For many applications, it must first be condensed and then held under pressure, and homes and offices that use it for heat occasionally explode. For the same reason, it is harder than oil to transport. To be shipped over long distances it is transformed into liquid natural gas, which also must be stored under pressure, a process that is vulnerable to large explosions that could have devastating effects on local populations.

Therefore, although natural gas is often found in the same places as oil, it serves a relatively limited market geographically. It is more

likely to compete as a fuel locally and regionally rather than internationally. Since most communities do not want a liquid natural gas
facility nearby, regulation also impacts whether the gas market is local
or global.

From a climate change perspective, it is often noted that an advantage of burning gas is that it produces fewer CO_2 emissions than
burning either coal or oil. This is one reason why gas is sometimes
touted as a transition fuel from oil and coal to renewables. There is a
lot of nuance to this argument, however.

For one thing, EROEI is a factor. Like oil, gas comes in conventional and unconventional forms. Conventional gas comes to the
surface under natural pressure and pumping after a well is drilled.
Because this sort of gas is increasingly difficult to find, energy companies are turning to unconventional gas, which is found in shale
formations and extracted by fracking that requires large amounts of
energy and water.

Some researchers suggest that across the full life cycle of unconventional gas production, from extracting by fracturing through
refining and delivery, unconventional gas, or "shale gas," is more
polluting than conventional gas, conventional oil, or coal (unconventional oil was not included in their study). This research assumes
that during extraction, 3.6 to 7.9 per cent of the natural gas – that is,
methane – is leaked, or perhaps deliberately "vented," into the air.[35]
Other research, using different assumptions about the extent of leak-
age and flaring that appear to reflect recent technological improvements, has found that burning shale gas produces about the same
greenhouse gas emissions as burning conventional gas, but produces
more greenhouse gas emissions than burning conventional oil. In
comparison, burning coal produces about two times the greenhouse
gas emissions as burning either type of gas.[36]

A final reason why gas is called a transition fuel is that, for the
moment, it is relatively plentiful in the United States. One source
suggests that the US gas reserves can last about eighty-six years.[37]

However, because energy availability is discussed by government sources like the US Energy Information Administration in terms of "proven reserves," which are defined in part as reserves that can be economically recovered under current prices, and because the unconventional gas industry is in the early stages of development, it is challenging to predict how long the gas resources will last. Meanwhile, commercial interests want the public to see natural gas as a transition fuel so they will buy more of it.

4. COAL

Finally, coal. In many circles it is considered to be the fossil fuel of yesterday, and environmentalists believe it should be left in the ground. But coal is still very much with us. In China, 70 per cent of total energy consumption is based on coal.[38] It is the greatest current contributor to global greenhouse gas emissions, and burning all the coal that exists in the ground would go a long way toward destroying Earth's climate as we know it.

Climate leaders have targeted how coal usage might be reduced, along with unconventional oil usage. In 2009, a group of prestigious scientists argued that "the global climate problem becomes tractable if CO_2 emissions from coal use are phased out rapidly and emissions from unconventional fossil fuels (e.g., oil shale and tar sands) are prohibited" and replaced with currently available technology for renewable energy.[39] Current efforts to scrub emissions from burning coal are experimental and, given its high sulfur content, they are not likely to succeed anytime soon. Likewise, the carbon capture and storage solution by which emissions from coal plants are injected underground is at this point experimental.

Of course, like the supplies of other fossil fuels, coal supplies will one day peak. As the late British scientist David MacKay has written, "if the world coal consumption rate is 6.3 [units] per year, and coal reserves are 1600 [units], people often say 'there's 250 years of coal left.'" But this calculation does not account for growth. (Nor do many resource projections, in fact.) He continues, "if the growth rate of coal consumption were to continue at 2% per year (which gives a reasonable fit to the data from 1930 to 2000), then all the coal would be gone in 2096. If the growth rate is 3.4% per year (the growth rate over the last decade), the end of business-as-usual is coming before 2072. Not 250 years, but 60!"[40]

In the saga of energy evolution, one day coal may play the role of comeback kid. Again, MacKay argues that "the price of emitting carbon dioxide should be big enough such that every running coal power station has carbon capture technology fitted to it ... Solving climate change is a complex topic, but in a single crude brushstroke, here is the solution: The price of carbon dioxide must be such that people stop burning coal without capture. Most of the solution is captured in this one brushstroke because, in the long term, coal is the big fossil fuel."[41]

Why is that? Obviously, because coal pollutes heavily. But also because, given that supplies of oil and gas will decline steeply over the next fifty or so years, coal will almost certainly be the last fossil fuel left for us to burn. Or, not.

5. RENEWABLE ENERGY

Enter: renewable energy. In many ways the story of green energy follows a standard narrative of innovation. It is the story of creating new products through research, promoting and marketing those products, and bringing them to scale commercially. In each phase, renewable energy competes with the incumbent fossil fuel industries, with oil being the most powerful industry in history.

In the United States, renewable energy accounts for about 19 per cent of total energy usage. The United States already has so many dams that essentially it fully utilizes its hydroelectric resources. It also has abundant resources for solar, wind (on land and sea, and at high altitudes), hydrokinetic, and biofuel energy. Within the renewable energy usage figure, 9 per cent is nuclear power and the other 11 per cent is allocated among, in descending order of usage, biomass (including biofuels, wood, and biomass waste), hydroelectric, wind, solar, and geothermal energy.[42]

The prize for creating a breakthrough technology, such as an improved energy storage system, will be extraordinary, and scientist-entrepreneurs are hotly pursuing it. Some are famous, like Elon Musk creating better batteries for electric cars at Tesla. Others are beavering away more quietly in government, academic, and private laboratories, capturing the energy of waves or turning algae into oil or attempting to tap the earth's core heat. To date, the role of government has been limited, and government investment in basic research on energy has been small. In 2015, the *Christian Science Monitor* called that investment "detrimentally modest,"[43] and it has not grown appreciably.

Bringing their inventions to scale commercially is a major challenge for these entrepreneurs. In addition to their investment in basic research, interested governments can help by enacting direct subsidies for the products in commercial markets, and by applying their own massive purchasing power to bolster early sales.

Success is building for both solar and wind. Solar silicon prices dropped 94 per cent from early 2008 to the end of 2011, and the price of crystalline silicon fell an additional 47 per cent by 2015.[44] Employment in the US solar sector has grown much faster than overall job creation – at a rate of twelve times faster in 2015 – and solar jobs grew at a rate of 25 per cent from 2015 to 2016.[45] The International Renewable Energy Agency (IRENA) points out that green jobs are growing faster than jobs in oil and gas extraction, and predicts there may be 24 million jobs worldwide in clean energy by 2030.[46]

Wind energy usage exceeds solar and is growing. According to the US Department of Energy (DOE), America's current installed wind power capacity across all facets of wind energy (land-based, off-shore, and distributed, where "distributed" means non-concentrated sites like residential, agricultural, commercial, industrial, and community) tripled from 2008 to 2015. The DOE's *Wind Vision Report* describes the successes of the wind industry and predicts a strong wind energy future:

> Wind supports a strong domestic supply chain. Wind has the potential to support over 600,000 jobs in manufacturing, installation, maintenance, and supporting services by 2050.
>
> Wind is affordable. The price of wind energy is projected to be directly competitive with conventional energy technologies within the next decade.
>
> With more wind energy available, the electric utility sector is anticipated to be less sensitive to the volatility in natural gas pricing. By reducing our national vulnerability to price spikes and electrical supply disruptions, wind is anticipated to save consumers $280 billion in natural gas costs by 2050.
>
> Wind reduces air pollution emissions. Wind energy already helps the country avoid the emission of over 250,000 metric tons of air pollutants each year, which include sulfur dioxide, nitrogen oxides, and particulate matter. Wind is expected to offset the emission of more than 12.3 gigatonnes of greenhouse gases by 2050.
>
> Wind energy preserves water resources. By 2050, wind energy can save 260 billion gallons of water – the equivalent to roughly 400,000 Olympic-size swimming pools – that would have been used by the electric power sector.
>
> Wind deployment can increase community revenues. Local communities will be able to collect additional tax revenue from land lease payments and property taxes, reaching $3.2 billion annually by 2050.[47]

Eventually, every state will be able to make some use of wind energy. The report advises that wind can be a viable resource in all fifty states by 2050. Additional science suggests that offshore wind farming has even more potential than farming wind over land.[48]

Meanwhile, nuclear energy usage in the United States has stalled, in part because of concerns about plant safety and the disposal of nuclear waste, and in part because its prices are not competitive.[49] Its future as a renewable energy source is highly uncertain. The utilization of fusion (rather than fission) would solve the current issues, but research on applying it has so far been unsuccessful and is not likely to bear fruit for decades. At the same time, many thought leaders believe that utilizing nuclear energy will be necessary to quickly achieve reduced levels of carbon emissions.

A crucial factor in the renewable energy buildout is the electrical grid, that network of generating stations and power lines that transfers electrical power from suppliers to consumers. Although it is currently run primarily on fossil fuels, the grid could be decarbonized. Modernizing the grid is essential to moving the United States to an all-electric economy.

Critics point out various difficulties with plans to improve the grid. One argument is that any intermittent source of energy must be backed up with storage facilities like batteries, which at this time is impractical at any large scale. However, there is also some debate about this. Scientists from the NOAA's Earth System Research Laboratory and the Cooperative Institute for Research in Environmental Sciences have crunched the numbers to show that "contemporary wind, solar and transmission technologies could reduce CO_2 emissions by 80% compared with 1990 levels (or 81% compared with 2030 levels) with no storage, at a 9% lower cost than the baseline fossil fuel grid cost. Smaller CO_2 reductions can be obtained at even lower cost."[50] This innovative model shows how managing power output over large rather than small areas will help. The researchers assert that while intermittency is a significant concern in small geographical areas, intermittency problems can be overcome when the geographical area is larger and power is shared across a region.

Critics also note that the challenge of transforming the entire US electrical power system by the 2030s is "formidable."[51] Difficulties include integrating diverse generating systems, investing in a new high-voltage electric power transmission system, building new, efficient power plants, and negotiating the current regulatory, commercial, and legal system. On an optimistic note, critics do point out that although challenging, such a transition would not be dissimilar to the building of the American interstate highway system from the 1950s through the 1980s.

Based on current technology, it is clear that no one renewable source can replace fossil fuels. The world must adapt a mix of renewables, and the question is, What mix? It is impossible to compare the viability of all the potential green energy sources in the space of this book, and the picture will be different tomorrow anyhow. For leaders who might like to consume energy responsibly, or advocate for renewable energy, or invest in the most promising form, a major issue will be finding sound science.

Consider the tale of hydrogen. Some scientists believe hydrogen, which is plentiful in the atmosphere, can be burned to save the world; others dismiss it because it has a negative EROEI – burning it costs more in energy than it produces. Under the George W. Bush administration, hydrogen was touted as the fuel of the future and the salvation of humankind, and the government made significant investments.[52] It is true that hydrogen engines produce no harmful emissions. However, the process of manufacturing them does. Furthermore, the hydrogen burned is typically a by-product of methane in natural gas. Thus, without a research breakthrough, the process is not environmentally viable. Under the Obama administration, government investments in hydrogen were cancelled.

Sitting down to write about renewables here, I decided to update the hydrogen story. I started with a library search of peer-reviewed articles. Many of the articles I found were at least five years old, and from abroad. Interesting. Moving on, from a US government website

I learned that "the only federal laboratory dedicated to the research, development, commercialization, and deployment of renewable energy and energy efficiency technologies" is the National Renewable Energy Laboratory (NREL). This organization is a public–private partnership (which raises red flags about accountability) managed by the private Alliance for Sustainable Energy, LLC, in partnership with Battelle and MRIGlobal, for the US Department of Energy's Office of Energy Efficiency and Renewable Energy. NREL's goal is "to minimize the use of energy, materials, and water while carrying out the laboratory's mission of clean energy research. NREL analysis informs policy and investment decisions as energy-efficient and renewable energy technologies advance from concept to commercial application to market penetration."[53]

This site seemed to offer just what I was looking for. Searching further for recent research on hydrogen, I found this on their webpage: "Today, a new generation of transportation pioneers is hard at work reshaping transportation through the development of hydrogen fuel cell electric vehicles, or FCEVs. The benefits of the technology are clear."[54]

When I see inspirational language like "new generation" and "pioneers" along with incautious judgments like "clear," my System 1 paranoia gets a green light from my System 2 analyst. The article asserts:

They can fuel in just minutes for a more than 300 mile driving range. You never need to change the oil. And, other than water, they offer completely zero emissions from the tailpipe with no compromise in performance. Because a fuel cell can be more than twice as efficient as an internal combustion engine, you can get much farther on a tank of hydrogen than with a tank of gasoline. (And the journey will be much quieter along the way!)

The technology has made enormous strides over the past several years, with the cost of hydrogen fuel cells dropping by 50% since 2006 with the help of research and development efforts backed by our office and our collaborations with industry partners. That's why nearly every major automaker is now actively pursuing the development of FCEVs.[55]

Reading on, I learned that NREL performs technology validations, which are "confirmation that component and system technical targets have been met under realistic operating conditions ... Technology validation projects involve gathering extensive data from the systems and components under real-world conditions, analyzing this detailed data, and then comparing results to technical targets."[56] Inspiring, but what do the data say?

It turns out that the raw data from these studies are protected by NREL; results of their analyses are only aggregated into public results they call "composite data products." These public results show the status and progress of the technology, but don't identify individual companies. In other words – sorry, no raw data are available.

Back on the Internet, I discovered the following statement on hydrogen fuel from one of the founders of Tesla, which famously chose battery technology over hydrogen to fuel its innovative vehicles:

If your goal is to reduce energy consumption ... hydrogen is uniquely bad.

There's a saying in the auto industry that hydrogen is the future of transportation ... It's a scam as far as I can tell because the energy equation is terrible. It's just terrible ...

[Hydrogen] is ... bound up into water, wood and everything else. The only way that you get hydrogen requires you to pour energy into it to break it from the chemical bonds. ...

You have to compress it and that takes energy, and then you have to transport it to wherever you actually need it, which is really difficult because hydrogen is much harder to work with than gasoline or even natural gas ...

And then you ultimately have to place it into a car where you'll have a very high-pressure vessel which offers its own safety issues – and that's only to convert it back again to electricity to make the car go ...

When you add that all up, it turns out that the amount of energy per kilometer driven is just terrible. It's way worse than almost anything else you can come up with – *which I always suspected is one of the reasons why the energy companies have long been big proponents of it.*

When we were raising money the first time, we had very carefully gone through the math … We … went down the whole list [of energy sources] to figure out what the most energy efficient system was – which turned out to be battery electric cars. (Emphasis added)[57]

This is most likely the real story, and the reason why few legitimate scientists and innovators are promoting the study and application of hydrogen fuel cell technology.[58] The story illustrates once again that, when it comes to ascertaining the facts, leaders must keep their wits about them, and, as always, monitor System 1 hopes with System 2 analysis.

Marc Tarpenning, the former Tesla executive just quoted, also described how vested interests may react to threatening technological change. When trying to raise money from venture capitalists, Tesla founders included a slide about hydrogen fuel cells in their presentation: "The slide was of course about why Tesla would use batteries to power its vehicles and not hydrogen … Half of the VCs would ask them to skip the slide saying that they already ran their own cost analysis and they are aware of the inefficiency of the system, but the other half of the VCs would go really quiet and then start asking more questions. Marc explained that those VCs had already invested in fuel cell companies, which most [sic] went out of business by now."[59]

The moral of the story? Clean energy sells, but as with any new venture, one needs to approach it with sound science and an appreciation for what's at stake for owners, developers, and their potential customers. The debate goes on. For example, Toyota sold its stake in Tesla in order to compete with it in the growing market for clean energy vehicles; and "[Toyota] continues to invest heavily in hydrogen fuel cells," notes the *Financial Times*.[60]

6. COMMUNITIES

So far in this chapter we have weighed the competition and power relationships among the various energy sectors, including what their stakes are and what the future portends. Now let's look at how energy evolution is playing out where people live. We will compare two very different American communities, examine the job opportunities in the green energy sector, and discuss the world's most vulnerable nations.

Communities are the go-to sector for anticipating and managing climate and energy impacts on homes, businesses, and infrastructure, while also being concerned with jobs and the economy. For communities, the top stakes are safety in the face of damaging climate events and energy security in the face of energy evolution. Communities must take on the daunting task of predicting and planning for environmental change. They have to consider that the greener they are now, the better able they will be to deal with energy transitions later. Citizens and their representatives often want to do the right thing for the planet by investing today in the reduction of greenhouse gas emissions, but they must also monitor costs.

One way to understand the stakes at the local level, and what communities can and are doing today, is to visit a couple of them. We travel first to the Boston suburb of Lexington, Massachusetts (population about 32,000), and then to the sparsely populated state of North Dakota (population about 760,000). These two communities share many values, yet their approaches to climate and energy could not be more different.

Lexington is a suburb of Boston that is known for its excellent school system. Most of its tax revenue, nearly 80 per cent, is from residential property owners.[61] It votes heavily Democratic. Sustainable Lexington is an official committee appointed by the town's Select Board to "enhance Lexington's long-term sustainability and resilience in response to environmental resource and energy challenges."[62] The committee works to improve the quality of life and promote the desirability of living and working in their town. It is mainly composed of individuals who have expertise in built environments (including buildings, energy systems, and water infrastructure), land use (including agriculture and groundwater management), and community organizing.

This formal town committee is supported by more than a dozen local environmental groups. One of these, the Global Warming Action Coalition, educates citizens about climate change and promotes local action. It sponsors the Lexington Green Network, a website that coordinates the local efforts. It also supports other towns' initiatives, including nearby Weston's Mass Energize website, a pilot that allows the town to track what people are doing and encourages citizens to share contacts and resources.

The seven-person Sustainable Lexington committee recognizes that the Northeast is already experiencing a great increase in extreme storms. It is also aware of the prediction that within twenty-five to fifty years Massachusetts summers will be as warm as those of Virginia or South Carolina are now. This would mean more than two months of temperatures over 90° Fahrenheit and more than three weeks of temperatures over 100° each year.

In response, the committee has adopted two long-term climate goals. The first is to get to net zero emissions in the town by reducing greenhouse gas emissions and emissions from toxic and hazardous substances. The second is to be able to maintain essential services for ten days following extreme weather events by developing appropriate infrastructure. The intermediate goals of the many environmental programs in Lexington boil down to two basics: to save money by greening energy usage, and to promote human health.

For a decade, the town itself has followed a sustainable building policy, in which all renovations and new projects must conform to LEED Silver standards. Leadership in Energy and Environmental Design (LEED) is a popular private certification program that promotes resource-efficient buildings nationwide. Adhering to the standard has significantly reduced energy costs in Lexington, and now the town is debating how to improve upon even that standard. For instance, in public buildings, the town can maximize solar energy and install zero-emission heat pumps rather than natural gas boilers. In anticipation of millions of dollars in energy savings for the municipality itself, the town has installed solar panels on six major municipal buildings and has built a ground-mounted solar system on 4.5 acres. Most recently, the town has encouraged residents to use 100 per cent renewable electricity and contracted with its primary energy company to provide it; applying sound psychology, it has given residents the opportunity to opt out rather than opt in to this program.

Also concerned with indoor environmental quality, especially in schools, the town scores well on LEED Silver health points but strives to do better. For example, motivated by the correlation between higher levels of CO_2 and lower levels of student cognitive performance, local citizens figured out they could reduce CO_2 at a minimum cost simply by increasing ventilation and changing air filters in school buildings.

To engage citizens, Lexington representatives and town officials foster an attitude of "just ask." A new school was being designed and one citizen who knew about solar energy "just asked" whether the architect might move the gymnasium from the south side of the building to the north side. Putting it on the south side would shadow the classroom building on the north side and prevent the future deployment of solar panels there. "Yes, of course," was the answer.

The town also partners with state and private programs. It participates in Community Choice Aggregation (CCA), a state-level policy that allows local governments to combine their residential and commercial retail electricity demand to buy electricity that is greener, cheaper, and more local. Other states that participate in CCA include California, Illinois, New Jersey, Ohio, and Rhode Island. The town has also worked with one of its major energy suppliers, the private

British company National Grid, to foster conservation. The company has offered the town an incentive program through which it can earn tens of thousands of dollars by doing home energy assessments and installing insulation and automated thermostats. The town partners with local companies that provide such services.

Not surprisingly, the town's state senator is a leader in promoting a carbon fee for the Commonwealth of Massachusetts. Also, following the lead of nearby towns, in 2020 Lexington sought a full-time sustainability director to coordinate green energy initiatives across town departments and within the community. One of the director's main responsibilities will be to apply for grant money offered by the state and federal governments.

North Dakota is a heavily agricultural state in the High Plains region of the United States. Farms and ranches cover 89 per cent of the total land of the state.[63]

In the ten years from 2010 to 2019, North Dakota experienced exceptional storms, including nearly 25 per cent more tornados per year than during the period from 1950 to 2019.[64] In recent years it has also suffered devastating spring floods. North Dakota has been moderately affected by the drought conditions that have plagued the states to the south of it in the High Plains region. Those states have been experiencing cyclically dry and moderately dry conditions, with some pockets of severe drought.[65]

North Dakota has a population of about 760,000 people. A sparsely populated state, it has an abundance of energy. When oil and gas prices are high, it has a low unemployment rate and a significant influx of workers. It also has a strong farm lobby. It votes heavily Republican.

North Dakota includes a significant portion of the Bakken shale oil formation. At times it has been one of the largest crude oil–producing states, accounting for more than 12 per cent of total US crude oil production. Its 251 per cent increase in production from 2010 to 2014 was driven by horizontal drilling and hydraulic fracturing.

However, when the price of oil sinks, so does the state's economy. With oil prices below \$40 per barrel, unemployment and bankruptcies grow.[66] The state also has about 5 per cent of the country's coal reserves, in surface mines that are easily exploited.[67]

Not surprisingly, the state is a strong supporter of fossil fuel extraction. North Dakota was the first state to sue the Environmental Protection Agency over new rules that would require shale oil and gas producers to reduce methane leaks at new or modified drilling sites. Methane is an even more powerful greenhouse gas than carbon dioxide, warming the planet eighty-six times as fast as CO_2.[68] However, it does not remain in the atmosphere for nearly as long.

The state's energy consumption per capita is among the highest in the country. Energy is cheap, the industrial sector is energy-intensive, and cold winters create high heating demand. About two-thirds of the state's electricity generation comes from coal, 25 per cent from wind, and 5 per cent from hydroelectric power.[69]

North Dakota was the second-largest crude oil–producing state after Texas in 2017. It is also among the top states in the nation in wind energy potential.[70]

Apart from the failed protests against the Dakota Access Pipeline that now carries crude oil out of the state, in North Dakota there is little going on to slow climate change or reduce its impacts. As the National Climate Assessment puts it, "Although there is tremendous adaptive potential among the diverse communities of the Great Plains, many local government officials do not yet recognize climate change as a problem that requires proactive planning."[71] On the climate advocacy side, the North Dakota Game and Fish Department is studying the impacts on plants and wildlife. Also, a chapter of the nonpartisan Citizens Climate Lobby, which advocates nationally for a carbon fee, opened in Fargo, the state's most populous city, in 2015. The Oglala Lakota tribe is developing climate change adaptation and mitigation planning that includes such factors as transportation and housing.

As described by a spokesperson for the North Dakota Game and Fish Department, climate change is seen as a "slow moving, relatively unpredictable crisis over which people, particularly in North Dakota, have little influence or control," whereas the turbulent economy fueled by an oil boom and bust is another story.[72] The department is concerned that, with a warmer climate, the region will support a new range of crops, especially corn and winter wheat. This opportunity is likely to spur development, but it will also drive habitat loss for many plants and animals that depend on the state's large swaths of inter-connected grasslands and wetlands.

The Yale Climate Opinion Maps offer a fascinating interactive option for exploring such climate attitudes at the state level.[73] Their data from 2018 inform us that, within the fifty states, the people of North Dakota are among those least likely to believe that global warm-ing is happening (60 per cent of a large sample there believe that it is). Across the United States, 70 per cent of the population believes in global warming. People in North Dakota don't worry about global warming much, either. The percent of worriers there is only 49 per cent, in contrast with 66 per cent in Massachusetts, 70 per cent in New York State, 60 per cent in Florida, 68 per cent in California, and a national average of 61 per cent.

In some ways, the people of North Dakota see climate change as normal, a fact of life to which they have already adapted successfully. They say that their weather has always been unpredictable, on aver-age the coldest in the lower forty-eight states and the driest in winter. Whatever happens, they have ample and diverse energy sources. A rancher who advocates holistic techniques like rotating his cows over the land is typical. He says, "Was I specifically thinking about climate change? ... No. But I know [the ranching practices] would be benefi-cial. And if, indeed, those things were to happen, my system would be more resilient economically and environmentally."[74]

While these communities take different approaches to energy utilization, one thing they can agree on is the nationwide need for good jobs. Across a variety of communities, green energy development creates such work. In the United States in 2010, the federal Bureau of Labor Statistics was funded to promote green careers, which it did in part by publishing developments in green job creation. The Bureau defines green jobs as "jobs in businesses that produce goods or provide services that benefit the environment or conserve natural resources, and jobs in which workers' duties involve making their establishment's production processes more environmentally friendly or use fewer natural resources." Unfortunately, the funding for this project was eliminated in 2013, and the Bureau stopped collecting data.

This left data collection to the states. At the time, some thirty-five states and Washington, D.C., had targets in place for the use of renewable energy in electricity generation. Progressive analysts, using data from the US Energy Information Administration, the American Council on Renewable Energy, and the NREL, suggested that these programs alone would create more than 2 million jobs nationwide. They predicted that in California, wind and solar development would create over half a million construction phase jobs and close to 3,000 permanent jobs. Colorado, which passed the first renewable energy standards in 2004, was on the path to creating 15,546 wind-related jobs in the construction and manufacturing industries, and 604 jobs in operating and maintaining these facilities. The contribution of solar would be 18,330 jobs in installation, construction, and manufacturing, and 122 in permanent jobs.[75]

As of 2016, according to the International Renewable Energy Agency of the US Bureau of Statistics, there were more US jobs in solar than in either oil and gas extraction or coal mining. Worldwide, renewable energy employed nearly 10 million people.[76]

These figures are in line with other research at the state level and internationally. They led Greg Kats, managing director of ARENA Investments, a fund that invests in early stage renewable energy, to conclude that "renewable energy and energy efficiency clearly are several times more labor-intensive than fossil fuels. Clean energy jobs also generally are more distributed and are largely higher quality jobs. For these reasons, the ongoing shift to clean energy is very good news for employment and workers, and any politician interested in creating jobs should embrace and support the clean energy transition."[77]

Numerous job sites have emerged to serve the needs of businesses and job seekers in clean energy. They include Eco.org (www.eco.org); Environmental Career Opportunities (www.ecojobs.com); Eco-Employ (www.ecoemploy.com); Environmental Career Center (www .environmentalcareer.com); Green Jobs Network (www.greenjobs.net); SustainableBusiness.com (www.sustainablebusiness.com); and the US Green Building Council (www.usgbc.org).[78]

As climate change progresses, providing energy for the world's most vulnerable communities will be essential. Globally, the regions most susceptible to climate change are also among the most underdeveloped. They include large parts of Africa and South Asia, including India. These regions are not responsible for causing the problem. Historically, the United States is responsible for more of the world's cumulative emissions than any other country. Today it is the second largest emitter of greenhouse gases, behind China.[79]

So it is not surprising that at the Paris climate meetings in late 2015, the more vulnerable countries argued that global warming must be held to 1.5° Celsius, rather than the 2° Celsius that other countries had targeted. Developing countries also argue that those countries that have built their economies on burning fossil fuels should now assist them in growing their economies. India has taken a leadership role, refusing to agree to limiting its own greenhouse gas emissions except as they reflect an improving national gross domestic product. It hopes to avoid burning more fossil fuels and to move directly to utilizing green energy, but argues that this change requires foreign investment.[80]

The 2015 Paris accords reiterated developed countries' previous commitments to provide billions of dollars to build green energy for communities in developing countries. The United Nations Green Climate Fund sponsors projects like the development of irrigation and groundwater replenishment systems in India, a hydropower plant in the Solomon Islands to eliminate diesel generators, and the protection of wetlands used by subsistence farmers in Uganda.[81]

The United States has pledged to pay into the fund about $9.41 per person in the American population, while Norway, Luxembourg, and Sweden have each pledged more than $50 per person.[82] However, the mechanisms for paying into the Green Climate Fund and related initiatives are neither clear nor binding. Why not?

7. COOPERATE? OR COMPETE?

The previous sections have laid out some of the key stakes for energy sectors and communities. Now let's think about which human factors contribute to bringing sectors and communities together, and which are likely to drive them apart. To delve into this complex topic, we turn first to two classic parables on inter-group relationships and conflict.

To understand cooperation and competition at the sector level, people often turn to the "tragedy of the commons." In this classic scenario, community members all graze their animals on land held in common. Eventually, their growing herds deplete the supply of forage and the community economy collapses. How does society prevent the tragedy of the commons? The prevalent view is that effective communities create regulations that require people to share the commons without ruining it. Of course, another perspective is that of the survival of the fittest: Community members compete to take whatever they can from the commons while it is still a viable resource, and then the strongest among them simply move on to exploit the next resource. These perspectives establish the essential arguments behind regulated capitalism and so-called free-market capitalism.

Today the globe is humanity's commons, and it is being overrun by us and our domestic animals, crops, and pollution. The atmosphere itself is a commons into which we are dumping pollutants like CO_2. For those who imagine a societal system that can be called civilization, it stands to reason that since the atmospheric commons is global, it requires global regulation. This much is clear.

What is not so clear is how people will organize globally to regulate the use of the global commons. Regulation is needed, yes, but what kind of regulation, created by whom? To begin to define this challenge, consider the classic ethics puzzle known as the stag hunt dilemma:

> A group of hunters tracks a stag, and they learn that it often takes a certain path. If they work together, the hunters can hide near the path and kill the stag, and everyone will eat. However, if the hunters spook the stag or fail to cooperate in the kill, their quarry will escape, and everyone will go hungry. The hunters wait on the path for many hungry hours. Suddenly, they all see a hare coming down the path. Each hunter knows that if he kills the hare, he himself will have enough to eat, but the trap laid for the stag will be sprung and the others will go hungry. On the other hand, if he does not kill the hare, someone else might. The hunter reasons that the stag might never come, but the hare is there right now. What should the hunter do?[83]

A simple way to frame the hunter's decision is in terms of the risks of punishment and reward. On the one hand, the hunter who kills the hare risks being punished: He must estimate the risk that, if he kills the hare himself, the other hunters will ostracize him or hurt him. At the same time, he has a chance to grab a reward: eating the hare. If he does not kill the hare, on the other hand, or if he shares it, his hunting group may reward his loyalty, perhaps with gifts. Assessing risks and rewards is a straightforward, often mathematical, approach to framing complex decisions. It helps the decision-maker clarify questions like: Who is at risk here? What are the risks? How high are the risks? Using the punishment–reward frame, the hunter's decision boils down to choosing among an array of risks and rewards.

A second way to frame the hunter's decision is in terms of the psychology of group cohesion. Applying this frame, the hunter who is loyal to the hunting group will not kill the hare, while the hunter who is disloyal to the group will. The hunter's choice, his loyalty or disloyalty, will bring consequences to both himself and his group. Being loyal builds group trust that generates advantages over time. Being disloyal advantages the individual over the group (at least in the short term), and it reduces group cohesion.

Next, in light of the dynamics of group cohesion, let's consider a more complex version of the stag hunt dilemma. This version is actually more true to life. We'll call it the sociological version:

> As before, a group of hunters is stalking the stag. This time, the hunting group is made up of the very best hunter selected by each of several tribes. When the hare comes down the path, each hungry hunter knows that if he kills the hare, not only the hunting group, but his own tribe back home, may reward or punish him. Now what should the hunter do?

In the first version of the stag hunt, the hunter weighed his individual gain against the benefits of group loyalty. In the sociological version, he weighs in-group loyalty to his tribe against out-group loyalty to the group of hunters. You can see that when he is embedded in not just one but two groups, the hunter's potential punishments and rewards become dramatically more complex. If he does not kill the hare, the group of hunters will praise him, but his own tribe may disown him (especially if he cannot convincingly explain to them why he chose not to bring them this food source). If, knowing how desperately hungry his tribe is, he does kill the hare and bring it to them for even its meagre calories, the group of hunters may fall on him and kill him (or whatever) before he can escape to his tribe. Of course, if he takes the selfish route and eats the hare himself, the hunter faces two groups that may punish him.

There is no right answer to the stag hunter's dilemma, which is used mainly to tease out the interpersonal and ethical aspects of choice under scarcity. In real life, we are all embedded in groups and in systems that are composed of groups. We are aware (if at times dimly) that we mostly exist not as lone hunters, but as hunters for our tribes – for our families, companies, and countries. Because of this systemic embeddedness, we strive to understand our group's norms so we can fit in. We cultivate group allegiances and cohesion. We take a special interest in individuals who leave one group for another: When a cult member quits, we wonder about what their new allegiance bodes for the power of the spurned group. We cultivate in-group loyalty in others and we discourage valuable group members from leaving our group.

One might argue that when we belong to a cohesive group, which is defined as a group that shares emotional ties, killing the hare for that group becomes a virtue. In this scenario, personal success means getting there first and feeding the family. Success is collective, and it's tribal: Kill the hare. Run to the castle. Eat together. Repeat. The hunter finds himself embedded in circumstances in which he can be greedy with a good conscience. Or so it seems.

Displaying in-group loyalty is popular in modern societies. Indeed, it is so well regarded that psychologists have identified it with a rather friendly name: They call it "parochial altruism," rather than, for instance, "group greed." They define it as the act of being unselfish toward in-groups while at the same time being aggressive toward out-groups. For thousands of years, we humans have feared strangers from other tribes, and our fear has been eminently reasonable.[84] Our very brains have been influenced: When members of one's in-group are threatened by an out-group, known brain patterns for empathy and concern for one's in-group members are strong. At the very same time, one's tendency to aggress against the out-group grows.

Parochial altruism is System 1 in action. Decisions to sacrifice the self for the group, endangering oneself to save a person under threat, are often made instinctively and quickly. They are "relatively automatic and intuitive."[85] Often such self-sacrifice is triggered when the concentrated thinking of System 2 is thwarted because an individual is stressed – he or she is overly busy, or is in a noisy environment, or is under social pressure.

Research suggests that the more competitive a person is, the more likely he is to engage in parochial altruism. Being in competition with other groups motivates competitive people to perform. When their group is competing with another group, competitive individuals become especially cooperative with their own group members, and simultaneously, they become particularly flexible in their thinking.[86] Research suggests that parochial altruism is particularly strong in individuals who have high levels of testosterone. Such individuals exhibit high prosocial attitudes toward members of their in-group and, when threatened by an out-group, they are likely to escalate hostility toward the members of that out-group.[87]

Here's the rub. If the hunter kills the hare for his tribe, his action leads logically to war with the other tribe. Each tribe will hunker down to protect its own. Thus, the sociological version of the stag hunt dilemma points to the limits of altruism, and these human limits threaten the future of the planet.

Bringing these findings to the climate and energy conversation, we can see the challenge that faces superordinate groups like the United Nations and the European Union. Competing nation-states faced with the depletion of the global commons may not be able to cooperate to fix the problem.

Like all human beings, those who work in the energy sectors operate by the principles of parochial altruism. They are loyal to their tribe, be it oil or solar energy. Although many humans are competitive, let's assume for the sake of argument that individuals in the energy business are a tad more competitive than most. Researchers tell us that individuals who score high on the personality trait of competitiveness, which is related to extraversion, see relationships in terms of power, and they like to win.[88] So they are likely to want their sector to win. Competitive people also tend to view cooperating as weak and unintelligent, while competing is seen as strong and smart.[89] Such competitors are likely to disrespect other sectors, and, most likely, they will try to dominate them. Thus, individuals in the competing energy sectors, each loyal to their own tribe and aggressive toward the others, are not likely to be part of the global climate solution.

Unless, of course, an enlightened Team Humanity can develop systemic leadership that guides them and the world toward cooperation and friendly competition. Much as we humans love competition, we also know instinctively that we need to contain it. The late T. Boone Pickens, who was both a gas mogul and a wind power entrepreneur, and without doubt a quintessential competitor, said it well: "Competition is good, but play by the rules. I love to compete and win. I don't want the other guy to do badly; I just want to do a little better than he does."[90]

Thus far, we have viewed the stag hunt dilemma through the lenses of individual risk and group membership. Leaders with systemic aspirations should also view it through the lens of ethics: What is the *right* thing for the hunter to do? This may be the most evocative approach, and, in fact, the essential question to pose. The answer should consider the needs of the individual, his or her tribe, and all the other tribes in the universe. It goes without saying that it will not neglect the welfare of the hare and the stag.

Recent social science sheds light on the connection between people's willingness to act and their tendency to envision ethical dilemmas in complex social situations. Interestingly, a major factor that predicts the tendency to act is whether a person is a systems thinker – defined as whether he or she can imagine the world in terms of systems. Psychologists Adam Davis and Mirella Stroink have found an association between individuals' tendency to think in terms of social and ecological systems and their degree of emotional connectedness to nature. Systems thinkers are more likely to agree that the Earth's systems, from the climate to the economy, are interconnected, and also that the small choices we all make can ultimately have major consequences. In addition, the more a person can see beyond themselves to understand higher-level interactions like inter-sector conflicts, the more likely that person is to "feel a sense of oneness with the natural world."[91] Importantly, making this connection predicts that a person is also more likely to act to protect that world.[92] Perhaps systems thinking also predicts an individual's tendency to take on a leadership role. On that idea, more research is needed.

Certainly, systemic leaders must be able to imagine the interplay of the societal and global institutions through which they must create change. How will the sectors of society, from industrial sectors to different communities, find ways to share crucial and scarce resources? Climate change and energy evolution will bring punishments and rewards to humanity. Leaders must imagine how those rewards and punishments might be distributed. Which tribe, or tribes, *should* eat the hare? Which tribe *will* eat the hare? What kind of tribe is most likely to wait for the stag? How can leaders induce all tribes to wait for the stag? Who will be willing to delay fine dining now so that many others can eat decently in the future?

Applying systemic imagination, climate leaders can develop goals and initiatives that make psychological, sociological, and ethical sense. They must overcome parochial altruism to step outside their own sector and its interests; they must lead as cosmopolitans and globalists. To develop climate solutions, they must figure out how business and government can join to develop and implement broad environmental policies, and how countries and regions of the world

can work together. They must push and inspire at the systems level –
in communities, states, countries, and the world – a tall order.

It is crucial that climate leaders understand compelling sector
interests and power struggles and not hide these conflicts under a
cloak of imagined, idealized cooperation. Thus, while encouraging
cooperation, climate leaders must also pay attention to the processes
that referee competition.

In a democracy, government is the sector that monitors and
mediates sector competition. At the same time, it also competes as
a sector.

Government is, by definition, the way people operationalize their
values, and it is how systemic leaders bring societal change. Ideally,
the processes by which governments broker compromise are democratic. Yet, democrats always face the opposition of powerful, competitive actors who, as we have just noted, may see collaboration as a
foolish, win-lose proposition and who will work hard to defend their
tribe. In the United States today, these actors are likely to be driven
by the enduring neoliberal philosophy of the novelist Ayn Rand, who
romanticized extreme individualism, imagined power in the hands of
elites, promoted free-market capitalism, and sought a minimal role
for government. By her way of thinking, dominance is a matter of survival of the fittest, including fit elites in business and science, and government power should be subordinated to economic power. Further,
market forces like supply and demand should dominate interactions
in and among all sectors.

In reality, at the institutional level, government itself is a competitor, and the business and government sectors often compete for the
same slice of the pie. Both want to rebuild our infrastructure, for
instance. Both want to control natural resources like fossil fuels and
water. In a world with a finite set of opportunities to make money,
entrepreneurs see what is currently in the government domain – pris-
ons, schools, the military, the electrical grid, water resources – and try
to monetize and control it. As natural resources like energy decrease,

pressure to privatize them will increase, and so will the counter-pressure to maintain government control.

In this business–government competition, both sides cultivate the public's favor. Business and government compete to be seen as the sector that rewards, and to avoid being seen as the sector that punishes. Business points out that it provides jobs and also creates new jobs, while government points out that it educates everyone for jobs and reduces unemployment through sound job policies. These days, citizens are likely to view business as the sector that rewards (provides jobs and income) and government as the sector that punishes (spends money and regulates).

In the United States, the business sector tries to delegate the nasty business of punishment to the government whenever possible. Rather than clean up its own environmental messes and raise prices to cover its costs, business makes government the bad guy by continuing to pollute and then complaining about government regulation of that pollution. Businesses coordinate together to these ends. Meanwhile, government, by convention and at times by law, does not blow its horn as loudly, and few stakeholders know how to talk positively about how effective government is.[93]

The complexity of modern society contributes to such separations and misunderstandings. In large countries, there are so many levels of society that a citizen cannot see through them to either the top or the bottom. It is hard to see what is really going on, let alone understand it.

In addition to being complex, many countries are highly diverse, comprising various ethnic groups, economic stakeholders, and ecological regions. In America, such diversity is both a strength and a weakness. Different communities make different choices based on their local values and the realities on the ground. Their diversity increases innovation and opportunity, but it also reduces possibilities for clarity, predictability, and compromise. Issues that arise out of diversity and complexity will be magnified as climate change begins to affect different regions in a multitude of ways. For example, it is predicted that states in the Midwest and South will suffer more economically than will those in the Northeast and the West, and that the United States will suffer more than Canada. Thus, there will be no one-size-fits-all solution, but rather a need for continual balancing and compromise.

A related governance problem is America's sheer numbers. When the US Constitution was ratified in 1790, the population of the country was less than 4 million, and Congress consisted of ninety-one representatives and senators. In 2010, the population was 309 million, and Congress consisted of 435 people. Thus, in 1790 the ratio of citizens to congressional representatives was 44,000 : 1, whereas in 2010 it was 710,000 : 1. Today it is sixteen times more difficult for Americans to know their representatives and to be known by them. Even given advanced communications, effective governance is influenced by these numbers: The 435-person Congress receives 300,000,000 emails a year.[94] Contrast this, for example, with Canada and its 37 million residents.

When people don't interact with each other, they don't support each other. Research confirms that although the public sees and accepts that national, state, and local governments have different responsibilities,[95] the higher the level of government, the less likely they are to trust it. That is, they trust local government more than state government,[96] and local and state government more than federal government.[97] At this writing, the federal government in the United States is polarized and systemically ineffective with respect to the issue of climate change. To psychologists and sociologists, it comes as no surprise that the more localized efforts are finding more support.

• • •

The main stakeholders in climate and energy are the various sectors that provide energy and the communities that depend on them. To understand how these sectors compete, climate leaders must be aware of in-group altruism and the realities of inter-group competitiveness. Going forward, they might attempt to envision more substantially how the sectors could cooperate.

In the end, all roads lead to government. Not only is government the legitimate compromiser, it has significant latitude to plan for and invest in a sustainable future.

PRACTICE 4

Define the Business of Business

All of us benefit from having an effective business sector. Yet, while we are enjoying the latest products, we must grapple with the reality that it is the business sector that turns the natural resources of the planet into products, profits, and problems. Individuals who work in the business sector are on the front lines of climate and energy concerns. Thus, the fourth practice of climate leaders is to inspire their own organizations toward global solutions.

These days it is not unusual for a company to promote sustainability – for example, to green its supply chain or install solar panels. Much less typical is the company that connects such green initiatives to a systemic vision for the planet and to the specific goals of stopping global warming and promoting a sustainable energy future.

Think of company sustainability initiatives as ranging from company-oriented to community-oriented to systems-oriented. Company-oriented interventions operate within the company and typically focus on the short term; community-oriented interventions include both the company's stakeholders and its business sector; systemic interventions pursue global societal and natural systems with a long-term emphasis. In this chapter we examine what companies are focusing on now, and how their leaders can promote the transition from local strategies to a global vision.

We begin with an analysis of typical company sustainability goals, the foremost among them being saving money. We then explore how companies move through different stages of sustainability, and how new management roles and company cultures can foster this transition. We conclude this chapter with a look at why the education of future business leaders is only beginning to address the global sustainability challenge.

1. TRADITIONAL BUSINESS GOALS VERSUS PLANETARY GOALS

As the saying goes, the business of business is business.[1] It is certainly true that companies need to make a profit, or at least break even, in order to survive. Yet, this constraint does not mean that businesses must make excessive profits, or that they cannot legally spend money and other resources to be socially and environmentally proactive. The business of business can include leading to preserve the planet, and companies may legally apply their profits to that end.

Some business people are surprised to learn this. Many graduate from business school having been taught the simplistic notion that the business of business is strictly business. Typically, this doctrine is taken to mean that a company must serve its stockholders before it serves any other stakeholders. This is in itself incorrect, since legally any company can choose to protect itself before it protects its stockholders. Also, within the American legal system, and in many other nations as well, even publicly traded companies have considerable latitude to serve the public interest.

In a major book on corporate altruism, the late Lynn Stout, a legal scholar at Cornell University, summarized the situation: "United States corporate law does not, and never has, required directors of public corporations to maximize either share price or shareholder wealth. To the contrary, as long as boards do not use their power to enrich themselves, the law gives them a wide range of discretion to run public corporations with other goals in mind, including growing the firm, creating quality products, protecting employees, and serving the public interest."[2] Interested in promoting social and environmental justice, some business leaders have engaged with the recent notion of social enterprise, which is, fundamentally, the idea that businesses can do well by doing good. Some believe, erroneously, that new legal forms are needed to promote such business altruism. In large part, the social enterprise movement is itself based on the false premise that the business of business is strictly business. Taken to an extreme, this point of view can be a costly distraction from the real picture, and the real opportunities.

There are sound business reasons why corporations should not slavishly adhere to the bottom line. As put by practicing attorney Steven Munch, "Some corporations have long supported social initiatives as a means of enhancing their own profits and long-term viability ... There is some evidence that these strategies are successful. Recognizing the potential benefits to shareholders, courts have upheld corporate social actions with even the most tenuous of supposed business purposes."[3] In the past, responsible companies often focused on social initiatives. Today, many recognize that environmental initiatives *are* social initiatives. Or, as put by the sustainable business advocacy group Ceres, "Sustainability is the bottom line."[4] Like their social initiatives, a company's environmental initiatives pay off in goodwill and may contribute indirectly to a company's profits and, indeed, its survival.

By pursuing sustainability, an organization hopes to (1) achieve cost savings; (2) motivate and retain employees; (3) obtain marketing advantage; or (4) gain strategic advantage. Climate leaders often work with these standard initiatives to learn how such change happens locally before encouraging their organization in a more systemic direction that focuses externally, on the planet. Top-level management, chief sustainability officers, and concerned employees can all contribute to this evolution.

Early on, companies are likely to entertain initiatives that help them save money by adopting sustainable technologies and practices. Two of their most important approaches are designing or retrofitting buildings and greening their supply chain.

According to the US Department of Energy, commercial buildings account for about 18 per cent of America's total energy consumption, and residential and commercial buildings together contribute 38 per cent of the country's carbon dioxide emissions.[5] The US Green Building Council (USGBC) is a private nonprofit that advocates for sustainable building practices. By its reckoning, buildings account for 72 per cent of electricity consumption, 39 per cent of energy use, 38 per cent of all carbon dioxide (CO_2) emissions, 40 per cent of raw materials use, 30 per cent of waste output (136 million tons annually), and 14 per cent of potable water consumption.[6] By improving buildings' heating, cooling, and air conditioning systems, changing lighting systems, and managing electrical consumption by computers and electronics, along with other smaller tweaks, USGBC shows companies how to improve their profits while protecting the environment.

To help with their planning and promote their successes, some companies pursue third-party endorsement of their green initiatives. LEED (Leadership in Energy and Environmental Design), the famous certification process created and managed by the USGBC, covers all aspects of building, including design and construction, interior design, operations and maintenance, and neighborhood development. It certifies new buildings on four levels, beginning at simply Certified and ranging upward through Silver, Gold or Platinum, based on their performance on such measures as energy savings, water efficiency, CO_2 emissions reduction, and indoor environmental quality.[7]

Some organizations also credential individual professionals to bring their expertise to their organization's building projects. This is the approach of the International Facility Management Association, which offers the credential of Sustainability Facility Professional.

LEED offers a similar service in its Green Associate program. Having a professional on board allows companies to monitor and maintain their green systems over time.

Although LEED certification has achieved a strong reputation in the field of building design and construction, it is not without its critics.[8] A building may initially achieve a high standard, yet after construction its performance may not be monitored. In contrast, Energy Star, a building rating system of the US Government's Environmental Protection Agency, requires submission of utility bills to prove a building continues to meet its standard. Another concern is that, as a nonprofit, USGBC can invite memberships and accept donations, suggesting possible conflicts of interest when customers are also donors. Also, a platinum LEED membership, not to be confused with a platinum building rating, costs tens of thousands of dollars. Finally, the certification itself is also expensive.

The other important way that companies save money is by greening their supply chains. Moving and storing raw materials, inventory, and finished products consumes a lot of energy and represents much of the cost of running a business. Companies can save along their entire supply chain, from sourcing and moving raw materials all the way to sending products to consumers. The major professional organization for supply chain specialists is the Institute for Supply Management (ISM), which aims to "support environmental precaution, promote environmental responsibility and encourage environmentally friendly technologies and processes." The ISM promotes supply chain sustainability through the development of "more sustainable business practices, products and services, and the embedding of sustainability throughout supply chains."[9]

In particular, supply chain professionals who are knowledgeable about energy evolution can have significant impacts on both promoting sustainable energy and cutting costs. For example, they must factor the cost of oil into their supply chain analyses. Larry Lapide, a forecaster and previous director of demand management at MIT's

Center for Transportation and Logistics, observes: "I believe that the
trend toward higher oil prices is the single most important macro
factor that supply managers will have to contend with over the next
couple of decades. Specifically, managers will be required to continually evolve their supply chains to align them to an increasingly expensive oil regime. However, it seems that the volatility in oil prices we've
seen over the past seven years has masked this critical trend for most
shippers. They simply have not heard the warning shot."[10]

Lapide was writing in 2012, before the 2015–16 decline and partial
recovery in oil prices. He was wrong for the short term but is probably
correct in terms of how energy usage will evolve over the next decades.
He further argues that companies should begin to align their supply
chains with rising oil prices by finding substitutes for plastics-based
materials, reducing plastics-based packaging, and shortening supply lines by favoring domestic and other close sources. He also suggests adjusting just-in-time thinking in favor of adopting slower, more
energy-efficient supply chains. For example, in the future, companies
might favor ocean shipping over airfreight, and trains over trucks.

The second way companies pursue traditional sustainability goals is
by establishing a green company culture that motivates their employees. Managers green their cultures to attract and keep good workers.
They especially want workers who are committed to their company –
who are involved with it, identify with it, and even have an emotional
attachment to it. By greening their cultures, companies hope to
attract workers with similar values. At the same time, companies hope
to prevent employee *dis*satisfaction. While some dissatisfied employees try to improve their situation, others withdraw to minimal performance levels, leave, or even actively try to sabotage the company.
Again, sharing similar values can help prevent such problems. Of
course, managers also want to improve their workers' performance,
and, thereby, overall organizational productivity. They even hope to
inspire organizational citizenship behaviors, those acts of kindness
and leadership that improve group cohesion and decision-making.

Citizenship behaviors contribute not only to employees' organizational commitment but also, at the end of the day, to customer satisfaction and financial results.[11]

How do managers pursue these goals for employee motivation using green initiatives? A leader's work starts with building a strong organizational culture that emphasizes sustainability. Culture is the system of shared values and norms, along with related behaviors, that defines what is important in an organization. A company's culture suggests to employees what attitudes, beliefs, and behaviors are appropriate. For example, if a job candidate notices that, over several hours of interviews, a potential employer offers him a refillable flask instead of several plastic water bottles, he might deduce that the company favors sustainable approaches to doing business.

Having what is termed a "strong" company culture provides a competitive advantage. Research suggests that having a strong culture enhances individuals' performance by offering them identity and meaning, and by shaping and coordinating their behaviors. Evidence suggests that having a strong culture helps companies improve their long-term economic performance.[12]

Consider, for example, what we'll call "Company X," a real company that promotes a strong, green corporate culture. Company X exists in an innovative, hyper-evolving business sector. It favors innovation, intelligence, and community. Company X is more of a clan than a bureaucracy, in part because among its employees there is a deep understanding about the organization's goals and values. Although it continues to grow, this large company hopes to maintain a small company feel. Company X also makes a point of collaborating with the surrounding community, including governments, nonprofits, and businesses.

It is not surprising that Company X has built a worldwide reputation around its corporate culture, in part because of its emphasis on environmental sustainability. Most of its green initiatives have been started by employees. They include using solar panels and wind

energy for electricity, having many LEED certified buildings, and serving organic, locally sourced food in the cafeterias. Company X also
supports a bike to work program and offers employees bicycles and
scooters for travel between office buildings. The company's highly
efficient data centers are world famous for their innovative technologies and strategic site development. To spend less energy on air conditioning, for instance, the company encourages employees in the
data centers to wear shorts to work.

To address climate change, the company has adopted a three-step
approach to being carbon neutral: (1) be as efficient as possible;
(2) maximize renewable energy; and (3) use carbon offsets to neutralize
the rest. The company also empowers employees to join in grassroots
groups with other employees, including environmental groups that
have some say in greening the corporation and improving employee
health. There is a clear fit between this company's values on innovation and its ideals about environmental sustainability. Among the
company's slogans are: "You can be serious without a suit" and "Don't
be evil." Experiencing this fit allows employees to reconcile their professional values with their personal values. They can contribute at
work to causes they care about.

You have probably guessed that Company X is ... Google. And do
you imagine that this laudatory description of the company is true?[13]
Well, yes, it is true; but then again, it is not systemic. Let's consider
next an additional perspective that situates Google in the broader
community of which it is a part.

Yes, it is true that if an employee goes to work by walking, running,
or biking, the company will donate to a charity of their choice. Also,
if an employee lives in downtown San Francisco, the company will
transport them the thirty-six miles to work on one of its own Wi-Fi
equipped biodiesel buses.[14] But it is also the case that some people in
the local communities believe that the Google buses undermine public transportation. The introduction of the buses has affected public
ridership on the local bus system, and the Google buses add to traffic

congestion.[15] These concerns are part of the larger transportation situation in San Francisco, where companies like Facebook, YouTube, and Apple all hire private transportation companies to provide bus service for their employees.[16]

So, yes, Google's culture attracts, motivates, and retains some of the best employees in the world. At the same time, the company, like all companies, also affects communities and the environment beyond its borders. An accurate assessment of a company's impact requires a cradle-to-grave, local-to-worldwide analysis of their products and operations. Only climate leaders who recognize systems can work on this broad canvas. It takes leaders who understand not only company attributes but also the place of the company in the organizational and natural ecosystem to work effectively with emerging and changing power relationships.

The third reason companies pursue climate and energy initiatives is to create a marketing advantage and thereby increase income. Supporting the triple bottom line of people, profit, and planet gives a favorable impression to outside stakeholders, and, perhaps most importantly, to customers.

Green initiatives strengthen several types of branding that give a company a unique image. The first type is corporate branding. Corporate branding as green is especially effective if a company is already working in a business sector that shares similar values on sustainability, such as the solar energy sector. Green initiatives also promote a company's employer branding: prospective employees, especially the younger, tech-sophisticated talents many companies hope to attract, may identify with and be attracted to a group-oriented, green culture that provides a healthy work environment. Finally, identifying with an environmental issue, such as rain forest protection, promotes image improvement through cause branding.

Another way that companies gain branding advantage is by joining together to share information and promote their interests in green issues. For example, the Environmental Business Council of New

England (EBC) represents businesses that specialize in environmental and energy technology, services, and products. Members include manufacturers, engineering consultants, and solid and hazardous waste management professionals, along with some institutions in investment, lending, financial, education, and governmental agencies. Among other initiatives, the EBC produces a Green Guide that educates companies and their employees about taking basic steps on energy reduction and waste management. The organization also gives their executive members technical and business information they need to manage and expand their companies. It reaches out to other businesses to support their efforts to conserve resources. In general, the EBC raises the visibility of these industries in New England to attract capital and customers.

Finally, being knowledgeable about climate and energy issues helps companies gain strategic advantage. Gaining advantage may mean simply that a company gets out ahead of any problems that might come its way; company leaders always want to anticipate and manage their risks. For instance, in anticipation of future transportation limitations, a company might move its offices from the suburbs to the city. Facing energy evolution, it might reduce its dependence on oil, gas, and coal, and plan its future consumption around electricity. If it is very rich, like Google or Apple, it might purchase wind farms. Of course, acting on such concerns gives a company an advantage over those of its competitors who fail to act.

In their role as change agents, senior managers ensure that their company has eyes and ears. So, they establish environmental scanning systems to stay on top of the complexities of climate and energy, and then inject that information into organizational decision-making. An organization's sustainability strategy must be based on reliable information about pertinent external factors. Performing a thorough environmental scan establishes a firm foundation for its risk analysis and decision-making. For this purpose, companies can use the PESTEL framework, a simple scanning tool that guides them to develop a systemic environmental analysis across six areas: politics, economics, sociocultural factors, technology, the natural environment, and legal frameworks.[17]

In the PESTEL framework as applied to climate and energy, understanding a company's political context requires investigating such factors as environmental policy, the power of vested interests, and government stability. Economic factors include the investment potential of sustainable energy versus fossil fuel energy, the job creation potential of the various types of energy, and the potential for economic disruption as fossil fuel availability declines. Examining sociocultural factors includes understanding and predicting public attitudes toward science, business, and government; resistance from disadvantaged communities; and education about science and energy.

In the PESTEL framework, technological factors include the rate of technological change and the hope for a breakthrough innovation on energy, and the possibilities for rapid dissemination of information through the Internet. Beyond climate influences and energy consumption, environmental factors include climate feedbacks, many of which are currently unpredictable but which may change the climate quickly and drastically. Finally, the PESTEL framework encourages examination of the law, including regulations on climate and energy and related areas like eminent domain and provisions for public health and safety.

A company integrates data from its PESTEL survey into a standard SWOT analysis to highlight climate- and energy-related strengths, weaknesses, opportunities, and threats. Since companies often focus on climate and energy issues as threats, they then pursue risk analysis. Of course, some see risks as opportunities to pursue interesting markets, or to outthink their competitors.

Coca-Cola routinely projects threats to the company from climate change. It attempts to predict where and how climate change will affect the water supply on which it heavily depends to produce its beverages. According to Jeffrey Seabright, vice president for environment

and water resources, "increased droughts, more unpredictable variability, 100-year floods every two years ... when we look at our most
essential ingredients, we see those events as threats."[18] What does
Coke do about it? It investigates, among other things, how to apply
water conservation technologies, and then it applies these technologies in its divisions worldwide.

Nike likewise analyzes how it may be affected down the road. Many
of its hundreds of factories are in Southeast Asia, where extreme
weather makes them vulnerable to flooding. Extreme weather also
disrupts Nike's supply chain: droughts affect regions that produce
the cotton it requires in some of its clothing. In response, the company makes many adjustments, such as switching away from using
cotton. The company also joins with like-minded companies in the
national organization Business for Innovative Climate and Energy
Policy (BICEP), discussed later in this chapter.

After problem identification, leaders address organizational
change. Management theorists earn their livings thinking about
change,[19] and change theory comes in many forms. Often it is grounded
in stages of development that are logical and driven from the top: In
this way of thinking, company leaders identify a problem, research the
problem, research solutions, and test the solutions. Some change theorists believe change is caused by seminal events, such as environmental
threats. Others emphasize that change occurs in a company's vision,
culture, governance, or learning, or in some combination of these.

MIT's systems dynamics expert John Sterman argues that, when
it comes to greening a company, most company change initiatives
are ideas for improving business processes. He notes that process
improvements can be problematic because innovative green processes
must compete internally with other process improvement ideas, and,
unfortunately, they may not measure up. In his article entitled "Stumbling Towards Sustainability: Why Organizational Learning and Radical Innovation Are Necessary to Build a More Sustainable World – But
Not Sufficient," Sterman reasons that "the primary difference is

that traditional improvement initiatives are justified and marketed to employees, supply chain partners, customers, and investors as critical for competitive advantage, profitability, or firm survival – that is, they are seen as central to the core business – while sustainability initiatives are framed as (also) helping to heal the world."[20] Furthermore, he notes, even traditional process improvement ideas that aim to improve cost, quality, or productivity "commonly fail."[21]

Technically and organizationally simple actions provide large returns quickly, while complex initiatives like improving the carbon footprint of the supply chain, or promoting low-carbon production methods, are likely to yield smaller returns over longer periods. Unfortunately, like maintenance, the more complex projects can be deferred. Sterman points out that today few organizations have a lot of slack, that workers are working hard already, and that sustainability initiatives add to that workload.

For those climate leaders not deterred by Sterman's somewhat pessimistic analysis, there are some tested ways to minimize problems with sustainability initiatives. One tactic is to frame the startup expenses of the change not as costs but as an investment. Also, to avoid an improvement becoming a one-off initiative, earmark at least some of the savings to fund further improvements. Some organizations create green loan funds that use such returns to finance more green improvements.

Effective green leaders work hard to estimate how complex a project will really be, and to set realistic goals. They avoid rewarding merely cutting corners. They hold managers accountable not only for delivering projects on time and within budget but for enhancing the firm's development overall. They reward improvements not only in costs but in employees' capabilities and skills.

While pessimistic about process improvements, Sterman also argues that developments in climate and energy offer the greatest entrepreneurial opportunity since the Industrial Revolution. He writes: "We cannot expect traditional business firms to promote policies that

would cause their growth to stop, to cease the marketing and adver-
tising campaigns that urge people to buy ever more, to unilaterally
internalize environmental and social costs when their competitors do
not. The leverage points for action on overconsumption do not lie
within business organizations, but in the beliefs, goals, and values of
the public, and in public policies that would both enact and reinforce
those values."[22] Climate leaders working at the intersection of business and public policy will play an essential role in building out the
opportunities created by such new values.

Most people want to work for organizations they can respect, and,
ideally, care about, and they can see that even humble green initiatives are at least steps in the right direction. Even if a company is primarily trying to save money by reducing its energy usage, its initiative
is worth something to the planet. Just as it is hard to know whether
your partner really loves you or your cheesecake, it is hard to tease out
whether your company's sustainability initiative is self-serving or pro-
society. Probably, it is some of each. Leaders must depend on their
System 1 instincts and System 2 fact-finding proclivities to figure out
what a given organization is "really" up to.

Based on observational studies, researchers suggest that, when
developing a commitment to sustainability, companies move through
predictable stages. Each stage represents an increased commitment
that builds toward embracing change for a more sustainable and just
society. Increasingly, employees support companies that attempt to
be part of climate and energy solutions at the highest level.

One model suggests that companies go through the stages of compliance, efficiency, and innovation.[23] Companies are likely to begin
their involvement when they face regulation that forces them to collect data on their processes. In the process of self-examination, they
become more aware of their environmental impacts. At this point,
their leaders are thinking mainly in terms of compliance. They are
worrying about things like what the regulations require, how that will
be measured, and whether they need technical and legal advice to

meet the requirements. But they also begin to be concerned about possible regulation changes and how they should plan for them.

Companies enter the second stage, efficiency, when they begin to think more broadly and strategically. They pursue organizational efficiency not merely to comply with regulation but to reduce their costs across the board. They begin to compare themselves with other companies to see where efficiency can create a competitive advantage. Sustainability, previously defined as the ability of the company to survive and thrive, comes to mean that a company must learn to survive and thrive in an era of increasing disruption of natural systems.

In the innovation stage, companies do all of the above, but also consider how they can contribute to the sustainability of society and natural systems. They move far beyond cost-cutting to develop systems that promote long-term profitability while reducing their environmental impact. In this stage, the research suggests, company leaders are challenged to convince their stakeholders of their good intentions, and to fend off accusations of greenwashing.

Of course, leaders who think globally believe that this model should be extended to a fourth stage, in which companies consider not only their role but also their sector's role in the preservation of the planet. In this stage, business leaders rethink not only their own business model but the model of business in the world. They reflect on the assumption that growth is endless. They realize that no manufacturing operation can truly have zero environmental impact and weigh the implications of this reality for social and natural systems.

2. OPERATIONAL LEADERSHIP

Companies implement change through leadership. As a company moves from the compliance stage to the efficiency stage of sustainability, it often creates the position of chief sustainability officer (CSO).[24] "Companies are monitoring the impact they're having environmentally and on society, and the appointment of the CSO reflects an underlying need for companies to not only monitor but also improve their performance," says George Serafeim of the Harvard Business School. "Many organizations are afraid to raise the stakes and make bigger bets," he notes. "It's not easy to make that transition. That's why you need the CSO to make a push to move on, become more ambitious."[25]

The CSO is an organizational change agent dedicated to a goal, much like a corporate officer devoted to diversity and inclusion. Some companies create the position simply to determine internal needs and opportunities and to help employees meet these needs. Other companies want the CSO to be an ongoing voice that monitors sustainability issues internally within the organization and externally among its stakeholders, and to ensure the inclusion of that information in high-level decision-making. Most studies indicate that being involved in strategic development is a focal activity for most CSOs, although their other important activities vary widely by company.[26]

The first CSOs began to appear around 2004, when the conglomerate E.I. DuPont created the first known position in a publicly traded American company. Today, however, an Internet search finds more job openings for CSOs in government than in business. Consider the following example of what such positions entail. The city of Westminster, Colorado, advertises for a CSO to develop "an innovative and consensus-building Sustainability Plan that accelerates the achievement of the City's vision to become the next urban center of the Colorado Front Range and one of the most sustainable cities in America." The CSO reports to the Deputy City Manager and works with the City Council, the city organization, the community, and other stakeholders. Requirements for the job include a bachelor's degree in sustainability, natural or environmental science, public administration, or a related field and seven years of related experience. Also required are "municipal, public sector or institutional experience addressing complex social, environmental, and economic issues including public education, outreach, and consensus building," and credentials like the LEED professional certification.[27]

In the business sector, the CSO position is often filled internally. One data set puts the percentage of internal hires in the position at 55 per cent; another puts it at 86 per cent. Candidates are drawn from such departments as external affairs, operations, marketing, and environmental, health, and safety. About half of those in a position to hire the CSO believe that a business and financial background is required. Others point to an MBA, or experience in communications, operations, basic science, or product development, as prerequisites.[28]

Research suggests that the CSO's role evolves over time. In the early compliance and efficiency stages of sustainability, almost all CSOs do things like formulate and execute strategy, work with ongoing internal projects, report data, manage stakeholder relations, and educate employees.

When a company moves into the innovation stage, the CSO's role includes even more emphasis on strategy and strategic innovation but less learning from external sources, less educating employees, and less working with stakeholders. At this stage in an organization's development, many employees have been brought on board through internal education. Sustainability initiatives have probably been decentralized, and the company supports change champions companywide. Departments are likely to report sustainability data to the chief financial officer rather than to the CSO.[29] Now the CSO's role is to continue to deepen strategy as it applies to the company's unique position to face global challenges or effect social change. The CSO also works to deepen the sustainability culture and unify subcultures inside the company. It is at this point that the CSO is most likely to join the company's executive team.

In organizations today, climate leaders are the latest candidates for emotional labor and burnout. Some jobs require a lot of it. For example, teachers, call-center workers, nurses, and flight attendants all experience emotions on the job that they dare not express.

Emotional dissonance – the inconsistency they experience between their felt emotions and their forced emotional expression – is a significant factor in their job stress.

Emotional labor involves repressing emotions, or repressing core beliefs that themselves give rise to emotions. For example, the beliefs espoused by a corporate sustainability manager may differ from those of the individual in the role. At work, sustainability managers typically aim to maximize profits and increase their corporation's competitiveness, while as environmentalists they might want to improve such planetary factors as ecological well-being and biodiversity. Also, while sustainability managers use corporate metrics to measure their success, environmentalists find corporate metrics to be inadequate for this purpose and advocate complicated ethical decision-making instead. It follows that sustainability managers who identify with environmentalists' beliefs and practices may be subject to burnout. Likewise, when corporate sustainability leaders begin to think systemically, they are likely to increase their emotional labor and stress.

In a major study of managers in Australian and various international businesses, Christopher Wright and Daniel Nyberg investigated emotional stress among climate leaders. In their sample of sustainability specialists and operational and senior managers concerned with sustainability strategies and practices, they identified repeated instances of emotional labor. One frustrated manager told them, "This is all about the shareholder return, and the directors' fiduciary duties and the executives' duties to the directors and to the shareholders are quite clear ... Mucking around sustainability things for society is not the work of companies."[30]

Across their subjects, Wright and Nyberg repeatedly found that corporate managers are "acutely aware that the promotion of the environment can only occur when accompanied by the promotion of the market" and that there is no space for reducing profit or slowing company growth.[31] They conclude: "Ironically, with environmental goals thus subsumed within the core demands of profitability and shareholder value, it is those managers who are the most environmentally aware who almost invariably find themselves at the forefront of the compromise process. This is 'noble corruption' in action. As nature itself is reconstructed into a commodity and a tool for profit, environmental and sustainability managers have to get their hands dirty – and they know it."[32] It follows that climate leaders need to be clear about their personal green identity, and how it fits or does not fit their organizational role. Then, in terms of their organizational role, they have three basic choices.

Their first choice is to assume the identity of rational manager, as seen in a traditional business. In this role, the rationale for pursuing environmental sustainability is solely to improve efficiency and reduce costs. Promoting environmental sustainability prevents risks to the corporation and provides opportunities to create value. It also does some good for the planet.

Their second choice is to become an internal change agent. In this role, an individual who is personally concerned about the environment and climate change is willing to push through internal resistance to advance an environmental agenda. As one internal sustainability manager put it, "I have a huge passion around climate change, around the change side of how you move this change through organizations." Another said, "Really what you're trying to do in this whole field – Get people to go: 'Oh, okay, there's another agenda, there's something bigger than just me and my job.'"[33]

A leader's third choice is to take on the overt role of a committed activist who is willing to take significant risks to change their organization. In this role, individuals' corporate engagement with climate change is visibly related to their personal values, and they are on a journey or mission to do whatever they can. As one such manager put it, "I guess we have to be the voice of the environment, which can't speak … So sometimes decisions are made and those considerations aren't there, and we've got to be the ones who stand up and say: No!"[34] Research suggests that such individuals are prone to burning out when their organizations fail to support change initiatives. However, they are also likely to be part of a sustainability community beyond their work organization.[35] One of Wright and Nyberg's interviewees felt he had to resign when his firm was taken over by an energy multinational. "70% of their revenue comes from hydrocarbons, and I just can't do it. I never had anybody who really came back to me and said: 'You're crazy.' A lot of them really admired me for taking a stand on this."[36]

Among the managers they interviewed, Wright and Nyberg uncovered a range of raw emotions. They report:

> The perceived shortcomings of wider social action on climate change and the everyday reminders of expanding consumption and environmental degradation led to feelings of disappointment, disillusionment, and sometimes even despair for many of those who participated in our study. One sustainability manager at an insurance corporation told us: "I oscillate. I hear those things, and then you just look at everything else and just go: 'It's all doomed.'" For some the desolation was almost crushing. Maybe the ultimate concession of noble futility, of raging against the dying of the light, came from the manager who confided: "Well, personally, I think it's the end of the world. I get the whole story, and I have got to just paralyze my fear about the whole thing. I have no doubt about what's going to happen."[37]

When such negative emotionality cannot be aired at work, individuals are left to deal with it outside.

Is there a solution to climate leader burnout? Leaders who want to minimize emotional labor around sustainability issues establish strong company cultures in which norms and values about sustainability are clear. They encourage employees to find value and meaning in pursuing sustainability initiatives, and reward employees for displaying appropriate emotions. They also try to hire people who are most likely to feel comfortable in the organization's level of green culture.[38]

However, these goals are not easy to implement. Nor is implementing them going to get any simpler as the role of business in causing climate change becomes clearer, the consequences become more dire, and employees' emotions become more intense.

One of a CEO's primary jobs is to frame issues in a way that promotes action. To promote environmental initiatives, encouraging employees to debate climate scenarios may help. Much as the IPCC builds scenarios for the planet, some companies use scenario methodology to help organizational members think broadly and practically about climate and energy. For example, a company might apply scenarios to imagine how rapid climate change might affect their consumers, or how it might influence government regulations.

Economist Rebecca Henderson, co-director of Harvard University's Business and Environment Initiative, suggests that under climate change there are two fundamental uncertainties that are driving organizations to use scenario building. The first is how quickly technological advances can address climate problems. The second is how quickly consumer demand and political pressure will react to climate change. Mapped against each other, these two uncertainties suggest four scenarios that business decision-makers need to contemplate.[39]

Two of the four scenarios assume that demand for green technologies will be high. The first, referred to as "Green Goes Mainstream," assumes strong demand for sustainable products and services, driven either by political pressure or consumer preferences, and fueled by accelerating technological innovation. Some industries, including solar energy, wind power, and alternative transportation like Zipcar and Uber, are already experiencing this scenario.

The second scenario, "Demand Driven Opportunity," assumes increasing demand for green products and services, even though technological progress in developing new products is slow or costly. The introduction of Tesla's mainstream electric car falls into this category.

Under the third and fourth scenarios, in contrast, demand for green technologies is predicted to be low. Under "Supply Driven Opportunity," technological innovation is significant, but consumers cling to old technologies because the new ones are expensive. Reduction in the supply of raw materials of all kinds helps drive prices up. This category includes burning oil or gas to heat homes in hot regions even though solar is a reasonable substitute.

Under the fourth scenario, "Business as Usual," there is no significant increase in demand for sustainable products and services either from consumers or regulators, in part because they continue to be relatively expensive, and because there is little technological innovation. This scenario reflects the belief that personal identity, mental models, and organizational culture change very slowly. Henderson observes that "this is the world that most firms experience at present, and it appears to be the future that is taken for granted by many business people ... Even those business people who do not believe that 'business as usual' is the most likely future often act as if it were."[40]

Henderson concludes that

> Mapping these examples to industries highlights the way in which the current case for sustainability differs enormously across the economy, with the major opportunities currently occurring in energy, buildings, water, agriculture, and consumer goods. In these cases, the uncertainties I have mapped are increasingly no longer uncertainties – firms can be sure that technological progress will occur, or the consumer or regulatory demand will enable them to offer a more highly priced product. But framing the strategic space in this way also focuses attention on the fact that for many industries, the case for becoming more sustainable rests on the assumptions one makes about how these uncertainties are likely to play out.[41]

The main opportunities will be in industries in which raw materials and energy make up a significant percentage of the value added.

Strategizing for a new business environment helps companies be proactive in terms of climate and energy. For instance, an organization may decide to develop customer and regulator relationships, along with practical knowledge that it deems strategically advantageous. Developing sustainability experience can set an organization up to take advantage of technological change in markets as it occurs. Henderson notes, for example, that Nissan's electric car, the Leaf, has developed strategic advantage for the company. Launched in 2010, by 2013 the all-electric, five-passenger compact car had not achieved profitability. Nevertheless, Nissan has viewed the Leaf as an asset to its brand, as a leg up on developing innovative technology, and as a successful strategic hedge.

How do leaders know that the people in their organization are ready to tackle the opportunities and risks posed by climate and energy initiatives? Assessing their organization's culture can be informative. In a time when most organizations assert that they are going green, leaders can find out just how green they really are by digging into what people actually think and do. By understanding where the people in their organization are coming from, concerned leaders can determine whether, and how, to intervene.

An organization's culture has four levels. The first is the level of the obvious – the behaviors and artifacts that are the visible indicators of underlying values and beliefs. This level is the face the organization presents to the world. It shows what the company wants its stakeholders, including employees, customers, and business partners, to believe about it. Does the company have a story to tell about why and how it is going green? Does it promote sustainability in both its external publicity and its internal publications? One can observe whether the company provides recycling bins and whether people are talking about environmental issues. Does the building demonstrate the company's commitment to energy conservation?

A deeper level of culture is found in the rules and norms that most people are aware of in their organization. A greener company recycles, but it also routinely discusses the contributions and limitations of recycling. In a responsible company, there would be some understanding that ethical decision-making combines the best aspects of System 1 and System 2 thinking. One norm might be to favor data-based problem-solving and group decision-making over merely following management directives. Another would be to routinely consider both the positive and the negative impacts of decisions on internal and external stakeholders.

The third level of culture consists of the ideals, standards, and goals of which most people in the organization are aware. These establish the foundation for the two more observable cultural levels just discussed. Sustainability ideals can range from the most basic, aimed at company cost reduction, to the most engaged, aimed at planetary survival.

In an organization that is concerned with climate and energy, a scientific approach to problem-solving is the standard and employee education is valued. Beyond that, being educated about systems is of interest. Individuals value knowledge of and experience with environmental systems. They also value knowledge of a variety of social systems, including the environmental policies of other sectors and countries. Individuals also value stakeholder input and are open to external communication and newcomers. At this level, people are also aware of potential conflicts, such as what their organization says versus what their organization does, and how these conflicts reflect existing power relationships.

Finally, the three previous levels of culture all derive from the fourth and deepest level – individuals' unconscious assumptions about the world. People make assumptions, for example, about the nature of truth and its origins: Today's green company culture values science and a realistic appraisal of the world's natural resources. Some companies naturally adopt a system view that encompasses other stakeholders and includes the natural world, while others cannot see beyond their own interests. Some gravitate toward systems that share power, while others gravitate toward systems that centralize it. Some gravitate toward competition and domination, while others gravitate toward compassion and responsibility for others.

A fundamental theme in a company's culture is how it utilizes science. Climate leaders should assess how their colleagues value science, how they use science, and how much their coworkers know about the science of climate and energy. People read science at different levels to achieve their unique goals. Some may skim peer-reviewed articles for their own general knowledge. Others may need to drill down to find specifics that will drive their recommendations and actions. Highly research-oriented individuals may want to dissect new findings in detail, often with the intent of improving or refuting them. Of course, many people do not read science at all. Even if individuals highly value science, they may nevertheless rely strictly on science interpreters to inform them. If their coworkers' knowledge is slim, leaders must be ready to face resistance to change, and plan to do some educating.

For many years, the EPA Center for Corporate Climate Leadership has recognized individuals and organizations that are change agents in their companies or sectors, and models for other organizations. Here are a few of their stories.[42]

As the director of sustainability at JetBlue Airways, Sophia Mendelsohn has worked to reduce the environmental impact of the airline and the aviation sector. She helped imagine and implement a ten-year binding agreement for millions of gallons of renewable jet fuel, one of the largest biofuel purchase agreements in aviation history. The agreement permits the biofuel producer to raise capital for new refineries, which will allow them to expand their scale and eventually lower the price of biofuel for the entire industry. Mendelsohn consults extensively with JetBlue's crew members to identify opportunities for emissions reductions. These conversations have contributed to such innovations as transitioning ground support equipment to electric vehicles; reducing fuel costs and saving CO_2 emissions by filling potable water tanks to only 75 per cent; and reducing aircraft idling times and thus lowering fuel usage by millions of pounds annually.

In the government sector, as a member of the California State Assembly, Eduardo Garcia has represented an inland district that has one of the highest unemployment rates in the state. He has served on numerous environmentally oriented committees of the Assembly, including chairing the Committee on Water, Parks and Wildlife and the Joint Select Committee on Climate Change Policies. He has reached out extensively in his district and other low-income California districts to create dialogue about climate change, even though it is an issue that must compete with health and jobs as local concerns. To do this, he has partnered with organizations that include business, labor, faith, environmental justice, and traditional environmental groups. Based on his representation and networking, he can intervene effectively at the state level to ensure that state climate policies benefit low-income communities.

Among organizations, an EPA award winner is Procter & Gamble (P&G), the consumer goods company from Cincinnati, Ohio, that operates in some seventy countries. P&G has already made its mark on energy consumption by encouraging the use of cold-water laundry detergent. It has also set sustainability goals for a ten-year period, which include reducing greenhouse gases by 30 per cent for its global operations; using at least 30 per cent renewable energy; reducing truck transportation by 20 per cent; and doubling its use of recycled resin in plastic packaging. It is partnering to build one of the largest renewable combined heat and power facilities in the United States, and a wind farm in Texas that will provide 100 per cent of the electricity for one division's manufacturing sites in the United States and Canada.

3. SYSTEMIC LEADERSHIP

The late Ray Anderson, founder and CEO of Interface, was an early adopter and champion of business practices that are practices for the planet and not just for the company. In fact, many consider him to be the father of the business sustainability movement. Certainly, his example of transformational leadership inside Interface, and his engagement with the wider business community, are instructive and inspiring.

Interface is an international company that produces modular carpets and high-quality broadloom carpets; it is the world's largest designer and maker of carpet tile. It was in 1994 that a potential customer suggested to Interface management that the company should pay attention to the environment. The customer told Interface's West Coast sales manager that when it came to the environment, Interface "just doesn't get it." As Anderson wrote in his book, *Business Lessons from a Radical Industrialist,* "I was not happy. My only thought was, Interface doesn't get *what?* ... I knew we stood to lose other sales. How many? I had no idea. But I did know that telling our customers, 'we comply with all environmental laws,' wasn't going to cut it."[43]

At the suggestion of a senior manager, Anderson convened an environmental task force of managers from divisions around the world to see what they were currently doing and to develop a better way. You can appreciate Anderson's role as persuader-in-chief in his 2009 TED Talk, "The Business Logic of Sustainability."[44] There you can see how, with charm and authenticity, he sold sustainability as an ideal to his company and to businesses worldwide.

Anderson is a classic model of executive leadership that manages meaning for a company, which in his case meant suffusing sustainability thinking throughout the company culture. From 1994 on, he was a transformational leader who successfully engaged with his employees to move Interface radically toward specific sustainability goals. Anderson also became a national and international spokesperson for sustainability in modern manufacturing organizations. His work presaged later, more systemic efforts among business leaders.

One of the many initiatives Interface undertook was to aim for zero waste. As Anderson put it, "The truth is, attacking waste is the engine that will pull the whole train. If you're looking for a quick, profitable

[success], going after waste is the natural place to begin."[45] Interface
defined waste as any measurable cost that goes into their product but
doesn't add value for the customer. Their major areas of waste were
in yarn usage and product packaging. All fossil fuel, including gas,
oil, diesel, and electricity from a coal-fired plant, was also counted as
waste to be eliminated.

The company set measurable goals for waste reduction, and
at first they tied every manager's bonus to hitting a 10 per cent
annual reduction. Later, after finding that this approach didn't
particularly inspire employees, they switched to directly paying the
people who came up with good waste-cutting ideas. Over the first
ten years, Interface figured that eliminating waste saved the company $262 million.

Anderson's goal was to achieve what he dubbed "Mission Zero,"
driving Interface to a zero environmental footprint by 2020.[46] The
company has made significant progress. In 2018 it reported that even
though carpets are a petroleum-intensive product, since 1996 the
company has reduced the average carbon footprint of its carpet business by 69 per cent. It also reduced water consumption by 89 per cent,
and energy usage by 46 per cent. Of the energy used at carpeting
manufacturing sites in the United States and the United Kingdom,
99 per cent was from renewable sources.[47]

Anderson inspired his employees to be creative and strategic, and
to do everything possible to achieve environmental sustainability. Yet,
it is simultaneously a good thing and a bad thing that the company
has probably achieved everything that has been technologically possible. It is good, because of Anderson's inspiration, the employees'
effort, the company's demonstrable achievements for the environment. It is bad, because even with all of this, the company, like all
manufacturing companies, is still far from achieving net zero. The
Interface story of hard-earned but partial success is similar to that of
other smart and concerned manufacturing companies. They can do
a lot, but at the same time they can only do so much.

The Interface effort raises the fundamental issue of how society can really obtain a zero environmental footprint. Does a zero footprint mean zero manufacturing? What are the practical and ethical limits of excusing nonrenewable practices by purchasing carbon offsets? Should Interface limit its business to renewable hardwood (or, more renewable yet, dirt) floors?

Even Ray Anderson didn't have wise answers to such difficult questions. His important contribution was to open the door to the tough conversations we are having today.

Top managers today follow in Anderson's footsteps as both internal change agents and external company spokespeople. Some are stepping up even further, to work at the institutional level by taking on sector leadership and cultivating global influence.

A census of internal initiatives in several multinational companies suggests the practices that leaders are using today to advance corporate environmental responsibility.[48] Top managers generally:

- develop vision, strategy, and goals that incorporate environmental responsibility;
- integrate environmental responsibility into business decisions and operations;
- act as role models;
- engage a variety of stakeholders, internally and externally;
- develop and empower employees to take responsibility for the environment;
- systematically communicate about environmental responsibility;
- are accountable publicly;
- visibly support integrity in management decision-making.

Engaging in these practices helps leaders build internal support and establish green company cultures.

Importantly, some leaders are developing more external, systemic roles, and driving change not just for their companies and their immediate stakeholders but for the planet itself and the long term. Systemic leaders do things like building coalitions within and between the business and government sectors. They network with businesses and governments internationally, and fund the kinds of organizations that can help.

One such change maker is the US Climate Action Center, an organization that includes many businesses and has shadowed and influenced such world convocations as the United Nations–sponsored Paris talks and the subsequent conference in Bonn in late 2017.[49] At these conferences the Center has brought together American cities, states, and businesses to advance US climate policy and counteract the policy vacuum left by the Trump administration.

Another is BICEP, a coalition of businesses committed to "working with policy makers to pass meaningful energy and climate legislation that will enable a rapid transition to a low-carbon, 21st century economy that will create new jobs and stimulate economic growth while stabilizing our planet's fragile climate."[50] BICEP's members are mainly consumer companies like CA Technologies, Gap Inc., IKEA, Kellogg's, and Nestle. BICEP is a project of the nonprofit organization Ceres, which is itself a coalition of investors, environmental groups, and other public interest organizations that work with companies on building sustainability.

Ceres directs a large set of such integrative projects. In addition to BICEP, it runs the Investor Network on Sustainability and Climate Risk, which connects institutional investors with each other and with investment leaders globally, providing opportunities for collaboration and leadership. This group, in turn, works with the California Public Employees' Retirement System (CalPERS) and other organizations to promote Climate Action 100+, "a five-year initiative led by investors to engage systemically important greenhouse gas emitters and other companies across the global economy that have significant opportunities to drive the clean energy transition and achieve the goals of the Paris agreement." In 2020 this initiative had grown to more than 360 investors controlling more than $34 trillion in assets.[51] Also, in 2019 Ceres announced a new center, the Ceres Accelerator for Sustainable Capital Markets, to "transform the practices and policies that govern capital markets in order to accelerate action on reducing the worst financial impacts of the climate crisis and other sustainability threats."[52] The annual Ceres conference attracts thousands of high-level corporate officers to learn about and engage with such initiatives.

4. EDUCATING LEADERS FOR STRONG SUSTAINABILITY

These days there is a significant debate about how well universities, and in particular business schools, are teaching environmental sustainability. Should sustainability be integrated across the curriculum? Should it be taught in a series of electives? How useful are university sustainability centers?

In this debate the most important question is, What should be taught? Scholars of sustainability pedagogy rate sustainability content on a spectrum from weak to strong. Professors who teach weak sustainability advance the belief in infinite growth. They measure that growth in terms of gross domestic product. They are likely to advocate putting a strictly monetary value on natural resources. In contrast, professors who teach strong sustainability see growth as finite; measure development using economic and noneconomic, quality of life factors; and consider natural capital to be priceless. They advocate a humanistic, values-based approach to valuing natural resources.[53]

Research by professors Nancy Landrum and Brian Ohsowski, in a sample of fifty-one out of the hundreds of business school programs in the United States, found that only a few schools offer majors, minors, graduate degrees, or certificates in sustainability management or sustainable business.[54] In those that do, the subjects are offered mainly as electives in the curriculum. Even more important, in their sample,

Landrum and Ohsowski examined concept by concept the assigned readings in over eighty sustainability courses and found that 55 per cent were most closely aligned with a weak or very weak sustainability view, while 29 per cent were aligned with a strong or very strong sustainability view.

In other words, the majority of sustainability courses covered complying with the law and improving profits, while a minority discussed current scientific findings and the future of nature and humanity. The researchers also observed that there is as yet no commonly accepted body of knowledge in the academic field of sustainability, and that many of the publications in use today come from practitioners rather than from academics themselves.

Other academic observers point out that, "in recent years, business schools have come under scrutiny for their failure to instill a sufficiently deep sense of responsibility and to prepare graduates for the sustainability challenges of the modern business environment."[55] Some conclude that "recent debates on the role of business schools have highlighted the need for greater societal engagement and for incorporating sustainability and corporate social responsibility into business schools' activities, in particular, by embedding sustainability in the curriculum."[56]

Of course, these shortcomings may be because the field is relatively new. However, there are other possible explanations. One is that the weak sustainability approach reflects the dominant culture of business and business schools.[57] It may also be the case that adopting the weak sustainability approach reflects an inability or reluctance on the part of professors to teach from the controversial perspectives of finite growth, reduction in consumption, and changes in the quality of life. These are also topics with which they are likely to have little expertise, given the highly specialized research expected of today's business professors.

Whatever the particular reasons, Landrum and Ohsowski conclude that "the fact that US business schools are educating future business leaders from a weak sustainability paradigm is disconcerting and brings into question not only the ability of future USA business leaders to address or solve global sustainability challenges but also the implications this could have for the future competitiveness of the USA in a low carbon or post-growth society."[58]

A colleague who teaches business in a liberal arts college recently complained to me. "We can't hire business professors," he said. "They just don't get it." He explained that PhDs trained to teach in business schools see their research and theory as ending at the boundary of the organization. Aside from strategic considerations affecting their company, what happens outside of the organization is generally not that important to them. Neither is it methodologically accessible to them: Professors are not investigative reporters. Also, given sector complexities, it is difficult for them to stay current on developments not only in business but in government and other sectors. Thus, they study and teach about company survival and profit, and tend to gloss over or ignore the impact of the business sector on the planet.[59]

Business schools have been complicit in promoting blind optimism about market solutions to planetary problems. One reason may be that they face ambiguous demands, being asked by some stakeholders to promote profits and by other stakeholders to promote sustainability.[60] Another reason may be that, given companies' contributions to faculty rewards like endowed chairs, and, in general, to business schools, faculty lack incentives to tackle power relationships that reflect the more unfortunate impacts of the business sector. As my liberal arts colleague put it, business schools are in the business of training young people to work for companies; they are not concerned with educating citizens.

A related driver is that, since the middle of the twentieth century, business schools have sought intellectual legitimacy by adopting scientific methodologies from the natural sciences, with a focus on quantitative analysis of measurable phenomena. Yet, in climate and energy, so much is happening politically, and happening so fast, that it cannot be measured in these ways. Nor, most likely, can political interaction in real time ever be measured effectively using the traditional methods of social science.

Career-oriented business school professors in top research institutions study mainly what is observable and quantifiable, and therefore publishable. For example, applying the contingency theory of leadership, which focuses on individuals, both reflects and constrains the aspirations of management researchers. Studying traits and skills is unambiguous, lending itself more to the scientific method and to publishing than studying complex human behavior in the context of fast-changing, interactive social systems. Indeed, The Economist recently called management theory "a compendium of dead ideas," in part because it does not account for politics.[61]

Just as some processes in natural science cannot be measured because there are practical limits to acquiring observations, many social processes fall outside of the realm of practical observation. In addition, much of organizational decision-making happens behind doors that are closed to researchers for reasons of privacy and competition. This is nothing new; the doors of business have always been barred to any purpose other than promoting a company. Management scholars have always relied on privileged but limited access, and on informants, public accounts, and laboratory studies, to get at "the truth" about organizational decision-making. Published case studies, one of the most popular pedagogical tools in business schools, are often stories told by companies for companies.

Despite such problems, many university educators are working to improve sustainability education. For instance, a systemic change is developing in the more than 200 US Jesuit business schools. In 2010, a group of these schools decided their teaching was becoming complicit with secular but unethical paradigms. Since then – representing schools like the University of San Francisco, Gonzaga University, and Boston College – they have met often to improve their curricula. They set the long-term goal of doing more to include such values as social justice, human dignity, ethics, and sustainability. Among other initiatives, they now publish the *Journal of Management for Global Sustainability*, which examines a broad set of systems-wide issues like environmental preservation, social entrepreneurship, poverty eradication, social justice, desirable production and consumption patterns, species preservation, and spiritually rich lives.[62] Likewise, Babson College has initiated, and measured the impact of, the introduction of sustainability topics and modules across their curriculum.[63] Many schools have similar initiatives. Your author has taught a strong sustainability course to high-level undergraduates and MBA students for over a decade.[64]

Still, when hiring, companies devoted to global, systemic sustainability cannot assume that newly minted college graduates understand or value their initiatives. Since business schools themselves may not support such values, there is little reason to assume that their new graduates will. In the education sector, there remains a lot of room for innovation.

• • •

We have seen that leaders have many good reasons to foster sustainability in their organizations. Some companies pursue limited sustainability, focusing on increasing profits and strategic advantage, while others pursue systemic sustainability, hoping to help protect humanity and the natural systems on which we all depend. Understanding their organization's sustainability culture can help climate leaders to be effective. Likewise, evaluating the alignment between one's own assumptions and those of others in the organization can help committed environmentalists decide whether, and how, to lead. Climate leaders whose values do not match those of their employer face the possibility of burnout. On the other hand, by taking some risk, they may experience the deep satisfaction of leading their organizations toward meaningful change.

In the next chapter, we examine effective leadership on the global stage, in light of some additional social science on human psychology in systems.

PRACTICE 5

Engage Global Leadership

Is systemic, global leadership an oxymoron? Or can human beings successfully join across the planet to manage our climate and energy challenges?

The fifth practice of leaders for the planet is to develop perspectives and plans to drive global change. We saw in Practice 3 (Weigh the Stakes) that societal sectors compete, and that global leaders must think beyond their sector's interests to forge collaborative and/or competitive processes that integrate interests across sectors. They must build inter-organizational and inter-sector relationships, especially relationships between business and government, and among countries.

So global leaders must think big, and they must think smart. They must understand the psychology and politics of motivation, collaboration, and competition, including how to set motivating goals and turn those goals into action. They must be thoughtful about how humanity distributes resources – about economics, including ecological economics and the workings of capitalism itself. They must improve the long-term effectiveness of existing global institutions or develop new ones. They must spark the moral imagination of world citizens, encouraging us all to think and act beyond the confines of our own place and time.

And they must do all of this while facing up to psychological factors like human denial and political factors like national sovereignty. Is any of this realistic? In this chapter, we evaluate some of the strategies that are being tried.

1. DESIGNING PLANS THAT ADD UP

Motivating large parts of the world begins with setting goals we can all believe in. When it comes to climate and energy, Team Humanity has two such goals.

The first goal is to curb fossil fuel use by those in the developed world. Burning fossil fuels to run our refrigerators and fly our airplanes has been a lot of fun. Unfortunately, motivating us to stop doing these delightful things is going to require a dose of punishment. Probably, that punishment will be smaller if we take it now, and larger if we take it later. Key questions, the answers to which are beyond the scope of this book, are whether we will be a better people for the sacrifice, and whether we will ultimately be rewarded.

One major complication is that not everybody shares the goal of curbing fossil fuel use – not by a long shot. Most among the world's poor do not, since they rely on whatever energy is cheap. Important power holders do not, since they either own the fossil fuel companies or run economies that depend on them. In developing countries, the middle and upper classes claim the right to use fossil fuels to improve their lives, just as the developed countries have. This is truly a global motivational problem.

Also, working with punishment is tricky. Psychologists recommend pushing the use of reward to its limits before resorting to slapping hands. Every person in the world is understandably nervous about giving others the power to punish them. Certainly, we have seen from many attempts, including the failed Kyoto accords, that elected governments are highly unlikely to cede to an external group the right to punish their citizens (for instance, through regulation). In fact, in competitive cultures, the strong and entitled may view cooperation itself as a form of punishment and loss.

Whether people are motivated by a goal is determined by an interactive process between individuals and their environments. Show a customer an innovative product (an extrinsic goal) and suddenly they "need" it (an intrinsic goal).[1] Convince the most popular guy on the block to install solar panels and suddenly others in the neighborhood want them, too. At a systems level, intrinsic and extrinsic factors do interact. However, that China takes the lead in producing solar panels does not necessarily inspire their competitors. From a motivational standpoint, commercial and economic systems are highly complex.

Beyond curbing the use of fossil fuels, humanity's second goal is to create renewable, much less polluting energy ("much less" because all energy forms pollute as they are manufactured). This goal is psychologically easier, because it rewards rather than punishes. We will promote green energy by, first, replacing fossil fuel energy sources according to a greening plan and, second, by generating scientific innovation that improves upon existing technologies or creates new ones. Happily, such interventions engage positive mental states like imagination and curiosity.

Achieving these goals will require personal intensity and perseverance. Many people, especially scientists, find that the ability to solve problems is itself a reward. They expect to be intrinsically rewarded for their work, in part, by satisfying their innate curiosity. Innovation that succeeds is rewarding to them, but so are steps in the right direction. To such people, making money and climbing a career ladder are secondary considerations. Similarly, morally driven climate leaders are likely to find the work itself to be rewarding.

Perseverance in the face of adversity is based in part on a sense of self-efficacy – the belief that even if one fails at first, by rethinking the problem one can eventually succeed. In the face of impending climate change, maintaining a sense of self-efficacy may require individuals to change their goals from ones that they cannot accomplish to ones that they can. Scientists and citizens alike may face system disruptions that will require reorientation and adaptation.

Research tells us that we human beings – or perhaps more accurately, we American human beings, on whom most behavioral research has been performed – prefer to work toward specific rather than vague goals. We also enjoy working toward tough but achievable goals. We like outcomes to be measurable, so that we can determine our own progress and so we can hold others accountable. Setting goals for the use of clean energy clearly qualifies on all counts.

Effective goal setting for clean energy is exemplified by the delightful book *Sustainable Energy – Without the Hot Air* (available free online), by the late David J.C. MacKay. A physicist and mathematician, MacKay painstakingly laid out goals for sustainable energy usage, and at the same time set specific, achievable carbon emission targets. He invited readers of his book to consider the nitty-gritty specifics of energy change for Great Britain,[2] and then kindly converted those calculations into comparable projections for the rest of us – for Europe, the United States, and the rest of the world. In all of this, he was clear about advocating his own power-down philosophy: He argued that we will all have to live on less energy.[3]

MacKay dedicated his work to "those who will not have the benefit of two billion years' accumulated energy reserves" and shared his vision of a plan "that adds up" as follows:

Because Britain currently gets 90% of its energy from fossil fuels, it's no surprise that getting off fossil fuels requires big, big changes – a total change in the transport fleet; a complete change of most building heating systems; and a 10- or 20-fold increase in green power. Given the general tendency of the public to say "no" to wind farms, "no" to nuclear power, "no" to tidal barrages – "no" to anything other than fossil fuel power systems – I am worried that we won't actually get off fossil fuels when we need to. Instead, we'll settle for half-measures: slightly-more-efficient fossil-fuel power stations, cars, and home heating systems; a fig-leaf of a carbon trading system; a sprinkling of wind turbines; an inadequate number of nuclear power stations. *We need to choose a plan that adds up. It is possible to make a plan that adds up, but it's not going to be easy.* (Emphasis added)[4]

He then calculated the renewable energy contribution that is feasible in the United States. It is important to note that MacKay was writing in 2008, before some significant technological innovations and market developments; thus, his plan is more an exemplar than a precise reflection of current realities. At that time, the average American was using 250 kWh/d (kilowatt-hours per day). MacKay wondered if individual Americans would consider cutting their energy usage in half, to that of the average European or Japanese citizen. (Note that some of that cut would come not in the American home, but in electric cars and high-speed electric trains.) He concluded (again, in 2008) that the following specific goals would get them there:

(1) If Americans could increase their *onshore wind* hardware 200 times and would be willing to place it on acreage equivalent to the state of California, assuming a population of 300 million people, they could generate 42 kWh/d per person.
(2) They could generate an additional 4.8 kWh/d per person with fifteen times more *offshore wind* hardware than exists. This wind hardware would be placed in shallow waters off the East Coast in an area about the combined size of Delaware and Connecticut.
(3) *Geothermal* could contribute 8 kWh/d per person.
(4) If doubled from current output, *hydroelectric power* from Canada, the United States, and Mexico might provide 7.2 kWh/d per person.

At this point, MacKay comments, "the total so far is 42 + 4.8 + 8 + 7.2 = 62 kWh/d per person. Not enough for even a European existence! I could discuss various other options such as the sustainable burning of Canadian forests in power stations. But rather than prolong the agony, let's go immediately for a technology that adds up: concentrating solar power."

(5) Calculating America's potential for *solar*, MacKay found that an area about the size of Arizona would provide enough power to give 500 million people the average American's consumption of 250 kWh/d.[5]

Looking next to electricity needs worldwide, MacKay assumed a consumption rate of only 80 kWh/d per person. To meet this goal, he noted, the world must rely on non-solar renewables and one or more forms of solar power, or use nuclear power, or both.[6]

Obviously, all of this renewable energy is more than enough to meet basic needs, but, just as obviously, it poses major hurdles. For example, given how extensive solar and wind installations must be, Americans may need to consider using more nuclear energy. In his book, MacKay discusses these concerns, and more. Unfortunately, to date, his clear, detailed work has not been replicated.

In his 2012 TED Talk, aptly titled "A Reality Check on Renewables," MacKay invited what he called "a grown-up conversation" about the future of renewables. "We need a plan that adds up," he said, yet "most levers have popularity problems."[7] While he successfully debunked the idea that we can rely heavily on green energy in the near future, he also offered realistic numbers that could guide the transition.

From a psychological perspective, he was right on. He set data-based, challenging, but achievable goals for both energy consumption and energy availability. He also showed how making changes in one area contributes to broader change, thus motivating people who strive to make contributions locally that also matter globally. Finally, he showed us where both the scientific and political challenges lie.

That MacKay is no longer with us to push this motivating agenda is a considerable loss.

By 2017 the United Kingdom had reduced its greenhouse gas emissions 39 per cent below 1990 levels, a significant accomplishment on the way to its goal of 80 per cent reduction by 2050. The key measures that contributed to meeting that target include energy efficiency, the use of low-carbon power, more electric vehicles, some low-carbon heating, and some use of carbon capture usage and storage, along with electrification in industry, planting trees and changing farming practices, diverting waste from landfills, and phasing out fluorinated gases.

As noted earlier, in 2018 the United Kingdom was running its economy on an energy mix that included about 51 per cent from renewables and nuclear, and 41 per cent from gas.[8] Building on its success, the United Kingdom in 2019 announced a plan to achieve close to net zero emissions by 2050 as compared with the 1990 levels. To reach a 96 per cent greenhouse gas reduction would require all the measures already in place, along with what the plan refers to as a "significant low carbon hydrogen economy," in which carbon capture and storage would have a larger role in combination with biomass and major changes in farming.[9] To achieve 100 per cent reductions would require additional changes in diet and flying habits. For instance, it would require people to reduce their consumption of beef, lamb, and dairy by 20 per cent, and replace these with pork, poultry, and plant-based products. Radical shifts in land use would be necessary. Carbon capture and storage or successful development of synthetic fuels, for instance from algae, or renewable power, would also be required.

The report stated: "It is impossible to predict the exact mix of technologies and behaviors that will best meet the challenge of reaching net zero greenhouse gas emissions. [This analysis] is not intended to predict or prescribe the future technology mix, but it gives an understanding of what a sensible mix might look like and allows us to assess the potential challenges and costs in delivering it."[10]

Although encouraging on the face of it, such a plan is unlikely to motivate individuals or sectors.

Seen from a psychological perspective, this is a policy rather than a plan. On the one hand, it does name specific numerical targets for reductions in tons of carbon dioxide emitted. On the other hand, these targets are not presented systematically to allow readers to do the math. Without the math, policymakers cannot track progress and accountability goes out the window. Likewise, on the one hand, the report argues that it has new evidence on the potential to reduce emissions from industry. On the other hand, it finesses the prediction that cutting industrial emissions would cost 8 billion pounds per year in 2050, and would require "a fast pace of deployment of low carbon technology in comparison to the natural turnover rate of industrial assets."[11] In other words, business resistance will be likely. In addition to downplaying probable political resistance, the report also downplays the current lack of feasibility of carbon capture and storage and hydrogen technologies.

Unlike the MacKay plan, this current UK plan is not specific. And while one might fault the MacKay plan for ignoring politics, this plan does the opposite: It obfuscates goals by assuming politics. This approach is not bad as an invitation to improving policy, but it is not good as a motivator to action. Policymakers and other thought leaders would do well to heed environmentalist Edward Abbey, who wrote, "Sentiment without action is the ruin of the soul."[12] People need to see plans they can actually implement.

One plan that, like MacKay's, is specific and global, although without drilling down on consumption, is the carbon budget produced annually by the Global Carbon Project. The Project informs humanity where we are now in terms of overall carbon pollution, energy sources, and trends. It is a crucial foundation for estimating the time we have left before we set the stove too high (and it gets stuck there).

The Global Carbon Project is a partnership among groups of scientists to establish a common knowledge base about the causes and amount of greenhouse gases in the atmosphere. Every year since 2007, it has published comprehensive data on carbon emissions and their sources worldwide. It also estimates their absorption on the planet in "carbon sinks." For example, it notes that the atmosphere is a carbon sink that had absorbed carbon to the extent of 228 parts per million (ppm) in 1870, while in 2017 that figure was 405 ppm.

The Project reports that, in 2017 and again in 2018, CO_2 emissions from fossil fuel burning and cement production were the highest in human history.[13] In 2018 emissions come from coal (40 per cent), oil (34 per cent), gas (20 per cent), and making cement (4 per cent). The Project predicted in 2017 that there were four years left in the global carbon budget before warming might become extreme.[14]

While the Global Carbon Project points out sources of carbon pollution, and therefore suggests leverage points, it does not directly advocate for particular changes. One recent goal-setting effort sets some specific targets for reducing greenhouse gas emissions. Led by environmentalist Paul Hawken, Project Drawdown uses input from more than 200 scientists and researchers worldwide to rank interventions by how much greenhouse gas emissions each will cut. At this writing, the five most impactful interventions are capturing methane from landfills, retrofitting buildings, making new construction net zero, modernizing the electrical grid, and localizing electrical production and storage. On its website, Project Drawdown promises to update its rankings based on the latest data. Also, the project has produced a beautiful book to motivate action through, as they put it, novelty and human engagement.[15] One important limitation of Project Drawdown is that it does not show how individual goals add up to a total solution. Another limitation is that it does not thoroughly discuss how to reduce the emissions from major polluters like aviation and automobiles. Addressing projected aviation expansion, it suggests that technical developments will make planes more energy efficient but ignores the possibility of curtailing flying. Flying less is not listed as a way to reduce greenhouse gases. Similarly, although buying an electric car is listed, taking public transportation is not.[16]

Although they do set specific, challenging, and feasible goals, neither the Global Carbon Project nor Project Drawdown addresses how such changes will be both measured specifically and accomplished politically. One can hardly blame them, since achieving world change is an immodest goal at best. MacKay was more into the weeds of change. At the same time, the design of his plan motivates by showing individuals how their actions contribute to meeting an ultimate goal. Yet, he, too, concluded that "if you would like an honest, realistic energy policy that adds up, please tell all your political representatives and prospective political candidates."[17]

So, in addition to goals that are motivating, we also need leadership that simultaneously addresses pollution sources and carbon sinks. Tom Steyer, founder and president of NextGen Climate, points out the need for this level of leadership. As he writes in the introduction to Hawken's book, "Now we must ask how best to organize our coalition and govern our most selfish instincts ... using systems thinking and detailed analytics to tackle the biggest environmental challenge of our time."[18] Hawken himself notes the limitations of mere goal setting, while advocating for more global cooperation:

Our organization did not create or devise a plan. We do not have that capability or self-appointed mandate. In conducting our research, we found a plan, a blueprint that already exists in the world in the form of humanity's collective wisdom, made manifest in applied, hands-on practices and technologies that are commonly available, economically viable, and scientifically valid. Individual farmers, communities, cities, companies, and governments have shown that they care about this planet, its people, and its places. Engaged citizens the world over are doing something extraordinary ... Climate solutions depend on community, collaboration, and cooperation.[19]

Hawken joins activist Bill McKibben in advocating for individuals to join in a movement that "[helps] draw the threads and webs of humanity into a coherent and more effective network of people that can accelerate progress towards reversing climate change."[20]

2. PUNISHING CARBON USAGE: CARBON FEES AND CAP AND TRADE

While all these climate leaders exemplify systems thinking and goal setting, and have made important contributions to motivating change, there is a great deal of work to be done to effect that change. Implementation begins with motivating people to share a vision and act on it. From a psychological standpoint, this means applying principles of reward and punishment to motivate valued behaviors.

We have already noted that practicing punishment is problematic. Climate leaders are suggesting it today only because they believe the cause is urgent. Most likely, we cannot reward people into new behaviors quickly enough. For example, when towns offer energy-frugal homeowners bonuses that might also motivate their neighbors, the process is both expensive and slow. Governments simply do not have enough capacity to reward even such small changes. Therefore, to reduce greenhouse gases, politicians have proposed a variety of ways to charge individuals and companies for burning carbon.

Punishing carbon usage does have certain advantages. Implementing across-the-board surcharges reduces carbon usage across all of society, rather than in just one sector like transportation or industry. In this way, citizens perceive it to be fair. The practice is also acceptable to a wide audience because people can know in advance approximately what the price of the carbon will be. This facilitates planning, and, again, is likely to be seen as fair. At the sector level, putting a price on carbon is a positive because it creates a compelling green demand signal to businesses. Companies rise to the challenge and compete to meet the new demand for energy-efficient products and processes, thereby encouraging technological innovation and creating jobs.

From an environmental standpoint, surcharges are problematic because, although they foster conservation, they do not specify an overall emission reduction goal. Since policymakers cannot predict how much carbon reduction will be possible, they cannot reliably contribute to a systemic carbon reduction scheme like a regional, national, or international plan that adds up to a meaningful (and motivational) reduction in carbon emissions.

Carbon taxes and carbon fees are the two main types of surcharges in use today. A carbon tax is money collected by government that can be spent on whatever projects the law allows. Pretty much everyone acknowledges that a carbon tax, which is so visibly a new tax and is therefore immediately recognized as a punishment, waves a political red flag. Nevertheless, some have been passed.

Smart lawmakers have found ways to turn surcharges on everyone into rewards for at least some. Instead of a carbon tax, they propose a "carbon fee," the difference being that, with a fee, the surcharge on carbon is held in a specific fund and is returned directly to citizens. Sometimes these bills are referred to as "carbon fee and dividend" plans.

British Columbia is Canada's pioneer in this approach. They implemented a carbon fee (although they do, unfortunately, refer to it as a tax) that returns all carbon dollars to families and businesses through various means. As their provincial minister said when the program was designed, "If I had said, 'Give us the carbon tax and trust us,' I knew it would have been a failure."[21] British Columbia's Liberal Party (which, despite its name, leans to the right) introduced the fee in 2008. It covers the carbon emissions of families and businesses, homes and factories, and cars and trucks. The tax started out at $10 CAD per ton of carbon dioxide in 2008 and rose to $30 CAD in 2012. Simultaneously, the province cut corporate and personal income tax rates, and low-income families were given a tax credit. Under this formula, by 2016 the government was returning more to businesses and families than it was collecting through the tax.[22] Academic analysis has shown that, because of the nature of the household income that determines the fee, the fee has been highly progressive.[23]

Nevertheless, a poorly conceived carbon fee can be regressive, punishing certain disadvantaged populations, and legislators across the board have been addressing this problem. Back in the United States, in the Commonwealth of Massachusetts, early legislation proposed by State Senator Michael J. Barrett promoted a carbon fee program by which consumers and businesses would pay higher prices for transportation and heating and cooling fuels (punishment), but then all money would be returned in equal shares to individuals and businesses. If a family or company conserved, it could be rewarded by getting more back in rebates than it pays out in fees. This 2015 bill offered slightly larger returns to residents of certain communities, such as rural communities in the western part of the state who must drive long distances to work.[24] Barrett's bill also included provisions to protect business competitiveness by rebating fees paid to companies in proportion to their number of employees. For the purposes of the bill, carbon was priced initially at $10 per ton and increased by five dollars every year until the rate reached $40 per ton, after which a commission would set the rate. More recently, Barrett has argued that the price of carbon should rise to $60 per ton.

Today about forty countries and more than twenty cities, states, and provinces use either carbon taxes or carbon fees as pricing mechanisms, according to the World Bank. Other governments have plans to implement them. The existing programs cover about half of these governments' emissions, which together make up about 13 per cent of annual global greenhouse gas emissions.[25]

Everything is not roses in the fee department, however. At this writing, the British Columbia tax was the steepest and broadest in North America, and, as an early mover, the province has faced some pushback. The program places a cost burden on Canadian businesses, making them less competitive than their counterparts in neighboring jurisdictions. Having taken a leadership position, provincial officials hoped that other provinces, and also states within the United States, would step up to impose a carbon tax and thus create a level playing field for all regional businesses. However, their neighbors have not done so adequately. (In Massachusetts, businesses likewise unfavorably compare their energy costs to those of the Mid-Atlantic states and argue that what they need most is cheaper energy.)[26] Another issue is that the program may have set the price on carbon too low, so that the province will most likely miss its target of reducing emissions 80 per cent by 2050.

Voters' estimation of the tax gradually became more favorable. In 2009, 47 per cent of BC voters opposed the tax, while in 2015 only 32 per cent did. Emissions initially declined by 5 to 15 per cent, and the province's economy grew faster than its neighbors'.[27] However, 2015 figures showed that carbon emissions had increased 1.6 per cent over the previous year. This increase was met with concern by the Sierra Club of British Columbia, which saw the reductions as a token gesture and called for other measures, such as climate testing all major industrial projects, increasing protection for forests that store carbon, and a public inquiry into fracking in northeast British Columbia.[28]

Nevertheless, subsequently Alberta and Quebec also put a price on carbon, and Canada implemented a national carbon fee, a "revenue-neutral carbon tax," beginning in 2019. Ninety per cent of the national revenues are to be returned to individual taxpayers, and they are predicted to offset increased energy costs for about 70 per cent of Canadian households.[29] Meanwhile, conservative provincial governments newly elected in Alberta and Ontario continue to spar with the national government over all of these taxes. Alberta has overturned its own carbon tax on consumers, although as a province it continues to be subject to the national tax. Interestingly, one-third of Albertans, the highest level in history, think they would be better off economically if they were separated from Canada.[30]

One carbon fee proposal takes a different approach, taxing only producers and distributors nationwide in the United States. The non-partisan Citizens' Climate Lobby promotes a carbon fee and dividend program that puts a fee on fossil fuels where they are produced at their source, such as at the mine, the well, or the port. Governments would return 100 per cent of that revenue to US households. The organization estimates that this approach would cut greenhouse gas emissions by 50 per cent in twenty years. They predict it would create 2.8 million jobs, boost GDP, and save 200,000 lives.

The debates over carbon pricing and its implementation will continue, of course. Groups from Ontario (the conservative government of Doug Ford) to the State of Washington (voters defeating a referendum in 2018) to France (the Gilets Jaunes movement around the country) are pushing back. The issues are complex, and the trade-offs are unobvious.

Another solution that is being widely considered is "cap and trade." Cap and trade is a point sharing process that sets limits on carbon emissions in a region. The premise of this approach is that the amount of permitted polluting emissions should be measurable and finite. Motivationally, the idea is that companies should be rewarded for conservation and, at the same time, their growth should be only minimally punished. In a region, the amount of permitted carbon burning is fixed, or "capped," and carbon allowances are allotted to each polluting company. The companies can then sell their allowances or buy more. Hence, *cap* and *trade*. The process is also referred to as an emissions trading system.

This process creates a supply of, and a demand for, emissions allowances, thus establishing a market for greenhouse gas emissions. Some companies might need points to add manufacturing capacity. Companies that conserve well can increase their revenues by selling any unneeded allotment. In most such systems, the defined pool of emissions is set to shrink systematically over time. Thus, on the one hand, companies are encouraged to conserve, and on the other hand, they can adjust their business models to accommodate the reductions by a specific date.

A national cap and trade system for carbon emissions was considered at length by the United States Congress as recently as 2010, although it was ultimately rejected.[31] A regional version has been functioning in New England and the Mid-Atlantic states since 2009: The Regional Greenhouse Gas Initiative (RGGI) is the first mandatory program in the United States to reduce greenhouse gas emissions from the power sector (see https://www.rggi.org). States sell emission allowances through auctions and use the proceeds to invest in programs for energy efficiency and renewable energy.

Cap and trade has been criticized for allowing some companies to continue to create negative impacts rather than deal with their pollutants. Also, no competition model is ever perfect. For example, it is difficult for governments to impose the perfect cap on every company. Nevertheless, the recognition of the carbon emissions pollution problem, the collective attempts to solve it, and the smooth functioning of RGGI appear to be steps in the right direction. From a motivational standpoint, cap and trade allows for both punishment and reward. Also, it provides a stable, predictable regulatory regime for businesses.

From an environmental standpoint, the program offers a set emissions target that governments control. Collectively, companies and states seem to have accepted that enduring small punishments like administrative costs and inconvenience are worth the greater reward of slowing climate change and being seen to do so; they may also be able to make some money along the way. On the other hand, during the RGGI initiative, analysts contend, most emissions reductions could be chalked up to market forces and other clean energy initiatives, and only about 11 per cent of energy efficiencies could be attributed to the RGGI; such initiatives need to be significantly strengthened by such changes as extending trading beyond electricity and tightening emissions limits.[32]

3. ROADBLOCK: CLIMATE GOALS MEET GLOBAL POLITICS

As humanity has come to recognize and address climate change and energy evolution, the global political view of appropriate goals, as expressed by representatives of participating governments in several United Nations conferences, has evolved. The easiest way to see this is to contrast the goals of the Kyoto conference in 1997 with those set in Paris in 2015.

The Kyoto and Paris agreements were both negotiated under the auspices of the United Nations. They were designed to encourage countries to reduce their greenhouse gas emissions. These meetings of government representatives were held under the umbrella of the United Nations Framework Convention on Climate Change, an international environmental treaty established in 1992 to maintain the concentration of greenhouse gases at a level that would prevent dangerous human interference with the climate system.[33]

The Kyoto agreement covered countries that emitted, in total, less than 30 per cent of global emissions, and because even some of these countries withdrew, that percentage fell to about 13 per cent.[34] China was listed in the accord not as a major polluter required to reduce its emissions but as a developing country with minimal requirements. There was no provision for transitioning such an important emitter into the category of large polluters. The United States signed the agreement, but its Senate failed to ratify it. Within several years, shortly before the date on which they would become subject to binding penalties, Canada, Japan, and Russia all withdrew legally from the agreement.

Kyoto did have a lasting influence on global decision-making. It introduced the idea of a multinational carbon market, created supports for poorer countries, and influenced carbon usage legislation in some countries.[35] Because of the meetings, the world also got the message that powerful countries will not accept legally binding carbon caps. However, they could be convinced of the importance of reducing their carbon emissions, and they might be induced to help other countries to do so. The outcomes also made clear that all countries must be involved in any decision-making process that has a reasonable chance of being globally effective.

Although some parts of the Kyoto agreement run until 2020, as a whole it was essentially replaced by the Paris agreement of 2015. The core facts of the Paris agreement are these:

- The deal involves almost every country in the world – 195 countries. Only Syria and Nicaragua did not sign. The Trump administration announced in 2017 that it would withdraw the United States from the agreement.
- After initially proposing a goal of 2° C, governments agreed to attempt to limit the global average temperature increase to 1.5° C.
- Governments agreed to reduce total global emissions as soon as possible, while allowing developing countries a longer period to adapt to such changes.
- Each country submitted a national climate action plan to meet these goals. Although collectively these agreements do not keep global warming below 2° C, the agreement showed the path to this goal. For example, the United States pledged to reduce its emissions by 26 to 28 per cent from 2005 levels by 2025. Other developed countries made similar pledges. The achievement of these goals is not a legally binding commitment.
- The treaty does not include binding emissions targets or binding financial commitments.
- Governments agreed to meet every five years to set more ambitious targets based on the most recent scientific findings. Since

the agreement is considered a treaty under international law, this procedural agreement to meet is legally binding.

- Governments agreed to report their progress to each other using emissions inventories and other information that will be subject to independent review by technical experts and other governments.
- Compared with previous UN efforts, this agreement puts more of a focus on adaptation to cope with the impacts of climate change.
- The agreement also recognizes the role of stakeholders outside of the discussion, including cities and other subnational political groups, civil society, and the private sector. These groups are encouraged to reduce emissions, build resilience, and enhance regional and international cooperation.
- Developed countries agreed to mobilize $100 billion per year by 2020 to reduce emissions and build resilience in developing countries.[36]

Was Paris a good effort? Are these goals the best we can do to motivate global efforts? Are they enough?

Optimists see the Paris agreement as a bridge between current inadequate policies and the achievement of zero emissions by the end of the century. Historically, experiments with global cooperation among nations have been both promising and instructive. Witness the strengths and weaknesses of the United Nations and the European Union. Witness the inability of regions like Latin America to achieve economic coordination. Witness the contribution of the United Nations to peacekeeping efforts across the globe, if for no other reason than it promotes positive relationships and dialogue.

More hard-nosed behavioral analysts might argue that such global efforts are doomed to failure. In 1946, the year after the United Nations was chartered, thought leader George Orwell (author of

1984) argued that, without binding agreements, world cooperation will have no impact on peace keeping:

> In order to have any efficacy whatever, a world organization must be able to override big states as well as small ones. It must have power to inspect and limit armaments, which means that its officials must have access to every square inch of every country. It must also have at its disposal an armed force bigger than any other armed force and responsible only to the organization itself. The two or three great states that really matter have never even pretended to agree to any of these conditions, and they have so arranged the constitution of U.N.O. [United Nations Organization] that their own actions cannot even be discussed. In other words, U.N.O.'s usefulness as an instrument of world peace is nil. This was just as obvious before it began functioning as it is now.[37]

Time has shown that he was, in some ways, wrong. Today, United Nations peacekeeping efforts exist across the globe and have been active since 1948. Their current budgets run into the billions of dollars annually. One can argue whether they are enough, or worthwhile, and so on, but they are not nil. One might make the same arguments about the European Union.

Also in the pessimistic camp, Daniel Kahneman argues that attempts at such large-scale reforms often fail over time. This is because, according to the principle of loss aversion, people are more worried about potential losses than they are inspired by potential gains. For example, when institutions try to change their ways, he suggests, "plans for reform almost always produce many winners and some losers while achieving an overall improvement. If the affected parties have any political influence, however, potential losers will be more active and determined than potential winners; the outcome will be biased in their favor."[38] Moreover, research suggests that the defenders, rather than the reformers, generally win out.

From a psychological and political perspective, it is safe to say that for most citizens of the world, the idea of serving a global leader, whether an individual or a global body like the United Nations, is anathema. The risks of creating a structure that could facilitate world dictatorship are simply too high. For this reason alone, countries guard their sovereignty and avoid cooperation.

Where does that leave prospects for international cooperation for climate change? Country goals are highly disparate, and Paris leaves the adjustment of goals to individual countries on a handshake. Commercially, Australia is betting on selling huge amounts of coal to China, India is betting on using its own coal to become energy independent, and Russia and several Middle Eastern countries are selling their fossil fuels globally. It is hard to imagine that all or most of these countries will overcome self-interest to save the planet, even though they are all signatories to Paris.

On the other hand, soft power is certainly better than no power. Isolating countries to deal with the issues themselves would no doubt be even more tragic for the global commons. The Paris treaty is symbolically important, as the first time in history that the whole world has come together to acknowledge the impending threats of climate change. Also, countries may motivate each other by example. And, from the perspective of the business sector, the proposal that green energy should become more important is likely to motivate global entrepreneurs and create new markets.

Academics weighing in on the positive side of Paris include Oliver Geden of the German Institute of International and Security Affairs, who observes that "many segments contain very vague language, but this kind of 'constructive ambiguity' is often the only way to get a deal done. The actual meaning will only develop over time, as a result of ongoing power struggles."[39] MIT political scientist David Victor observes that "the encouraging precedent here is in trade – where you get a bicycle theory of cooperation. You build credibility and trust

over time and then [through momentum in subsequent talks] move
to bigger issues."[40]

But what about the goals set in Paris? Do they advance motivating,
actionable solutions? "It's a fraud really, a fake," scientist James Hansen says. "It's just bullshit for them to say: 'We'll have a 2C warming
target and then try to do a little better every five years.' It's just worth-
less words. There is no action, just promises. As long as fossil fuels
appear to be the cheapest fuels out there, they will be continued to
be burned."[41] Taken in context, Hansen is arguing that there is simply
not enough time to keep talking, and that we must act now, and act
radically. He supports a carbon fee that is rebated to the public.[42]

Are the goals of Paris even achievable? One collaborative scientific
report shows how national pledges would have to increase over time
to keep warming to 2° C: In comparison with 2005 levels, by 2050 the
EU would have to reduce its emissions by 80 per cent, and the United
States likewise would have to reduce its emissions by 80 per cent.[43] "To
even meet the Paris goals, by 2050, carbon emissions from energy and
industry, which are still rising, will have to fall by half each decade;
emissions from land-use (deforestation, cow farts, etc.) will have to
zero out; and we will need to have invented technologies to extract,
annually, twice as much carbon from the atmosphere as the entire
planet's plants now do."[44]

An intermediate goal for the United States is to reduce its 2005
levels 45 per cent by 2030. The comparable intermediate goal for the
European Union is to reduce its emissions below 47 per cent of 1990
by 2030. China's intermediate goal is to peak by 2030, or, better yet,
by 2025, and to reduce its emissions 2 per cent per year through 2040
and 4 per cent per year thereafter.[45]

Meanwhile, industries that operate across national boundaries are
exempt from the agreement. International shipping produces 2.4 per
cent of global greenhouse gas emissions,[46] and aviation contributes
about 2 per cent.[47] Both industries are expected to experience strong
growth in upcoming decades.

Paris is a mixed bag. On the one hand, it rewards countries that come to the table. Not only are they part of the solution, they may experience positive material impacts from the agreement, especially if they are in the developing world. The agreement informs, and it educates. It provides a forum for continuing negotiation. It appears to punish very little, if at all. It sets tough goals. On the other hand, the goals it sets for developed countries are probably not achievable. Also, it sets different goals for different countries, and it is not clear whether all see these goals as fair.

In December 2018, three years after Paris, representatives from 200 countries met for two weeks in Katowice, Poland, to hammer out a further agreement known as the "Paris Rulebook." This agreement nailed down some implementation details of the Paris conference. For example, it stated that all countries would be required to follow uniform reporting standards on emissions and policies. Also, rich countries are being encouraged, but not required, to specify exactly how they will aid poorer countries to install clean energy and forestall damage from national disasters.

Unfortunately, nations including the United States, Saudi Arabia, and Russia agreed only to "welcome" the new IPCC report, entitled "Global Warming of 1.5°C," that immediately preceded this conference, rather than to endorse its scientific findings.[48] The special report notably emphasizes moral considerations and world change across many systems, or, as it puts it, it integrates "climate change mitigation and adaptation with sustainable development."[49] (In this significant effort it integrates the previously established seventeen UN Sustainable Development Goals, which in addition to climate action include responsible consumption and production, no poverty, decent work and economic growth, life on land and below water, and reduced inequality.) It concludes that to reduce impacts on the most vulnerable nations and peoples, the world must cut carbon pollution 50 per cent by 2030, and by 100 per cent in 2050, to avoid 1.5° Celsius of warming.[50] Under Trump

administration policies, the United States was to fully pull out of
the Paris agreement as of 2020.

4. THE ECONOMICS OF FINITE RESOURCES

Let's back up from these initiatives for a moment to think more about
how leaders can motivate the allocation of scarce resources. Today
thought leaders are moving toward the belief that societies should
practice restraint in both their tendency to pollute and their use of
the remaining nonrenewable fossil fuels. When a society allocates
scarce resources among its members, it is said to ration them. Will
Team Humanity ration effectively?

As Stan Cox writes in his groundbreaking book *Any Way You Slice It:
The Past, Present, and Future of Rationing*, using the term "rationing" in
the United States is like shouting an obscenity in church. As a conversation starter, it is right up there with "socialism" (which is not to say
we should abandon that term).[51] To some, the idea of rationing oil or
gas or water is obviously un-American.

Right now, rationing is left mainly to markets. In economic jargon
this process is referred to as the allocation of scarce resources *by price*:
Whoever is willing to spend the most money gets the goods. A corollary is that goods are corralled by those who can make the most profit
from them. Today global society works on the assumption that markets are a very useful, if imperfect, way to manage scarcity.

Yet, human beings have created many other ways to ration that are
based on other assumptions, such as the ethical instinct to be fair
and humane. When a commodity is recognized as a human necessity,
societies often abandon market approaches.

In the 1970s, Americans experienced rationing by *straight quantity*,
for instance. During the oil embargo, Americans across the country
had to line up at gas pumps (they were not happy) to get a prede-
termined allotment of fuel. A similar process was used during the

Second World War for rationing necessities like gasoline, tires, and shoes. (Although people were willing to sacrifice for the cause, they also were not happy.) Americans in the South and Southwest are familiar with rationing by *time*, as they are only allowed to water their lawns every so often during a drought. Admission to clinical trials of scarce drugs is rationed by *lottery*. Emergency medicine and battle-field care are rationed by assigning degrees of urgency to the treatment, called *triage*.

The American experience with rationing during the Second World War suggests how leaders might design future rationing projects, writes Cox. Beginning in 1942, meats and canned goods were rationed by straight quantity, and people kept score with a notably nonmonetary process called the ration book. Policymakers learned from this experience that, when it comes to sharing necessities, the public likes to see rules applied equally to everyone, whether they are powerful or not, rich or not. Such universal policies are likely to be more acceptable than those that only target low-income families. However, during the war, less necessary but still scarce items that were termed "off the ration" were still allocated by ability to pay. According to historians, while this two-tier (e.g., market and non-market) policy accommodated people's desire for higher consumption, it also undermined the social acceptance of rationing.

When it comes to carbon pollution, as we have seen, global leaders are already addressing how to ration the burning of carbon. Most policymakers think we should ration carbon by price (called "putting a price on carbon"), and do so by using carbon fees and taxes denominated in either points or dollars. Rationing by price has the advantage of being familiar to citizens, and it appeals to those who think the process might save them money. As a global society, we do not yet see ourselves at the point at which rationing fossil fuel energy by straight quantity seems necessary, although that case might be made. In the future, we may change our minds. Rationing by straight quantity, for example, would give each person X gallons of oil per month, to be used for heating, transportation, or medicine – their choice.

As resources are deemed too polluting or are depleted, will we stick to rationing by price, or will we encourage our leaders to address rationing what remains more "fairly"? If the transition to green energy is not entirely successful, when it comes to rationing fossil fuels we will almost certainly face a crisis of moral conviction. Who will prioritize needs? Who will set allocations? The inevitable answer is governments; and we had better hope they are wise ones.

The success of all such plans depends on how citizens react to them. Are we the same kind of people as those who lived through rationing in the Second World War? David Orr, professor of Environmental Studies and Politics at Oberlin College, observes that we have changed as a society. "We have to reckon with the fact that from 1947 to 2008 we had a collision with affluence, and it changed us as a people. It changed our political expectations, it changed us morally, and we lost a sense of discipline. Try to impose a carbon tax, let alone rationing, today and you'll hear moaning and groaning from all over."[52]

Daniel Kahneman looks with a scientist's eye at the psychology of rationing and concludes that "negotiations over a shrinking pie are especially difficult, because they require an allocation of losses. People tend to be much more easygoing when they bargain over an expanding pie."[53]

Recall from Econ 101 that economics is defined as *the science of the allocation of scarce resources* among possible outcomes. Economists identify people's goals and study how best to allocate scarce resources to achieve them. One of their main roles in society is to advise governments and other policymakers on how to make critical allocation decisions about such resources as food, heat, and medical care. They also have a hand in measuring environmental justice across communities, determining from an economic perspective who will be able to live in healthy, non-polluted environments. Such resource allocation decisions define the core values of society.

Soon enough, policymakers will have to make critical allocation decisions about the use of dwindling fossil fuels. Should they be reserved for pharmaceuticals, heating, plastics, aviation? Decisions must also be made about managing growth under climate change. Should we allocate resources to mitigating climate change? On the adaptation side of the equation, what resources should be allocated to escaping droughts and sea level rise? What resources will the world allocate to help climate refugees?

Economic analysis will be increasingly important because it will help society to prioritize needs and conserve resources to meet them. In short, it will help us to ration well. Yet, we also have a fundamental conceptual problem, which is that modern economic theory is predicated on the assumption of growth.

As noted economist Kenneth E. Boulding wrote back in 1966, "Anyone who believes that exponential growth can go on forever in a finite world is either a madman or an economist."[54] He explained that "the closed economy of the future might ... be called the 'spaceman' economy, in which the earth has become a single spaceship, without unlimited reservoirs of anything, either for extraction or for pollution, and in which, therefore, man must find his place in a cyclical ecological system."[55] Enter ecological economics, a school of economic thinking that assumes resources are finite and denies the possibility of infinite growth. This approach challenges mainstream economic thinking and modern lifestyles with discussions of topics like rationing and collaboration.[56] To understand the importance of ecological economics, it is worth a couple of paragraphs to contextualize it within the history of economic thinking.

The main school of economics is neoclassical economics, which is based on the principle of supply and demand and the assumption that economies will grow. By this way of thinking, the size of the market defines what people want, and price and the ability to pay determine how scarce resources are allocated among them.

Within this main school is the branch of *environmental* economics, which, although a recent development, is also based on a market model. The two defining characteristics of environmental economics are, first, the assumption of growth; and second, the assignment of value to ecosystem pollution and ecosystem benefits. In practice, environmental economists attach costs to polluting practices and incorporate those costs into the cost of producing goods and the prices set for the consumer. Likewise, they price in the positive economic impact of replacing a forest that has been logged.

In contrast, the school of *ecological* economics is based on the principle that the human economic system is nested within a larger natural ecosystem that is finite. Unlike the other schools, it argues that the market is not necessarily the best mechanism for allocating scarce resources. As described by economists Herman E. Daly and Joshua Farley, there are several problems with the market as a mechanism for allocation within a global ecosystem.[57] One is that even the most talented System 2 decision-makers – that is, well-run organizations – sometimes produce knowledge and products that do not benefit humanity. Some of what they produce is simply wasteful. Some is actively harmful – unhealthy, ugly, or polluting. Furthermore, many of the things people need for their well-being are not marketable commodities and fall outside of the influence of the market.

The distinguishing feature of ecological economics is that it promotes development rather than growth. It studies improvements in the quality of goods and services according to their ability to increase human well-being within ecological constraints. While the theory views the market as useful for promoting this purpose, the market is considered to be insufficient. By its very nature, the market promotes overconsumption, pursuit of profit, and accumulation of capital over the development of well-being. Ecological economists are interested in identifying other motivators.

One of the main goals of ecological economics is to promote *sufficiency* rather than efficiency. Ecological economists spend less time studying efficient production and more time studying production that is adequate to meet human needs. In the tradition of ecological economics, the definition of sufficiency is determined through a society's political process.

Daly and Farley's interpretation of ecological economics highlights the importance of implementing humane values. One of their concerns is that "markets recognize demand only when it's expressed through purchases; they cannot 'see' actual wants, much less needs."[58] Ecological economists should distinguish between wants and needs and help citizens and policymakers to do the same. A related concern is that, as Joshua Farley puts it, when markets work as intended and at high efficiency, they allocate resources "toward those who have money and unmet wants, not toward those who have unmet needs."[59] In these ways, ecological economics promotes social justice. Will mainstream economists embrace the moral introspection that a philosophical change from growth to development will require?

Finally, Daly and Farley are also concerned with our ecological life support system. They argue that society should maintain the planet far from the edge of collapse. Pursuing this goal requires an end to the material growth of the economy as we know it. At the same time, they argue, it could support healthy, satisfied human populations that are working toward somewhat less materialistic goals.

How will capitalism evolve? In theory, an ecological economy satisfies the greatest possible number of needs using the smallest amount of labor, capital, and physical resources, and it does so through collective decision-making. This sounds pretty good. However, the theory has two important flaws – one economic and one political.

The economic flaw is pointed out by Farley himself, who argues that ecological economics cannot succeed without a major reform of the current financial system. The core role of money is critical: "A growing economy requires more money to chase more goods and services. Most money is created when the financial sector simply loans it into existence. The money is destroyed when the loans are repaid, but borrowers must also pay interest. If the economy is not growing, then interest payments are a zero-sum game: a transfer of resources to the financial sector, creating intense pressures for economic growth requiring yet more money creation, which is unsustainable on a finite planet." He points out that, furthermore, "money that must be repaid with interest can only be loaned for profit-generating market activities, and thus will not be used to finance the provision of public goods no matter how critically important they might be."[60]

So an important driver of policy change, and a major factor in the economic future of the world, is the competition between free-market (also called "laissez-faire" and "neoliberal") capitalism and regulated capitalism. Broadly speaking, this is a debate over the relative roles of markets and governments. Yet, even more fundamental than this debate, according to Daly and Farley, is the nature of money and exchange.

The political flaw in ecological economics as proposed by Daly and Farley is that it assumes a cooperative society that will make fair and reasonable decisions about resource allocation. For example, it assumes that rationing decisions will be made democratically and for the greater good rather than being dictated by a ruling elite that is self-serving.

Among sustainability thought leaders, the assumption of an ongoing democracy is common. Yet it is based on a projection of liberal values and ideas that can be reasonably disputed. As long as it recognizes and deals with scarcity, an ecological economy, like any economy, might just as well be led by an oligarchy. It could easily happen that it is dominated by a wealthy class, or by a dictatorship, that hoards resources for itself and impoverishes the weak. So, although ecological economics is a smart system for setting goals in a finite world, and although it has great promise among a citizenry that increasingly recognizes the world's finite nature, it lacks a rigorous discussion about how those goals will be implemented.

We are already experiencing a tendency toward governance by a small, elite group of the wealthy in the United States, most clearly under the Trump presidency. This reality brings us to consider the forces of capitalism in modern society. Many economists and political analysts have pointed out that, unchecked by government, successful capitalism inevitably centralizes economic power. Companies constantly seek to improve their market share, and as they are successful, economic power is concentrated in the winners. Small competitors are driven out. The owners of capital come to dominate society. It is for these reasons that democratic governments are concerned with breaking up monopolies.

This core systemic problem has long been an issue in American democracy. Abe Lincoln worried about what he called the "mobocratic spirit," by which he meant the development of authoritarian behavior within capitalist democracy.[61] That same concern is recognized widely today. For example, *The Economist* pointed out recently that, far from being entrepreneurial and competitive, American business has consolidated significantly and is stifling competition. It is a myth that business is more competitive than ever, they say, and a myth that we are in an age of entrepreneurism. In fact, industries are concentrating via mergers and acquisitions, and are driving out smaller companies. The creation of new companies has declined since the late 1970s.[62]

Although antidemocratic centralization and domination by the rich are not inevitable, they are difficult to avoid, particularly under free-market forms of capitalism. One knowledgeable voice on the subject was billionaire businessman J. Paul Getty. Back in the 1960s, just as large, global companies were beginning to come into their own, he pointed out that we live in an increasingly complex world, populated by more people and by more, and different types of, organizations. In this world, government oversight of business must inevitably increase, as he saw it, if society is to control the tendency of capitalism to centralize. Therefore, the freedom and autonomy enjoyed by early capitalists must inevitably be reduced.

Getty wrote, clearly with some nostalgia, that

> Today, the inherent nature of government in an increasingly complex civilization creates strong pressures toward systemization and standardization, which, in turn, serves to create vast bureaucratic complexes ... I do not suggest that there is a malevolent force behind any of this ... Government, law, control and regulation – and even concomitant bureaucracy – are essential ... if there is not to be utter chaos and eventual destruction.
>
> I would like to repeat and make it very clear that I am no antigovernment reactionary. I do not maintain that the restrictions I have cited are undesirable. They are, in my opinion, entirely necessary, in that their purpose is to make life safer and more pleasant for all.[63]

In the current era, our challenge as a society is certainly to manage capitalism and capitalistic pressures, including centralization. But it is also to manage annoying but necessary levels of bureaucracy. Going forward, we also must figure out how to curb growth. In fact, economists are beginning to weigh in on how a market economy might contract in a stable fashion.

The economist Farley has suggested three systemic changes. First, we should create institutions that declare and protect ownership of the commons. Scarce assets should be subject to rationing, and he advocates cap-and-auction systems (in this case, cap the amount of the resource to be used, and auction off the right to use it). Second, private financial sector institutions should be required to have 100 per cent reserves – they can only lend out money that they have, rather than money they can borrow – so they cannot loan money into existence. Third, we should develop a new international agreement, much like the Bretton Woods agreement that rebuilt the international economic system after the Great Depression and the Second World War, that would promote these two approaches and "the stable contraction of the market economy, the convergence of global consumption levels, and the improvement of global quality of life."[64] Such an institution would find ways to invest the revenues from a cap-and-auction system into renewable energy technologies that are owned not by particular companies but by the public.

As we come to accept that the currently dominant economic paradigm is wrong, while continuing to act as if it is right, we will experience cognitive dissonance. An example of a related behavior would be that, while believing that growth is finite, we continue to invest our retirement funds as though it is inevitable. Another example would be that we continue to consume as though resources are infinite, while at the same time feeling guilty about doing so. How we all resolve this will be, at the very least, interesting to watch. Psychological theory would predict that we will either stop investing as though growth is inevitable, or we will dispute the theories of ecological economics. Or, we will continue to consume blindly and turn away from environmentalism.

Will the immediate and concrete rewards of consuming outweigh the longer-term and more subtle rewards of personal growth and community – of "development," as the ecological economists would have it? Which sorts of people will choose growth? Which will favor slowing down? Stand by.

5. IT'S THE SYSTEM, STUPID

You can probably tick off a list of famous climate leaders. Such names as Bloomberg, Branson, Brown, Figueres Olsen, Pope Francis, Gates, Gore, Hansen, Heinberg, McKibben, Merkel, Musk, Oreskes, and Steyer immediately come to mind for American audiences. Other countries have other lists.

Clearly, we need systemic thinkers and doers like these. Individual leaders are important in part because we can identify with them. We can see them and judge whether we like them and decide whom we will follow. This kind of contact appeals in large part to our System 1 thinking.

But there are limitations to individual leadership. For one thing, leaders are individualistic and diverse in their approaches. Bill Gates prioritizes private and government investment in scientific innovation. Elon Musk is pushing all things electric. Bill McKibben and his movement promote stockholder divestment from fossil fuels. As a team with diverse political perspectives, Michael Bloomberg, Hank Paulson, and Tom Steyer educate businesspeople about economic risks and opportunities. In addition, government leaders across the world are developing national and local policies. But this creative diversity is also a weakness: It does not add up to a clear and compelling plan to save the planet.

Furthermore, individual leaders are too dispersed around the world to be known globally. At this point there is no one particular individual who is going to lead the world on climate and energy.

It may be that it is only the institutional world, composed of governments, businesses, and nonprofits and the representatives of all these sectors, that has a chance to solve our problems. We need people, yes ... We need corporate leaders, government leaders, nonprofit leaders, scientists, thought leaders, and philanthropists – and everyone else – working together ... But in what way should they organize? Imbued as the modern world is with the design of business organizations, relying on centralization and bureaucracy is our natural tendency. But, will the answer really be centralization? We have already seen that attempted and abandoned in Kyoto. Will the answer be networks? Creative disruption? A process as yet unimagined?

Certainly, the answer will include the notion of systemic intervention. We do know that we must prioritize the health of organizations and the systems in which they are embedded. We need institutions that are super System 2 decision-makers, and we need sound System 2 thinking to build them. It is argued, for instance, that with more data and resources – especially time – political and humanitarian decisions could be improved. For example, the Canadian nonprofit Evidence for Democracy fosters research and action using a data-driven approach.[65]

While it is relatively easy to identify talented leaders, it is relatively hard to embed them within effective social systems that give them real opportunities to implement change. A corollary of this is that it is all too easy for those who are following to depend on the existing leaders and experts of the world to solve their problems, while doing little themselves to get involved in building supportive systems.

Certainly, we need to design for continuity. We can't have Richard Branson's Climate War Room today and a substantially different initiative tomorrow. We can't have Obama's Clean Power Plan now but not next year. We need legal and administrative systems that are predictable enough that they allow for planning and investment of money and individual effort. This is the domain of government bureaucracy and partisan politics, a sector that, in the United States today, is in turmoil and stalemate.

To assure systems continuity, we must also plan for leader succession. When one leader fades, others should be in the wings, already trained and ready to carry on. Smart organizations know how to plan for leadership succession over time, even in the face of the organizational influence of individual charisma and powerful coalitions. Team Humanity needs to tap that expertise. Most prominent leaders today, having achieved influence over a lifetime, are older rather than younger. We must not let their ideas and initiatives quit when they do. We must develop a cohort of younger business, nonprofit, and political leaders and support them in their organizations to carry on.

We also need organizations that achieve global recognition and acceptance. It is unlikely that one international leader can get the job done on climate and energy. Who would that leader be? It is also unlikely that an organization like the bureaucratic and political

United Nations, an organization that also manages many missions, can get the job done. Can we imagine something better?

A meeting of scientists and policymakers produces not one megawatt of clean energy. In the end, whether all our talk of goals and planning, all our understanding of rationing and economics, is worth a dime comes down to who will implement them and what institutions they will design.

Together our global climate leaders face challenges in three main areas. First, they must envision a different future. Second, through persuasion and inspiration, they must drive the direction of humanity. Third, they must create plans for, and implement, specific changes.

To unite the world in action, humanity needs a vision for change, or possibly several compatible visions that can be fostered simultaneously. (One can argue that, by accepting that countries want to make individualized choices, a diverse set of visions is what was developed in Paris). Global leaders must be sensitive enough (System 1) and intelligent enough (System 2) to craft a vision of the future that not only makes sense but will sell to a global audience.

To creatively imagine alternative futures, climate leaders must be capable of developing visions outside of their own contexts. Each of us views the world from our unique position in the system, whether as an engineer who works for an oil company, a farmer who relies on petroleum-based fertilizer, or a parent who packs their child's lunch in plastic bags. The question is, How far beyond our own position can we see? What else can we empathize with and understand, really? Can the oil company employee see, and care about, how the fracking revolution is wrecking communities? Can the farmer understand the fragility of an agricultural system based on petroleum, and work against that? Can a parent see global pollution and swap out plastic bags for reusable containers, thus modeling responsible behavior for his or her children?

There is a tendency among sustainability leaders to frame the future in optimistic terms. Optimism does sell to certain audiences, but blind optimism eventually undermines the credibility of both the salesperson and the vision. When a leader is promoting climate mitigation, the ask is for action. But when actors find that their action has little connection with the realities of what is needed, and has little long-term influence, they will lose faith in the mission itself. Many leaders are extroverts, and extroverts tend to be optimists. Effective decision-makers must work with data and probabilities and avoid depending blindly on personality-driven optimism. Realists like scientists, data analysts, and data-driven planners must ensure that leaders' optimism is justified.

As an example of how optimism can undermine credibility, consider an annual report entitled *Global Trends in Renewable Energy Investment* that follows renewable energy investment trends.[66] On the one hand, the report offers an optimistic view of the broad investment picture for renewable energy. On the downside, it over-promises the contribution renewable energy will make to society over the next couple of decades.

The report notes that 2016 saw a record installation of renewable power capacity worldwide. In that year, renewables accounted for 55 per cent of all electrical generation that was added globally. Some green technologies also became more competitive because their costs went down. These included solar photovoltaics, onshore wind, and offshore wind. The average dollar capital expenditure per megawatt dropped by over 10 per cent for these sources. However, investment in other types of renewable energy was mixed.

The *Global Trends* report goes on to suggest that investment in solar was down in 2016 in large part because of cost reductions, rather than disinterest in the future of the technology itself. At the same time, some countries, notably China and Japan, did slow down their investments. Also of interest to investors, there was an unprecedented increase in financing of offshore wind projects, and a record amount of money spent in acquisition deals that include renewable energy generating plants, refinancing, and mergers. Finally, the report predicts that renewable energy will be the fastest-growing power source through 2040.[67]

Compare these facts with the ones in a US Energy Information Administration report that predicts a 48 per cent increase in energy usage worldwide by 2040, with the largest increases to be in nonfossil fuels.[68] This report points out that even though nonfossil fuels are expected to grow faster than fossil fuels, the latter will still account for more than three-fourths of world energy consumption in 2040. Natural gas is the fastest-growing fossil fuel in this outlook, with global natural gas consumption increasing by 1.9 per cent each year. Liquid fuels, mainly petroleum, will continue to be the world's largest energy source, although their share of world energy consumption is predicted to fall from 33 per cent in 2012 to 30 per cent in 2040. In a stab at optimism for renewables, the report notes that "as oil prices rise in the long term, many energy users will adopt more energy-efficient technologies and switch away from liquid fuels when feasible."[69]

The *Global Trends* report must be viewed in the context of the larger energy picture. Yes, renewable energy is growing, but it still faces staunch competition from fossil fuel energy, and it is not growing nearly fast enough to stop global warming. Yet, as so many environmental messengers are today, the report is more than a little optimistic: "It's a story being *repeated around the world* as public and private sectors grasp a *profitable and mutually beneficial* opportunity, which will help create *a more equitable, stable and peaceful world.* We urge investors, business leaders and policy makers to study this report, because profit does not have to be a dirty word. A *rapid shift* to clean renewable energy is not only slowing climate change, tackling pollution and *ending the suffering of vulnerable communities, but boosting long-term economic prosperity and stability*" (emphasis added).[70]

Really? One can forgive an investment report for encouraging investment in its specialty area. On the other hand, we should not listen to aspiring thought leaders when they take an unbalanced view.

After envisioning a progressive future, the second charge to global leaders is to convince the world to go along. Most leaders today believe in climate change and hope to solve the emerging problems, but they face indifference and denial from many among their followers. In the general population, only some are aware of the big picture of climate and energy. Many don't see a problem, perhaps because they are paying attention to other important things. Not seeing the problem can also be a personal coping mechanism, whether conscious or unconscious, to avoid dealing with it because it is unpalatable or unimaginable.

Other psychological factors likewise lead to denial. One influence is leaders' sense of powerlessness. They may feel helpless to change their own organizations, or to influence the government regulations that guide and control polluters. We may experience our company and its industry as locked without hope in an international competition that drives moral decisions to the lowest common denominator, so we move on to other issues. At the systems level, each individual denial contributes to society's denial of the moment.

Pursuing basic self-interest also leads to denial. Self-interest has many faces. It might mean making a personal commitment to living one's life well and ignoring everything else. It could mean expressing a personality-driven instinct to help others – or, conversely, to dominate others. Often, extreme self-interest leads to ignoring the influence that social and ecological systems have upon our lives. Certainly, it leads to denial of any need to promote the common good.

This moment in history requires leaders who can combat all such forms of denial. They will do so through promoting education and inspiring action, but also through personal example. We will know we have made progress when the rich voluntarily downsize to smaller homes instead of seeming to make a climate commitment by building their second home using state-of-the-art green technology. Part of being a world leader will be to personally demonstrate the concept of "enough."

In recent times, humankind's world vision has been to create a more prosperous and secure future. Now, as we create a society that may be less prosperous materially and must certainly be more environmentally and socially adaptable, that global vision must change. A major challenge will be to present a new vision to a skeptical and at times hostile public, a general public that rightfully or not suspects that under such extreme change they are likely to be the losers. Once again, psychology will be a factor. Since humans fear losses more than they value gains, losing status and other perks of modern life now is likely to outweigh the gain of saving the planet later.[71]

6. ARE HUMANS COOPERATIVE OR COMPETITIVE?

When we look out at the great arc of evolution that is before us, we can see two philosophies of change, each grounded in a different view of who we are psychologically and socially. The first is change based on the human predilection for competition and inspiration. The second is change based on our tendency toward collaboration and control. The former channels individuals like Elon Musk, T. Boone Pickens, and Al Gore (particularly in his role in Generation Investment Management). The latter channels Pope Francis, many thought leaders, and some scientists.

Some environmentalists' vision for the future assumes cooperative processes that work toward a cooperative society. Their rhetoric favors concepts like community, citizenry, and well-being. It may include thoughts about mutual monitoring and control. As many economists define it, cooperation means working together to the same end, and basic cooperation theory is predicated on the idea that competing interests can be induced to cooperate. Such theory suggests that "success requires a common commitment, not a patchwork of individual ones ... A common commitment can assure participants that others will match their efforts and not free-ride. A strategy of 'I will if you will' stabilizes higher levels of cooperation. This is the most robust pattern of cooperation seen in laboratory and field studies."[72]

How good are we at such cooperation? Climate scientists themselves are concerned that our inability to cooperate is likely to undermine efforts to deal with CO_2 pollution. For example, were geo-engineering to remove CO_2 from the atmosphere a viable technology to slow global warming (it is not, currently), it would still have to be implemented by people. A *New York Times* article reports that scientists wonder, "How could the world agree on the deployment of a technology that will have different impacts on different countries? How could the world balance the global benefit of a cooling atmosphere against a huge disruption of the monsoon on the Indian subcontinent? *Who would make the call?* Would the United States agree to this kind of thing if it brought drought to the Midwest? Would Russia let it happen if it froze over its northern ports?" Scott Barrett, an environmental economist at Columbia University, concludes that "the biggest challenge posed by geoengineering is unlikely to be technical, but rather [will] involve the way we govern the use of this unprecedented technology."[73]

We have seen that the Paris agreement does not rise to the level of cooperation as economists define it. The failure of the Paris agreement to develop mutually binding commitments suggests that a more realistic view is that, globally, humans will not "cooperate" in the sense of being mutually accountable. However, the agreement does demonstrate that we *will* collaborate. In collaborative processes, we talk together and work together, but we still maintain our distinct goals, powers, and boundaries. In collaboration, some forms of psychological reticence, some aspects of competition, remain part of the psychological task.

Behavioral economists first made their mark by pointing out that individuals are not merely self-interested operators, but do practice some forms of altruism. Behavioral economics knocked down the straw man that humans are entirely self-interested beings and established that they can be cooperative. It also advanced the theory that the ability to cooperate has contributed to our survival as a species. As a result, in recent years altruism has been heralded as both a fundamental characteristic of humans and an antidote to exploitive business practices. The economists are half right.

Also fundamental to human nature is competition. Indeed, it may be that competition is the more influential power. Direct experience with individuals, organizations, sectors, and countries suggests that competition is widespread, while cooperation is precious. Moreover, as we saw earlier, research suggests that, although humans do cooperate, they may not cooperate as much as we imagine. Psychologically, to some extent we are still tribal.[74] Perhaps the next straw man that behavioral economists will take on is our much-heralded altruism.

As we look over the current human systems for managing climate change, along with our systems for managing poverty, ignorance, and all the rest, we can easily find examples of parochial altruism. Willing to cooperate within our tribe but suspicious of other tribes, we resist cooperating at the inter-group, societal, and global levels. Indeed, after reviewing the psychology of issue management, the lead researchers on parochial altruism conclude that "whereas humans may have the evolved intuition to cooperate, it is unlikely such intuition brings world peace closer."[75]

Competitors take notice: Research in a variety of settings finds that aggression toward an out-group is often risky. Because the in-group on the other side is itself wary of outsiders, and prepares itself, about a third of such aggressions fail.[76] The flip side is that for the aggressors, parochial altruism is a win most of the time (66 per cent).

Charles Heckscher, author of *Trust in a Complex World: Enriching Community*, agrees. Based on an extensive analysis that includes factoring in new communication systems like the Internet, he concludes that

The positive lesson ... is that it is possible to build trust based on collaborative purpose. People can, at times, work together effectively even though they have no clear shared loyalty to a group, or even when they have a prior history of conflict and mutual suspicion. The negative, though, is that this is difficult and not yet reliable ...

I have argued that the complex problems of our age require collaboration – both because they require combinations of specialized knowledge, and because they require active commitment from diverse stakeholders. If that is the case, it doesn't leave us with an optimistic picture in the short run. We are not likely to be able to get the nations of the world to work together on climate change or the reduction of inequality; neither the needed attitudes nor skills are widely enough distributed.[77]

Although Heckscher is pessimistic, his analysis of human behavior does leave us an alternative – harnessing competition.

As we have seen, limitations on the human ability to cooperate abound. At the individual level, they include the proclivity to choose reward over punishment, a tendency toward parochial altruism, persisting emotional reactions to rationing, and the lack of ability to trust. At an institutional level, they include entrenched sector rivalries, weaknesses in both regulated and free-market capitalism, and reliance on imperfect global institutions. These limitations suggest that perhaps global leaders should turn toward a different side of human nature – toward competition. To harness competition would be to emphasize innovation over conservation, and change over adaptation, and to do so in business and in both the natural and the social sciences. To attempt this, it will be useful to understand what competitiveness is, and what it is not.

Consider the psychology of entrepreneurs. Many entrepreneurs are competitive. However, contrary to popular myth, they are not necessarily *ruthless* competitors. A research study in businesses large and small and across a variety of industries suggests that entrepreneurs often see themselves as pursuing self-actualization and personal growth through their companies. They are positive competitors, and they are likely to believe that most other entrepreneurs see the business world the same way they do.[78]

So even though entrepreneurs are in one sense competitors, that competitiveness is typically tempered. Most do not feel a need to dominate others, or to compete merely to win, or to avoid losing at any cost. These are all dominance traits that form a behavioral constellation known to psychologists as "hypercompetitive attitude" – call it simply "dominance." Of course, dominant competitors do exist. They are motivated to control others because they are psychologically driven to, or simply because they can.[79] Studies confirm that dominance is related to low self-esteem and neuroticism.[80]

However, most entrepreneurs see the need to dominate as abnormal. The majority of entrepreneurs are competitive in positive ways that don't require dominating as a goal in itself. True, when forced by competitive pressures to dominate a market, business owners will fight hard to protect their companies. It is also worth noting that even positive competitors tend to dislike soft-hearted (presumably, cooperative) people. Yet, positively competitive people tend to make friends easily, love action, and have a lot of fun. And unlike dominant competitors, they do feel sympathy for those who are worse off than themselves.[81] It is not a stretch to assume they are more likely to care about the planet.

It follows that when identifying climate leaders who care, we should look for the positive competitors. Interestingly, the very term "animal spirits," coined by John Maynard Keynes in 1936, suggests in part what we should be looking for:

A large proportion of our positive activities depend on spontaneous optimism rather than mathematical expectations, whether moral or hedonistic or economic. Most, probably, of our decisions to do something positive ... can only be taken as the result of animal spirits – a spontaneous urge to action rather than inaction, and not as the outcome of a weighted average of quantitative benefits multiplied by quantitative probabilities ...[82]

We should not conclude from this that everything depends on waves of irrational psychology ... We are merely reminding ourselves that human decisions affecting the future, whether personal or political or economic, cannot depend on strict mathematical expectation, since the basis for making such calculations does not exist; and that it is our innate urge to activity which makes the wheels go round, our rational selves choosing between the alternatives as best we are able, calculating where we can, but often falling back for our motive on whim or sentiment or chance.[83]

In Kahneman's terms, Keynes is describing the contribution of System 1 to innovation and the practical relationship between System 1 and System 2.

This is not to say that hypercompetitive entrepreneurs cannot create great innovations. Many have done so. Arguably, however, they are less likely to take a democratic and humane approach to creating and disseminating those innovations globally. Given that human competition comes in two main forms – the positive, self-actualizing competitor, and the less typical, dominant competitor – wise leaders and citizens will recognize the destructive tendencies of the latter, expect little interest from them in helping others, and anticipate their active resistance to change. As to the former, leaders should support their creative and innovative tendencies and find ways to reward those animal spirits.

Some global initiatives already emphasize competition. One approach has been to offer prizes for innovation and scientific excellence in climate and energy. For instance, the $4 million Zayed Future Energy Prize is presented annually by the government of the United Arab Emirates. It is reported that at least 200 million people have benefited from the green energy projects of the prize winners.[84] Another award with global impact is the MIT Clean Energy Prize, a multi-stage, student-organized business plan competition in which students submit projects in the categories of generating energy, delivering energy, improving energy usage, and energy for developing economies. Student entrepreneurial teams from universities across the United States compete for prizes up to the $100,000 Grand Prize.[85]

Similar incentives in other parts of the global system could help to bring out the best in climate and energy innovation. Both the private sector and governments should spend more resources to reward competitive proposals for basic research and build out tested innovations.

• • •

Climate leaders must be pragmatic about the impact of human factors in global, systemic change. They must utilize motivating goals and plans. They can be guided by our understanding of rationing as it has been used historically, and by new approaches to economics. To motivate followers and innovators alike, they must weigh the power of cooperation against that of competition.

Applying psychology in systems, this chapter has made some suggestions. As a matter of practice, climate leaders should build on these ideas to take them to the high level of applicability that we need now.

What's the Plan?

Given the urgency of climate and energy developments, we humans need to be as wise as we possibly can when it comes to making decisions for the planet. In this book we have begun to address where we will find that wisdom. We have covered a lot of ground in a short space, from characterizing human reaction to climate and energy concerns, to promoting climate leadership and systemic change in organizations and global institutions. Understanding psychology and human systems both theoretically and practically has been a major focus. Achieving trust has been a major theme. Building a narrative that leads directly to action has been our goal.

Each practice discussed here invites more investigation, which is up to you and the Internet and the natural and social science databases in your library – wherever your needs and curiosity take you. The notes to this book are a decent start. In the end, I can only add: Go lead. For we are not really at a conclusion, we are at a beginning.

In terms of someone in the world having a plan for leaders to implement, guess what?

You guessed it … There is no plan.

In a developed world characterized by efficient companies, mighty militaries, and collaborative institutions like the United Nations and the European Union, there is no regional plan and no global plan to save the planet. One might argue that the Paris agreement is a plan. Yet, as we have seen, the Paris agreement is a set of individual governmental aspirations, not regulations, for reducing CO_2. Nothing less, but nothing more. It says nothing about the power struggles between the fossil fuel sector and the renewable energy sector. It says nothing about promoting basic science funded by government, or boosting scientific innovation in the business sector, or supporting risk-taking entrepreneurs. It says nothing about reclaiming already devastated ecosystems. Paris says nothing about dealing with population growth or the agricultural contributions to CO_2. It says very little about how to help those developing countries that will be devastated by climate change.

Through Paris and similar initiatives, the United Nations keeps people talking, and that is hopeful. But to have a plan means to develop a collective vision, set specific goals, create an implementation strategy, design accountability strategies, identify resources, and follow through. A plan must have a leader, or leaders. It must have motivated followers. It must have organization and it must have continuity. To save the planet, it must be global: Local initiatives must add up to something that matters.

A decade ago there were some plans, or, at least, I should say, it *felt* like there were some plans. Perhaps we were more optimistic then, and certainly we were less bedazzled by thousands of vital facts coming at us very fast. There was *Plan B*, for instance – Lester Brown's book that set out in general terms what people need to accomplish for the planet. There was the Kyoto international protocol, which imposed financial penalties for carbon pollution and, as a result, was largely abandoned, country by country. There was (and still is) 350.org's plan to create a worldwide grassroots movement and encourage divestment in the stocks of fossil fuel companies. There was the US military's plan to keep the United States energy independent as fossil fuels dwindle. There were various organizations that recruited concerned business executives. These initiatives all helped. Now some of them have either morphed into something different or fallen away entirely. Such systemic evolution is not necessarily a bad thing, but neither is it a plan.

Fundamentally, the five practices identified in this book are practices for human decision-making. We humans decide what is true and what our risks are. We identify which stakeholders, institutions, and leaders will implement our plans. Reflecting back over the five practices, in what ways do you, yourself, believe that our human decision-making has been effective? In what ways has it been ineffective? What do you see as humanity's leverage points?

Take a moment to weigh these System 2 questions. Also, sense what your System 1 is telling you. What are your instincts about our capabilities? What grade would you give to Team Humanity so far?

Key factors include these:

1. **System 1 and System 2.** We humans have a ways to go when it comes to effectively integrating the System 1 and System 2 aspects of decision-making. Consider just this one problem: When it comes to climate change, there is no mastodon on our heels, only the specter of a very, very hot and perhaps uninhabitable planet of our own creation somewhere in the very distant, or maybe the not-so-distant-but-we're-not-sure-when future. One day, we may have to adjust to life in a very, very uncomfortable habitat, but we are uncertain about the attributes of that place. Will it be hot? Too hot? Too hot for what? Our deep uncertainty matters, and it is undermining our intent.

    The planet continues to warm rapidly, and yet we continue to rely heavily on fossil fuels. We need to be better decision-makers than we have been. Yes, we continue to require System 2 science data. But we also need to factor in System 1 and the psychology of risk, and we need to create and disseminate compelling narratives about power, politics, and change. We need to educate world citizens about climate and energy issues, but also about the human processes needed to address them. Our thought leaders should focus more on helping humanity *decide how to decide*, and how to design and implement plans.

2. **Altruism.** The research on the limits of altruism in inter-group relationships is robust, and the ethical issues raised by the stag hunt scenario are profound: We humans are tribal and clannish, and our natural tendency toward parochial altruism may be difficult to overcome. Yet, leaders can have an impact by developing widespread awareness of this tendency, and by explicitly educating all of us in cooperative alternatives.

   There has already been considerable real-world experimentation on bringing conflicting parties together, experiments that create some hope that we can nurture generosity of spirit.[1] Democracy itself is such an experiment, of course, and we would do well to study it and further it.

3. **Systemic engagement.** Implementing a plan requires political leadership. Hypothetically, it is possible for positive change to bubble up from the bottom of organizations, or to emerge spontaneously in a variety of venues in society, but this seldom happens. As suggested by historians, what one sees instead are violent overturnings. Thus, developing systemic leadership that inspires positive change will be vital.

   Systemic leaders must help their followers and stakeholders engage at the systems level. All of us should learn as much as we can about leadership and change across sectors, governments, and the world. To help us do this, we need education that targets civics and related systemic disciplines. We need to make media choices that structure our lives and our learning less around random details and more around broad issues and societal change. On a personal level, it follows that for every action one takes locally one should take an action systemically. Take public transportation to work this morning, but this afternoon support a candidate. Decide which levers you can pull: Should you spend your efforts on composting or on lobbying your utility to use green energy?

4. **Competitiveness.** Human beings have created a global society in which we routinely engage in organizational and sector power struggles. Often, we fight with each other not because resources are so limited that we cannot all survive comfortably (numerous sources say there is plenty of food on the planet), but because of who we are by nature and nurture. Many human beings are competitive. Extroverted leaders, in particular, are likely to display this trait. Their innate competitiveness is not going to be erased by other peoples' well-meaning aspirations for cooperation.

As a society we need to find ways to harness our competitive nature for the greater nurturance of community, humanity, and the planet. Directing competitiveness toward technological innovation is the most obvious way to do this. We should foster competition that leads to significant energy innovation – innovation at a level that can preserve society as we know it now. Another approach is to guide or regulate our competitive companies to deal with their own contributions to climate change and to account publicly for the climate change risks they face.[2]

We all might attempt to channel competitiveness toward new values. For example, we could encourage a system in which status comes from living in the smallest, lowest-energy home, or from mastering lifestyle minimalism.

5. **Innovation and curiosity.** The drive to innovate is closely related to competitiveness. Often this drive has been applied to developing new technologies, but it might also be leveled at improving social relationships and decision-making.

We might explore, certainly, how competing sectors can be induced to cooperate through joint incentives. We can ask more questions about how we can use reward and punishment to turn our innate curiosity and animal spirits away from projects that use up nonrenewable resources and toward projects that are thoroughly renewable.

6. **Dominance.** It is important to recognize that society as we know it has been a good thing. Namely, sensitivity to social status promotes hierarchy, and social hierarchy is a mode of organizing that has proven to be effective.[3] The best of all worlds may be a hierarchical system tempered by humane values and democratic institutions, led, of course, by empathetic individuals.

   Unfortunately, a not insignificant portion of humanity consists of individuals who want to dominate others. Sociopaths are people who lack empathy and have marked tendencies to manipulation. One authoritative estimate puts the percentage of sociopaths in the United States at 1 per cent.[4] In addition, a larger number of individuals have sociopathic tendencies. Among students in the United States and Sweden, one estimate of those who are sociopathic or almost sociopathic runs to between 5 and 15 per cent.[5] We must find ways to identify and limit the influence of toxic leaders who undermine interpersonal trust and trust in society and its institutions.

7. **Trust.** Despite widespread rhetoric about the value of cooperation, human beings have not found the path to global trust. Indeed, in some instances, we have not even found the path to trusting science. Leaders need to continue to identify these paths and to reinforce the people who walk in them.

8. **Hope.** Will human beings develop decision-making wisdom fast enough to save the planet? Optimism is a characteristic of extroverts; the rest of us like proof. We might develop something like optimism when we see renewable energy taking big leaps toward solving our climate problems. Such a leap would mean increasing the renewable energy market share considerably, for example, not by 25 per cent in twenty years, as is the stated goal of the Paris agreements, but – name your own figure? – personally, I would say to *at least* 50 per cent in twenty years.

Social scientists can help global leaders by nailing down what sorts of specific goals can inspire the kind of hope that motivates action. Judicious use of reward and punishment will be required.

Given the exigencies of climate and energy, we may not have time to improve ourselves as a species (although we can try). We must start where we are – with who we are – and, understanding that, decide what avenues of intervention are most likely to work.

As we have seen, social scientists suggest that we humans are situationally altruistic competitors driven by both emotion and intellect. Humans strongly prefer reward (consumption, social interaction) to punishment (cognitive dissonance, rationing) and will go a long way to avoid the latter. We care about each other and about building cooperative systems like democracy, but we also enjoy hierarchy and competition and the benefits they provide. We lack the imagination and motivation to care much for humanity's future, although we are aware that we should overcome this tendency.

Assuming this characterization is reasonably accurate, it follows that, to save the planet, a solely cooperative societal fix is not going to cut it. Even if we really do have all the technical solutions at hand, as some argue, we are unlikely to cooperate well enough to bring a global plan to fruition. In short, to face the climate crisis, humanity cannot afford to default to a knee-jerk dependence on fostering human cooperation. If anything, we should consider changing the default to fostering competition.

Our main strategy should be to foster competition that addresses a spectrum of technological and social solutions. In particular, we should incentivize research into new and improved energy technologies, including further developing renewable energy and energy storage, and capturing carbon. Also we should reward research teams who draw effectively on human talents: Some teams will be passionate and aggressive, others introverted and meticulous. Contemporary research on how to motivate such teams would be useful. In basic science, the work itself is often rewarding, but it is also true that commercially successful teams may make their members rich. What matters most to Team Humanity solving the climate crisis is that we engage innovators to foster the global transition to clean energy. Hopefully, we can do this by fostering friendly competition – the sort that encourages sharing methods and results.

At this point, basic climate and energy research is significantly underfunded. While global investment in the actual production of clean energy by the private sector is about one trillion dollars every three years, investment in basic research is much more modest. According to the research company BloombergNEF, in 2018 corporate research and development (R&D) spending was about $21 billion, and government R&D was about $15 billion.[6] How much research investment is needed? A lot more. As Bill Gates, founder of the Breakthrough Energy Coalition, dryly puts it, "huge uncertainties, huge underinvestment."[7]

It is interesting to note, from a psychological perspective, that, in 2019, fully 82 per cent of Americans supported funding research into renewable energy resources.[8] Meanwhile, only 60 per cent worried about global warming. It appears that, in our society, our leaders could reasonably develop an inspiring narrative about which types of energy are subsidized by governments and why, and about how to incentivize major investments in research on clean energy. How should we balance that investment with, say, investing in energy conservation and climate justice? These important questions are beyond the scope of this book. Thought leaders in industry, government, and academia should foster this necessary conversation.

All of this reasoning has come from this writer's System 2. My System 1 now has something to add.

Over the course of researching this book, I have routinely asked people I know and meet whether they think humanity will successfully fight climate change. Every single person I know well is pessimistic.

Almost everyone I ask just in passing is also pessimistic. We are too fractious, they say, and too self-occupied. They can't even imagine self-evident actions, like taxing fossil fuel usage or electing a Congress that works cooperatively. Perhaps you have had a similar experience.

As a social animal myself, my ideas and emotions are embedded in those of the people I meet. My own System 1 is telling me (not screaming at me just yet, but surely letting me know): "We are going to fry the planet, watch out."

You should know that in terms of personality, I am a "defensive pessimist," a person who enters situations expecting the worst because that approach has in the past yielded success for me. Expecting the worst protects a person by preparing them psychologically for possible failure while at the same time motivating them for success. As researchers put it, "Imagining negative scenarios may motivate the person to increase his or her efforts in order to prevent these scenarios from coming about ... Defensive pessimists harness their anxiety to motivate themselves."[9] In contrast, the researchers suggest, optimists set high expectations initially and, in the event of failure, retrospectively do whatever they can to protect their self-esteem – they are likely to rationalize, or reimagine their prior position. I immodestly offer that defensive pessimism may be the more effective approach to societal decision-making.

The exception I have found to our general pessimism is teachers of the young. Despite the facts, they stick to their optimism – in part, I suspect, because they identify with their students and love them and hope for the best for them. They also appear to believe that to learn and grow, the young *require* optimism. Perhaps, for certain age groups, they are right.

Yet, young adults realize the facts, and they grieve, along with the rest of us. As Greta Thunberg said at the UN Climate Action Summit in 2019:

How dare you pretend that this can be solved with just "business as usual" and some technical solutions? With today's emissions levels, that remaining CO_2 budget will be entirely gone within less than 8 1/2 years. There will not be any solutions or plans presented in line with these figures here today, because these numbers are too uncomfortable. And you are still not mature enough to *tell it like it is.* You are failing us. But the young people are starting to understand your betrayal. The eyes of all future generations are upon you. And if you choose to fail us, I say: We will never forgive you. (Emphasis added)[10]

Yes, young adults may challenge the hard truth more than the rest of us; after all, the truth about the future of the planet is hard to believe. They are more likely to see the threats because the threats will affect them personally. At the same time, they are likely to envision the amazing opportunities the climate crisis offers not only for saving the planet but for thriving while doing so. Also, they plan to be on the side of the good and join with others who want to do the same.

In the meantime, we need climate leaders; and whatever their age, people who are afraid of the truth are not likely to be those leaders.

So, no, I am not optimistic that we will halt significant climate change. Given a natural environment that is changing quickly and a psychology of human beings that is changing slowly, I don't think it likely that Team Humanity will get it done for the planet. Team Humanity fails the midterm.

At the same time, I am hopeful, and that hope is also based on who we are as decision-makers. Knowing what we today know about our decision-making weaknesses, we, the species of super-learners, really do have the potential to overcome them.

On what do I base this hope? Even though we have not managed them well so far, we do have many resources. In addition to our leadership, animal spirits, and individual resilience, we have extraordinary knowledge beyond any imagined by previous generations, we have amazing global communications systems, and, while we are not yet proficient, we do have some experience organizing globally.

We are not like civilizations of old that lived and died in isola-
tion and ignorance. We know their history, and we can learn from
it. We also have social science knowledge unlike any that has ever
existed. In a matter of decades, we have moved away from the canon
of patriarchal psychology-philosophers to a fact-based understanding
of human behavior and decision-making. We can imagine and even
demonstrate that it is useful to replace the centralized decision-
making of historical rulers with more collective, fact-based, and
decentralized decision-making. We communicate rapidly across
regions and across societal levels, and this communication empowers us to search the entire globe for the best decision-makers,
leaders, and ideas.

We need climate leaders who will attempt these things, and if you
have read this far, we certainly need people like you. Why should you
lead? You should lead because you wake up every day with a kind of
hope, the hope comes from who you are – caring and competitive,
analytical and innovative. Justin Marshall, an Australian biologist who
has studied the decline of the Great Barrier Reef under industrializa-
tion and climate change, personifies this brand of hope. "Yes, maybe
it's too late," he says, but "I'm not going to sit back and buy a Hum-
mer and just let it all slide."[11]

The great social philosopher Erich Fromm concluded *The Anatomy
of Human Destructiveness,* his classic work on evil and the Holocaust,
with this observation: "Hope is not passive and it is not patient; on
the contrary, it is impatient and active, looking for every possibility
of action within the realm of real possibilities ... Critical and radical
thought will only bear fruit when it is blended with the most precious
quality man is endowed with – the love of life."[12]

It is in a place of simultaneous joy and concern that inspired change
will take root. So, be happy. Be serious. Revel in your abilities. Enjoy
your work. Lead. Follow. Love your family and build your community.
Contribute to the systemic change that we certainly need but are only
beginning to create.

NOTES

Welcome to Team Humanity

1 Richard Whittington, "The Work of Strategizing and Organizing: For a Practice Perspective," *Strategic Organization* 1, no. 1 (2003): 117–25.
2 Richard Bolden and Jonathan Gosling, "Leadership Competencies: Time to Change the Tune?" *Leadership* 2, no. 2 (2006): 147–63.
3 Bolden and Gosling, "Leadership Competencies"; Brigid Carroll, Ester Levy, and David Richmond, "Leadership as Practice: Challenging the Competency Paradigm," *Leadership* 4, no. 4 (2008): 363–79; Ellen Van Velsor and Laura Quinn, "Leadership and Environmental Sustainability," in *Managing Human Resources for Environmental Sustainability*, ed. Susan E. Jackson, Deniz S. Ones, and Stephan Dilchert (San Francisco: Jossey-Bass, 2012), 241–61.
4 Rae André, *Organizational Behavior: An Introduction to Your Life in Organizations* (Upper Saddle River, NJ: Prentice Hall, 2008), 96.
5 Kleio Akrivou and Hilary Bradbury-Huang, "Educating Integrated Catalysts: Transforming Business Schools toward Ethics and Sustainability," *Academy of Management Learning & Education* 14, no. 2 (2015): 222–40.

Practice 1 • Get the Truth

1 Daniel Kahneman, *Thinking, Fast and Slow* (New York: Farrar, Straus and Giroux, 2011), 20–1.
2 Kahneman, *Thinking, Fast and Slow*, 20–1.
3 Kahneman, *Thinking, Fast and Slow*, 21.
4 Kahneman, *Thinking, Fast and Slow*, 21.

5 Comedy Central, "The Colbert Report: The Word – Truthiness," October 17, 2005, video, 02:40, http://www.cc.com/video-clips/63ite2/the-colbert-report -the-word—truthiness.

6 Brian Kennedy, "Most Americans Trust the Military and Scientists to Act in the Public Interest," Pew Research Center, October 18, 2016, http://www.pewresearch .org/fact-tank/2016/10/18/most-americans-trust-the-military-and-scientists -to-act-in-the-publics-interest/.

7 Peter Achterberg, Willem de Koster, and Jeroen van der Waal, "A Science Confidence Gap: Education, Trust in Scientific Methods, and Trust in Scientific Institutions in the United States, 2014," *Public Understanding of Science* 26, no. 6 (2017): 711.

8 Achterberg, de Koster, and van der Waal, "A Science Confidence Gap," 711.

9 Dan M. Kahan, Hank Jenkins-Smith, and Donald Bramen, "Cultural Cognition of Scientific Consensus," *Journal of Risk Research* 14, no. 2 (2011): 147–74.

10 Jay D. Hmielowski, Lauren Feldman, Teresa A. Myers, Anthony Leiserowitz, and Edward Maibach, "An Attack on Science? Media Use, Trust in Scientists, and Perceptions of Global Warming," *Public Understanding of Science* 23, no. 7 (2014): 866–83, https://doi.org/10.1177/0963662513480091.

11 Gordon Gauchat, "Politicization of Science in the Public Sphere: A Study of Public Trust in the United States, 1974 to 2010," *American Sociological Review* 77, no. 2 (2012): 167–87.

12 Anthony Leiserowitz, Nicholas Smith, and Jennifer R. Marlon, *Americans' Knowledge of Climate Change* (New Haven, CT: Yale Project on Climate Change Communication, 2010), http://environment.yale.edu/climate-communication -OFF/files/ClimateChangeKnowledge2010.pdf.

13 Gregory J. Feist, "Predicting Interest in and Attitudes toward Science from Personality and Need for Cognition," *Personality and Individual Differences* 52 (2012): 772.

14 Kim Witte, "Putting the Fear Back into Fear Appeals: The Extended Parallel Process Model," *Communication Monographs* 59 (1992): 329–49, https://doi .org/10.1080/03637759209376276.

15 Andrea L. Hinds, Erik Z. Woody, Ana Drandic, Louis A. Schmidt, Michael Van Ameringen, Marie Coroneos, and Henry Szechtman, "The Psychology of Potential Threat: Properties of the Security Motivation System," *Biological Psychology* 85, no. 2 (2010): 331–7; Natascha de Hoog, Wolfgang Stroebe, and John B.F. de Wit, "The Impact of Fear Appeals on Processing and Acceptance of Action Recommendations," *Personality and Social Psychology Bulletin* 31, no. 1 (2005): 24–33; Jocelyn Bélanger, Marc-André Lafrenière, Robert Vallerand, and Arie Kruglanski, "Driven by Fear: The Effect of Success and Failure Information on Passionate Individuals' Performance," *Journal of Personality and Social Psychology* 104, no. 1 (2013): 180–95.

16 P. Sol Hart and Lauren Feldman, "Threat without Efficacy? Climate Change on U.S. Network News," *Science Communication* 36, no. 3 (2014): 328.

17 Kahneman, *Thinking, Fast and Slow*, 418.

18 Kahneman, *Thinking, Fast and Slow*, 264.

19 Kahneman, *Thinking, Fast and Slow*, 418.

20 Nate Hagens, "A Guide to Being Human in the 21st Century," Earth Week Speakers Series at the University of Wisconsin, Stevens Point, posted April 21, 2016, YouTube video, 1:17:40, https://www.youtube.com/watch?v=EMlDuNH59c.

21 Adam Simon, Andrew Volmert, Alexis Bunten, and Nathaniel Kendall-Taylor, *The Value of Explanation: Using Values and Causal Explanations to Reframe Climate and Ocean Change* (Washington, DC: Frameworks Institute, 2014), 3.

22 Simon et al., *The Value of Explanation*, 3.

23 Henry David Thoreau, "Conclusion," in *Walden; or, Life in the Woods* (Boston: Ticknor and Fields, 1854), http://www.gutenberg.org/files/205/205-h/205-h.htm.

24 Charles Spurgeon, British Clergyman, quote taken from https://www.brainyquote.com/quotes/quotes/c/charlesspu105835.html, accessed March 26, 2020.

25 Stuart Brody, "Impact Factor: Imperfect But Not Yet Replaceable," *Scientometrics* 96 (2013): 255, https://doi.org/10.1007/s11192-012-0863-x.

26 The Economist, "The Heat Is On: A New Analysis of the Temperature Record Leaves Little Room for the Doubters: The World Is Warming," *The Economist*, October 22, 2011, http://www.economist.com/node/21533360.

27 The Economist, "The Heat Is On."

28 Christopher Leonard, "David Koch Was the Ultimate Climate Change Denier," *New York Times*, August 23, 2019, https://www.nytimes.com/2019/08/23/opinion/sunday/david-koch-climate-change.html.

29 NASA, "Earth Observatory," n.d., https://earthobservatory.nasa.gov/world-of-change/DecadalTemp, accessed December 19, 2019.

30 European Environmental Agency, "Climate Change, Impacts and Vulnerability in Europe 2016: An Indicator-Based Report," November 1, 2017, http://www.eea.europa.eu/publications/climate-change-impacts-and-vulnerability-2016.

31 NASA, "How Is Today's Warming Different from the Past?" June 3, 2010, http://earthobservatory.nasa.gov/Features/GlobalWarming/page3.php.

32 Ben Kentish, "Arctic Is Warming at Twice the Rate of the Rest of the Planet, Scientists Warn," *The Independent*, April 30, 2017, https://www.independent.co.uk/environment/arctic-warming-twice-rate-rest-of-planet-global-warming-snow-water-ice-permafrost-arctic-monitoring-a7710701.html.

33 Robert McSweeny and Roz Pidcock, "Scientists Discuss the 1.5C Limit to Temperature Rise," Carbon Brief, December 10, 2015, https://www.carbonbrief.org/scientists-discuss-the-1-5c-limit-to-global-temperature-rise.

34 Joeri Rogelj, Gunnar Luderer, Robert C. Pietzcker, Elmar Kriegler, Michiel
    Schaeffer, Volker Krey, and Keywan Riahi, "Energy System Transformations
    for Limiting End-of-Century Warming to Below 1.5 °C," *Nature Climate Change*
    5 (2015): 519–27, https://doi.org/10.1038/nclimate2572; Intergovernmental
    Panel on Climate Change, "Global Warming of 1.5°C," 2018, https://ipcc.ch
    /sr15/.
35 See Holli Riebeek, "The Carbon Cycle," NASA Earth Observatory, June 16, 2011,
    https://earthobservatory.nasa.gov/Features/CarbonCycle/.
36 Casey Forrestal, Pei Xu, and Zhiyong Ren, "Sustainable Desalination Using a
    Microbial Capacitive Desalination Cell," *Energy & Environmental Science* 5, no. 5
    (2012): 7161–7; John S. Woods, Karin Veltman, Mark A. Huijbregts, Francesca
    Verones, and Edgar Hertwich, "Towards a Meaningful Assessment of Marine
    Ecological Impacts in Life Cycle Assessment (LCA)," *Environment International*
    89–90 (2016): 48–61, 89–90; Veera Gude, "Desalination and Sustainability: An
    Appraisal and Current Perspective," *Water Research* 89 (2016): 87–106.
37 James Hansen, Makiko Sato, Paul Hearty, Reto Ruedy, Maxwell Kelley, Valerie
    Masson-Delmotte, Gary Russell, et al., "Ice Melt, Sea Level Rise and Superstorms:
    Evidence from Paleoclimate Data, Climate Modeling, and Modern Observations
    That 2 °C Global Warming Could Be Dangerous," *Atmospheric Chemistry and
    Physics* 16 (2016): 3761, https://doi.org/10.5194/acp-16-3761-2016.
38 Daniel J. Alberts, "Stakeholders or Subject Matter Experts: Who Should Be
    Consulted?" *Energy Policy* 35 (2007): 2336–46.
39 Alberts, "Stakeholders or Subject Matter Experts."
40 Mark Bowen, *Censoring Science: Inside the Political Attack on Dr. James Hansen and
    the Truth of Global Warming* (New York: Dutton Adult, 2008).
41 Timothy M. O'Donnell, "Of Loaded Dice and Heated Arguments: Putting the
    Hansen-Michaels Global Warming Debate in Context," *Social Epistemology* 14,
    no. 2–3 (2000): 109–27, https://doi.org/10.1080/02691720050199199.
42 Andrew C. Revkin, "Bush Aide Softened Greenhouse Gas Links to Gas
    Warming," *New York Times*, June 8, 2005, http://www.nytimes.com/2005/06/08
    /politics/bush-aide-softened-greenhouse-gas-links-to-global-warming.html.
43 Brady Dennis, "Scientists Are Frantically Copying U.S. Climate Data, Fearing It
    Might Vanish under Trump," *Washington Post*, December 13, 2016, https://www
    .washingtonpost.com/news/energy-environment/wp/2016/12/13/scientists
    -are-frantically-copying-u-s-climate-data-fearing-it-might-vanish-under-trump.
44 Amy Harmon, "Activists Rushed to Save Government Science Data: If They Can
    Find It," *New York Times*, March 6, 2017, https://www.nytimes.com/2017/03/06
    /science/donald-trump-data-rescue-science.html.
45 Yiqing Yuan, Xueli Gao, Yi Wei, Xinyan Wang, Jian Wang, Yushan Zhang, and
    Congjie Gao, "Enhanced Desalination Performance of Carboxyl Functionalized
    Graphene Oxide Nanofiltration Membranes," *Desalination* 405 (2017): 29–39,

https://doi.org/10.1016/j.desal.2016.11.024. All dollar figures in this book are USD unless otherwise indicated.

46 Justin Fox, "Academic Publishing Can't Remain Such a Great Business," *Bloomberg View*, November 3, 2015, https://www.bloomberg.com/view /articles/2015-11-03/academic-publishing-can-t-remain-such-a-great -business.

47 Jason Schmitt, "Can't Disrupt This: Elsevier and the 25.2 Billion Dollar a Year Academic Publishing Business," December 22, 2015, https://medium.com /@jasonschmitt/can-t-disrupt-this-elsevier-and-the-25-2-billion-dollar-a-year -academic-publishing-business-aa3b9618d40a#.z6988lk6e.

48 Gretchen Goldman, Genna Reed, Michael Halpern, Charise Johnson, Emily Berman, Yogin Kothari, and Andrew Rosenberg, "Preserving Scientific Integrity in Federal Policymaking: Lessons from the Past Two Administrations and What's at Stake under the Trump Administration," Union of Concerned Scientists, January 2017, https://www.ucsusa.org/sites/default/files/attach/2017/01 /preserving-scientific-integrity-in-federal-policymaking-ucs-2017.pdf.

49 Climate Science Legal Defense Fund, *Handling Political Harassment and Intimidation: A Pocket Guide for Scientists*, November 2018, https://www.csldf.org /pocketguide/.

50 Maxwell T. Boykoff, *Who Speaks for the Climate? Making Sense of Media Reporting on Climate Change* (Cambridge: Cambridge University Press, 2011).

51 Maxwell T. Boykoff and Jules M. Boykoff, "Balance as Bias: Global Warming and the US Prestige Press," *Global Environmental Change* 14 (2004): 125–36.

52 National Public Radio, "Completeness in Reporting: Guideline: Be Able to Hold Your Own with Sources," *NPR Ethics Handbook*, n.d., http://ethics.npr.org /category/c-completeness, accessed January 19, 2016.

53 Bill O'Reilly, "The Climate Feud" [Television Series Episode], in *The O'Reilly Factor* (New York, NY: Fox News, December 9, 2009). Cited in Maxwell T. Boykoff, "Public Enemy No. 1? Understanding Media Representations of Outlier Views on Climate Change," *American Behavioral Scientist* 57, no. 6 (2013): 796–817.

54 National Public Radio, "Completeness in Reporting."

55 Kathleen Quinn, "Courting the Great Gray Lady," *Lingua Franca* (April/May, 1992): 27–9. Cited in Maxwell Boykoff and Tom Yulsman, "Political Economy, Media, and Climate Change: Sinews of Modern Life," *WIREs Climate Change* (2013), https://doi.org/10.1002/wcc.233, also available at http://sciencepolicy .colorado.edu/admin/publication_files/2013.19.pdf.

56 Hart and Feldman, "Threat without Efficacy?"

57 Lauren Feldman, P. Sol Hart, and Tijana Milosevic, "Polarizing News? Representations of Threat and Efficacy in Leading US Newspapers' Coverage of Climate Change," *Public Understanding of Science* 26, no. 4 (2017), https://doi. org/10.1177/0963662515595348.

58 Chris Nelder, "Why Energy Journalism Is So Bad," ZDNet, November 30, 2011, http://www.zdnet.com/article/why-energy-journalism-is-so-bad/.
59 See the International Energy Agency's regularly issued Oil Market Report, at https://www.iea.org/oilmarketreport/omrpublic/.
60 Matthew L. Wald, "Fossil Fuels as the Whale Oil of the Future," Green: Energy, the Environment and the Bottom Line (blog), October 27, 2011, https://green .blogs.nytimes.com/2011/10/27/fossil-fuels-as-the-whale-oil-of-the-future/; Nelder, "Why Energy Journalism Is So Bad."
61 Nelder, "Why Energy Journalism Is So Bad."
62 Michael W. Wagner and Timothy P. Collins, "Does Ownership Matter?" *Journalism Practice* 8, no. 6 (2014): 758–71, https://doi.org/10.1080 /17512786.2014.882063; Matthew Gentzkow and Jesse M. Shapiro, "What Drives Media Slant? Evidence from U.S. Daily Newspapers," *Econometrica* 78, no. 1 (January 2010): 35–71.
63 Jim Waterson, "Uncovered: Reality of How Smartphones Turned Election News into Chaos," *The Guardian*, December 5, 2019, https://www.theguardian.com /politics/2019/dec/05/uncovered-reality-of-how-smartphones-turned-election -news-into-chaos.

Practice 2 • Assess the Risks

1 Paul Slovic, "Perception of Risk," *Science New Series*, 236, no. 4799 (1987): 280–5.
2 Daniel Kahneman, *Thinking, Fast and Slow* (New York: Farrar, Straus and Giroux, 2011), 20–1.
3 Slovic, "Perception of Risk."
4 Paul Slovic and Elke U. Weber, "Perception of Risk Posed by Extreme Events," paper presented at the conference "Risk Management Strategies in an Uncertain World," Palisades, New York, April 12–13, 2002, http://www.ldeo .columbia.edu/chrr/documents/meetings/roundtable/white_papers/slovic _wp.pdf.
5 Leon Festinger, *A Theory of Cognitive Dissonance* (Stanford, CA: Stanford University Press, 1957); Andrew Elliott and Patricia Devine, "On the Motivational Nature of Cognitive Dissonance: Dissonance as Psychological Discomfort," *Journal of Personality & Social Psychology* 67 (1994): 382–94.
6 David Fetherstonhaugh, Paul Slovik, Stephen Johnson, and James Friedrich, "Insensitivity to the Value of Human Life: A Study of Psychophysical Numbing," *Journal of Risk and Uncertainty* 14, no. 3 (1997): 282–300.
7 Elke Weber, "Perception and Expectation of Climate Change: Precondition for Economic and Technological Adaptation," in *Psychological Perspectives to*

Environmental and Ethical Issues in Management, ed. Max Bazerman, David Messick, Ann Tenbrunsel, and Kimberley Wade-Benzoni (San Francisco, CA: Jossey-Bass, 1997), 314–41.

8 Jennifer Marlon, Peter Howe, Matto Mildenberger, Anthony Leiserowitz, and Xinran Wang, "Yale Climate Opinion Maps 2019," Yale Program on Climate Change Communication, September 17, 2019, https://climatecommunication.yale.edu /visualizations-data/ycom-us/.

9 Charlotte Jones, Donald Hine, and Anthony D.G. Marks, "The Future Is Now: Reducing Psychological Distance to Increase Public Engagement with Climate Change," *Risk Analysis* 37, no. 2 (2017): 5, https://doi.org/10.1111/risa.12601.

10 *Merriam-Webster,* s.v. "risk," accessed February 26, 2020, https://www.merriam -webster.com/dictionary/risk.

11 Cynthia Hardy and Steve Maguire, "Organizing Risk: Discourse, Power, and Riskification," *Academy of Management Review* 41, no. 1 (2016): 80–108, http:// dx.doi.org/10.5465/amr.2013.0106.

12 Earth System Research Laboratory, Global Monitoring Division, NOAA, "Trends in Atmospheric Carbon Dioxide: Monthly Average Mauna Loa CO_2," NOAA Earth System Research Laboratory, Global Monitoring Division, n.d., https:// www.esrl.noaa.gov/gmd/ccgg/trends/, accessed December 7, 2019.

13 "Graphic: Carbon Dioxide Hits New High," NASA Global Climate Change: Vital Signs of the Planet, n.d., https://climate.nasa.gov/climate_resources /7/graphic-carbon-dioxide-hits-new-high/, accessed February 26, 2020.

14 James Hansen, "Rolling Stones," Earth Institute, Columbia University, January 11, 2017, http://www.columbia.edu/~jeh1/mailings/2017/20170111 _RollingStones.pdf.

15 Brian Palmer, "One Million, Two Million, Three Million Years Ago," NRDC, May 8, 2015, https://www.nrdc.org/onearth/one-million-two-million-three-million -years-ago.

16 Earth System Research Laboratory, "Trends in Atmospheric Carbon Dioxide."

17 Earth System Research Laboratory, Global Monitoring Division, NOAA, "Carbon Dioxide at NOAA's Mauna Loa Observatory Reaches New Milestone: Tops 400 ppm," May 10, 2013, https://www.esrl.noaa.gov/gmd/news/pdfs/7074.pdf; Earth System Research Laboratory, "Trends in Atmospheric Carbon Dioxide."

18 Bob Berwin, "Second Biggest Jump in Annual CO_2 Levels Reported as Trump Leaves Paris Climate Agreement," Inside Climate News, June 1, 2017, https:// insideclimatenews.org/news/01062017/donald-trump-noaa-CO2-paris-climate -change-agreement.

19 Al Gore and David Blood, "The Coming Carbon Asset Bubble: Fossil-Fuel Investments Are Destined to Lose Their Economic Value: Investors Need to Adjust Now," *Wall Street Journal,* October 30, 2013, https://www.wsj.com /articles/SB10001424052702304655104579163663464339836.

20 Quoted in James Bennet, "We Need an Energy Miracle," *The Atlantic*, November 2015, https://www.theatlantic.com/magazine/archive/2015/11/we-need-an-energy-miracle/407881/.

21 The Economist, "Breaking the Habit: Special Report on Oil, 4," *The Economist*, November 26, 2016, http://www.economist.com/news/special-report/21710628-worlds-use-oil-approaching-tipping-point-writes-henry-tricks-dont-expect.

22 Gore and Blood, "The Coming Carbon Asset Bubble."

23 Neil Gershenfeld, "Science Uses Models to Explain Aspects of the Real World," January 17, 2011, https://scienceornot.net/2012/01/17/science-uses-models-to-explain-aspects-of-the-real-world.

24 William H. Glick, C. Chet Miller, and Laura B. Cardinal, "Making a Life in the Field of Organization Science," *Journal of Organizational Behavior* 28 (2007): 817–35.

25 For a simple model of the carbon cycle, see Holli Riebeek, "The Carbon Cycle," NASA Earth Observatory, June 16, 2011, http://earthobservatory.nasa.gov/Features/CarbonCycle/page1.php.

26 Colin N. Waters, Jan Zalasiewicz, Colin Summerhayes, Anthony D. Barnosky, Clément Poirier, Agnieska Galuszka, Alejandro Cearreta, et al., "The Anthropocene Is Functionally and Stratigraphically Distinct from the Holocene," *Science* 351 (2016): 137, https://doi.org/10.1126/science.aad2622.

27 Andrew Freedman, "The Last Time CO2 Was This High, Humans Did Not Exist," Climate Central, May 3, 2013, http://www.climatecentral.org/news/the-last-time-co2-was-this-high-humans-didnt-exist-15938.

28 Aradhna K. Tripati, Christopher D. Roberts, and Robert A. Eagle, "Coupling of CO_2 and Ice Sheet Stability over Major Climate Transitions of the Last 20 Million Years," *Science* 326, no. 5958 (2009): 1394–7, https://doi.org/10.1126/science.1178296.

29 Kristina Pistone, Ian Eisenman, and V. Ramanathan, "Observational Determination of Albedo Decrease Caused by Vanishing Arctic Sea Ice," *Proceedings of the National Academy of Science, USA* 111, no. 9 (2014): 3322–6, https://doi.org/10.1073/pnas.1318201111.

30 Atul Gawande, *The Checklist Manifesto: How to Get Things Right* (New York: Henry Holt, 2009), 22.

31 U.S. Global Change Research Project, "National Climate Assessment: Climate Impacts in the United States," 2014, http://nca2014.globalchange.gov/.

32 Kerry Emanuel, *What We Know about Climate Change*, 2nd ed. (Cambridge, MA: MIT Press, 2012), 46.

33 Emanuel, *What We Know about Climate Change*, 42–4.

34 Emanuel, *What We Know about Climate Change*, 46–7.

35 IPCC, "Climate Change 2014 Synthesis Report of the IPCC Fifth Assessment Report,"
    2014, https://www.ipcc.ch/site/assets/uploads/2018/02/SYR_AR5_FINAL_full.pdf.
36 IPCC, "Summary for Policymakers," in *Climate Change 2013: The Physical
    Science Basis.* Contribution of Working Group I to the Fifth Assessment
    Report of the Intergovernmental Panel on Climate Change, ed. T.F. Stocker,
    D. Qin, G.-K. Plattner, M. Tignor, S.K. Allen, J. Boschung, A. Nauels, Y.
    Xia, V. Bex, and P.M. Midgley (Cambridge, UK and New York, NY, USA:
    Cambridge University Press, 2013), http://www.climatechange2013.org
    /images/report/WG1AR5_SPM_FINAL.pdf.
37 Detlef P. van Vuuren, Jae Edmonds, Mikiko Kainuma, Keywan Riahi, Allison
    Thomson, Kathy Hibbard, George C. Hurtt, et al., "The Representative
    Concentration Pathways: An Overview," *Climatic Change* 109 (2011): 5, https://
    doi.org/10.1007/s10584-011-0148-z.
38 Kahneman, *Thinking, Fast and Slow*, 333.
39 IPCC, "Summary for Policymakers."
40 IPCC, "Summary for Policymakers."
41 Scripps Institute of Oceanography, "Climate Model Suggests Collapse of Atlantic
    Circulation Is Possible," January 4, 2017, https://scripps.ucsd.edu/news
    /climate-model-suggests-collapse-atlantic-circulation-possible.
42 Stefan Rahmstorf, Jason E. Box, Georg Feulner, Michael E. Mann, Alexander
    Robinson, Scott Rutherford, and Erik J. Schaernicht, "Exceptional Twentieth-
    Century Slowdown in Atlantic Ocean Overturning Circulation," *Nature Climate
    Change* 5 (2015): 475–81, https://doi.org/10.1038/NCLIMATE2554.
43 James Hansen, Makiko Sato, Paul Hearty, Reto Ruedy, Maxwell Kelley, Valerie
    Masson-Delmotte, Gary Russell, et al., "Ice Melt, Sea Level Rise and Superstorms:
    Evidence from Paleoclimate Data, Climate Modeling, and Modern Observations
    that 2 °C Global Warming Could Be Dangerous," *Atmospheric Chemistry and
    Physics* 16 (2016): 3761, https://doi.org/10.5194/acp-16-3761-2016.
44 Hansen et al., "Ice Melt, Sea Level Rise and Superstorms," 3761.
45 Hansen et al., "Ice Melt, Sea Level Rise and Superstorms," 3761.
46 OECD Secretariat, "The Netherlands: Climate Change Impacts on Water Systems,"
    2013, https://www.oecd.org/env/resources/Netherlands.pdf.
47 Gavin Miller, "Rotterdam: Adapting to Climate Changes," Institution of Civil
    Engineers, February 27, 2016, https://www.ice.org.uk/disciplines-and-resources
    /case-studies/rotterdam-adapting-to-climate-change.
48 Miller, "Rotterdam: Adapting to Climate Changes."
49 Miller, "Rotterdam: Adapting to Climate Changes."
50 Andrew Rice, "When Will New York City Sink?" *Daily Intelligencer*, September 7,
    2016, http://nymag.com/daily/intelligencer/2016/09/new-york-future
    -flooding-climate-change.html.

51 Michalis Diakakis, Georgios Deligiannakis, Katerina Katsetsiadou, and Efthymios Lekkas, "Hurricane Sandy Mortality in the Caribbean and Continental North America," *Disaster Prevention and Management: An International Journal* 24, no. 1 (2015): 132, https://doi.org/10.1108/DPM-05-2014-0082.

52 Lenny Bernstein, "After Sandy, New York Aims to Fortify Itself against Next Big Storm, Climate Change," *Washington Post,* July 14, 2013, https://www .washingtonpost.com/national/health-science/after-sandy-new-york-aims-to -fortify-itself-against-next-big-storm-climate-change/2013/07/14/8c8c2eca-e9d9 -11e2-a301-ea5a8116d211_story.html.

53 Bernstein, "After Sandy, New York Aims to Fortify." See also https://msc.fema .gov/portal.

54 Rice, "When Will New York City Sink?"

55 Bernstein, "After Sandy, New York Aims to Fortify."

56 NYC Recovery, "Sandy Funding Tracker," n.d, https://www1.nyc.gov/content /sandytracker/pages/, accessed March 15, 2020.

57 Alix Schroder, "Lessons of Climate Resilience in New York City," State of the Planet: Earth Institute, Columbia University, October 24, 2016, http://blogs .ei.columbia.edu/2016/10/24/lessons-of-climate-resilience-in-new-york-city/.

58 Bernstein, "After Sandy, New York Aims to Fortify."

59 David Miller, *Solved: How the World's Great Cities Are Fixing the Climate Crisis* (Toronto: University of Toronto Press, 2020), xii.

60 "About the Under2 Coalition," Under2 Coalition, http://under2mou.org /coalition/, accessed February 26, 2020.

61 Warren Buffett, "Berkshire Hathaway Inc.," letter to shareholders, February 27, 2016, 26, http://www.berkshirehathaway.com/letters/2015ltr.pdf.

62 Warren Buffett, "Berkshire Hathaway Inc."

63 Willie Drye, "2017 Hurricane Season Was the Most Expensive in History," *National Geographic,* November 30, 2017, https://news.nationalgeographic.com/2017 /11/2017-hurricane-season-most-expensive-us-history-spd/.

64 Melissa Cronin, "Don't Be Like Exxon, Says Bloomberg-Led Task Force to Big Oil," Grist, April 6, 2016, http://grist.org/business-technology/dont -be-like-exxon-says-bloomberg-task-force-to-big-oil/.

65 NPR Staff, All Things Considered, "How Could a Drought Spark a Civil War?" September 8, 2013, http://www.npr.org/2013/09/08/220438728 /how-could-a-drought-spark-a-civil-war.

66 James Crugnale, "The 9 Most Endangered Islands in the World," The Weather Channel, February 18, 2016, https://weather.com/science/environment /news/9-most-endangered-islands-in-the-world, accessed July 14, 2017.

67 Gavin L. Foster and Eelco J. Rohling, "Relationship between Sea Level and Climate Forcing by CO_2 on Geological Timescales," *Proceedings of the National Academy of Sciences USA* 110, no. 4 (2013): 1209–14, https://doi.org/10.1073 /pnas.1216073110.

68 James Hansen, Pushker Kharecha, Makiko Sato, Valerie Masson-Delmotte, Frank Ackerman, David J. Beerling, Paul J. Hearty, et al., "Assessing 'Dangerous Climate Change': Required Reduction of Carbon Emissions to Protect Young People, Future Generations and Nature," *PLoS One* 8, no. 12 (2013): e81648, https://doi.org/10.1371/journal.pone.0081648.

69 Jared Diamond, *Collapse: How Societies Choose to Fail or Succeed* (New York: Viking, 2005), 438.

70 Diamond, *Collapse*, 419.

71 Terry L. Hunt and Carl P. Lipo, "Late Colonization of Easter Island," *Science* (March 9, 2006): 9.

72 Stéphane Hallegatte, Ankur Shah, Robert Lempert, Casey Brown, and Stuart Gill, "Investment Decision Making under Deep Uncertainty: Application to Climate Change," Policy Research Working Papers, The World Bank, September 2012, http://elibrary.worldbank.org/doi/abs/10.1596/1813-9450-6193.

73 Christopher Wright and Daniel Nyberg, *Climate Change, Capitalism, and Corporations: Processes of Creative Self-Destruction* (Cambridge, UK: Cambridge University Press, 2015), 72.

74 Michael Bloomberg, Hank Paulson, and Tom Steyer, "A Climate-Change Risk Assessment," *Washington Post*, October 3, 2013, https://www.washingtonpost.com/opinions/a-climate-change-risk-assessment/2013/10/03/d4f70e3c-2bb5-11e3-8ade-a1f23cda135e_story.html.

75 http://riskybusiness.com/, accessed February 7, 2017.

76 Cronin, "Don't Be Like Exxon."

77 Kate Gordon and James Barbra, "Proposition 39: Investing in California's Future," Next Generation, December 10, 2012, http://thenextgeneration.org/publications/prop39-investing-in-california.

78 The Economist, "Breaking the Habit: Special Report: Oil," *The Economist*, November 26, 2016, 5.

79 Diamond, *Collapse*, 522–4.

Practice 3 • Weigh the Stakes

1 Jonathan Ford, "A Green Economy Is Possible, But at What Cost?" *Financial Times*, July 9, 2017, https://www.ft.com/content/1c849b9a-6486-11e7-8526-7b38dcaef614.

2 For example, some scientists say it is possible to configure the power grid to fix the problems of intermittency, should we be willing to invest heavily in new electricity infrastructure. See the debate in Eduardo Porter, "Fisticuffs over the Route to a Clean Energy Future," *New York Times*, June 20, 2017, https://www.nytimes.com/2017/06/20/business/energy-environment/renewable-energy

-national-academy-matt-jacobson.html. Also see Richard Heinberg, "Controversy Explodes over Renewable Energy," Post Carbon Institute, July 11, 2017, http://www.postcarbon.org/controversy-explodes-over-renewable-energy/.

3 U.S. Energy Information Administration, "Petroleum, Natural Gas, and Coal Still Dominate US Consumption," July 3, 2018, https://www.eia.gov/todayinenergy/detail.php?id=36612.

4 Anjii Raval and Leslie Hook, "Renewable Energy Push Barely Dents Fossil Fuel Dependence," *Financial Times*, August 2, 2019, https://www.ft.com/content/4c77a13a-b50b-11e9-8cb2-799a3a8cf37b.

5 U.S. Energy Information Administration, "Oil: Crude and Petroleum Products Explained," last updated October 3 2019, https://www.eia.gov/energyexplained/oil-and-petroleum-products/use-of-oil.php.

6 U.S. Energy Information Administration, "Natural Gas Explained," last updated December 18, 2019, https://www.eia.gov/energyexplained/index.php?page=natural_gas_use.

7 U.S. Energy Information Administration, "Coal Explained," last updated May 9, 2019, https://www.eia.gov/energyexplained/index.php?page=coal_use.

8 James Conca, "EROI: A Tool to Predict the Best Energy Mix," *Forbes*, February 11, 2015, https://www.forbes.com/sites/jamesconca/2015/02/11/eroi-a-tool-to-predict-the-best-energy-mix.

9 Michael Dale, Susan Krumdieck, and Pat Bodger, "Net Energy Yield from Production of Conventional Oil," *Energy Policy* 39, no. 12 (2011), 8202.

10 U.S. Energy Information Administration, "United States Remains Largest Producer of Petroleum and Natural Gas Hydrocarbons," May 23, 2016, http://www.eia.gov/todayinenergy/detail.php?id=26352.

11 U.S. Energy Information Administration, "How Much Petroleum Does the United States Import and Export?" http://www.eia.gov/tools/faqs/faq.cfm?id=727&t=6, accessed February 20, 2017.

12 U.S. EIA, "How Much Petroleum Does the United States Import and Export?"

13 U.S. Energy Information Administration, "How Much Oil Is Consumed in the United States?" last updated September 4, 2019, https://www.eia.gov/tools/faqs/faq.php?id=33&t=6. Note that the U.S. Energy Information Administration includes biofuel in the consumption of petroleum products, of which it accounts for about 1 per cent.

14 U.S. Energy Information Administration, "What Countries Are the Top Producers and Consumers of Oil?" last updated February 3, 2020, https://www.eia.gov/tools/faqs/faq.php?id=709&t=6.

15 Art Berman, "The Crude Oil Export Ban: What, Me Worry about Peak Oil?," *Forbes*, December 27, 2015, http://www.forbes.com/sites/arthurberman/2015/12/27/the-crude-oil-export-ban-what-me-worry-about-peak-oil.

16 Berman, "Crude Oil Export Ban."

17 Berman, "Crude Oil Export Ban."
18 Nick A. Owen, Oliver R. Inderwildi and David A. King, "The Status of Conventional World Oil Reserves: Hype or Cause for Concern?" *Energy Policy* 20 (2010): 4743.
19 Jeffrey Ball, "Why the Saudis Are Going Solar," *The Atlantic*, July/August 2015, https://www.theatlantic.com/magazine/archive/2015/07/saudis-solar -energy/395315/; Anjli Raval and Andrew Ward, "Saudi Aramco Plans for a Life after Oil," *Financial Times*, December 10, 2017, https://www.ft.com /content/e46162ca-d9a6-11e7-a039-c64b1c09b482.
20 Wikipedia, "Rashid Bin Saeed Al Maktoum," https://en.wikipedia.org /wiki/Rashid_bin_Saeed_Al_Maktoum#cite_ref-gluckman_4-0, accessed February 26, 2020; cited in Ron Gluckman, "Hong Kong of the Desert?" n.d., http://www.gluckman.com/DubaiBiz.html, accessed February 26, 2020.
21 Raval and Ward, "Saudi Aramco Prepares for a Life after Oil."
22 United States Joint Forces Command, *The JOE 2010* (Suffolk, VA: United States Joint Forces Command, 2010), 24.
23 Joint Forces Command, *JOE 2010*, 24.
24 Joint Forces Command, *JOE 2010*, 27.
25 Joint Forces Command, *JOE 2010*, 27.
26 Stefan Schultz, "Military Study Warns of a Potentially Drastic Oil Crisis," *Der Spiegel*, January 9, 2010, http://www.spiegel.de/international/germany /0,1518,715138,00.html.
27 United States Joint Forces Command, *Joint Operating Environment 2035: The Joint Force in a Contested and Disordered World*, July 14, 2016, 19, https://fas.org/man /eprint/joe2035.pdf.
28 Eric Roston, "Exxon Predicted Today's Cheap Solar Boom Back in the 1980s," *Bloomberg*, November 4, 2015, https://www.bloomberg.com/news/articles /2015-11-04/exxon-predicted-today-s-cheap-solar-boom-back-in-the-1980s.
29 David Kaiser and Lee Wasserman, "The Rockefeller Family Fund vs. Exxon," *New York Review of Books*, December 8, 2016, http://www.nybooks .com/articles/2016/12/08/the-rockefeller-family-fund-vs-exxon/.
30 Terry Macalister, "Green Really Is the New Black as Big Oil Gets a Taste for Renewables," *The Guardian*, May 21, 2016, https://www.theguardian.com /business/2016/may/21/oil-majors-investments-renewable-energy-solar -wind.
31 Emily Gosden, "Shell Chief Ben van Beurden: You Cannot Expect Us to Act against Our Economic Interest," *The Telegraph*, July 2, 2016, http://www .telegraph.co.uk/business/2016/07/02/shell-chief-ben-van-beurden -you-cannot-expect-us-to-act-against/.
32 Steve Coll, *Private Empire: ExxonMobil and American Power* (New York: Penguin, 2012), 348.

33 Smarter Business, "UK Renewable Energy Percentage 2018," July 18, 2018, https://smarterbusiness.co.uk/blogs/uk-renewable-energy-percentage-2018/.

34 Sarah Miller Llana and Whitney Eulich, "Brazil, Venezuela, and Mexico: Three Ways to Nationalize Oil," *Christian Science Monitor*, May 12, 2012, http://www.csmonitor.com/World/Americas/2012/0512/Brazil-Venezuela-and-Mexico-three-ways-to-nationalize-oil.

35 Robert W. Howarth, Renee Santoro, and Anthony Ingraffea, "Methane and the Greenhouse-Gas Footprint of Natural Gas from Shale Formations (a Letter)," *Climatic Change* 106 (2011): 679–90.

36 Garvin A. Heath, Patrick O'Donoughue, Douglas J. Arent, and Morgan Bazilian, "Harmonization of Initial Estimates of Shale Gas Life Cycle Greenhouse Gas Emissions for Electric Power Generation," *PNAS* 111, no. 31 (2014): E3167–E3176, https://doi.org/10.1073/pnas.1309334111.

37 U.S. Energy Information Administration, "How Much Gas Does the United States Have, and How Long Will It Last?" last updated February 4, 2020, https://www.eia.gov/tools/faqs/faq.php?id=58&t=8.

38 U.S. Energy Information Administration, "Today in Energy: China Produces and Consumes Almost as Much Coal as the Rest of the World Combined," May 14, 2014, https://www.eia.gov/todayinenergy/detail.php?id=16271.

39 Pushker A. Kharecha, Charles F. Kutscher, James E. Hansen, and Edward Mazria, "Options for Near-Term Phaseout of CO_2 Emissions from Coal Use in the United States," *Environmental Science and Technology* 44 (2010): 4050.

40 David J.C. MacKay, *Sustainable Energy without the Hot Air* (Cambridge: UIT, 2008), https://www.withouthotair.com/about.html, 158–9.

41 MacKay, "Sustainable Energy without the Hot Air," 235.

42 U.S. Energy Information Administration, "US Energy Facts Explained," http://www.eia.gov/energyexplained/?page=us_energy_home, last updated August 28, 2019.

43 Calvin Chilcoat, "How Much Does the US Spend on Energy Research? Not a Lot," *Christian Science Monitor*, March 5, 2015, https://www.csmonitor.com/Environment/Energy-Voices/2015/0305/How-much-does-the-US-spend-on-energy-research-Not-a-lot.

44 Roston, "Exxon Predicted Today's Cheap Solar Boom."

45 Kirsten Korosec, "U.S. Solar Jobs Jumped Almost 25% in the Last Year," *Fortune*, February 7, 2017, http://fortune.com/2017/02/07/us-solar-jobs-2016/.

46 Anna Hirtenstein, "Clean Energy Jobs Surpass Oil Drilling for First Time in U.S.," *Bloomberg*, May 25, 2016, https://www.bloomberg.com/news/articles/2016-05-25/clean-energy-jobs-surpass-oil-drilling-for-first-time-in-u-s.

47 U.S. Department of Energy, Office of Energy Efficiency & Renewable Energy, "EERE Success Story-Wind Vision: Continuing the Success of Wind Energy," April 2, 2015, https://energy.gov/eere/success-stories/articles/eere-success

-story-wind-vision-continuing-success-wind-energy; U.S. Department of Energy, Office of Energy Efficiency & Renewable Energy, *Wind Vision: A New Era for Windpower in the United States*, March 12, 2015, https://energy.gov/eere/wind /maps/wind-vision.

48 Anna Possner and Ken Caldeira, "Geophysical Potential for Wind Energy over the Open Oceans," *Proceedings of the National Academy of Scientists* 114 (2017): 11338–43.

49 Eduardo Porter, "How Renewable Energy Is Blowing Climate Change Efforts Off Course," *New York Times*, July 19, 2016, https://www.nytimes.com/2016/07/20 /business/energy-environment/how-renewable-energy-is-blowing-climate -change-efforts-off-course.html.

50 Alexander E. MacDonald, Christopher T.M. Clack, Anneliese Alexander, Adam Dunbar, James Wilczak, and Yuanfu Xie, "Future Cost Competitive Electricity Systems and Their Impact on US CO_2 Emissions," *Nature Climate Change* 6 (2016): 526–31, https://doi.org/10.1038/nclimate2921; see also Mark Z. Jackobson, "Energy Modelling: Clean Grids with Current Technology," *Nature Climate Change* 6 (2016): 441–2, https://doi.org/10.1038/nclimate2926.

51 MacDonald et al., "Future Cost Competitive Electricity Systems," 530.

52 Jason Plautz, "George W. Bush's Favorite Green Car Is Making a Comeback: Automakers Are Pushing Hydrogen Fuel Cell Vehicles, But Want the Government to Chip in," *The Atlantic*, January 28, 2015, https://www.theatlantic .com/amp/article/452646/.

53 David Friedman, "D.C. Showcases Cutting Edge Hydrogen Fueling Station Demo," Energy.gov: Office of Energy Efficiency & Renewable Energy, July 11, 2016, https://energy.gov/eere/articles/dc-showcases-cutting-edge-hydrogen -fueling-station-demo.

54 Friedman, "D.C. Showcases Cutting Edge Hydrogen Fueling Station Demo."

55 Friedman, "D.C. Showcases Cutting Edge Hydrogen Fueling Station Demo."

56 Friedman, "D.C. Showcases Cutting Edge Hydrogen Fueling Station Demo."

57 Fred Lambert, "Tesla Co-Founder Says Hydrogen Fuel Cells Are a 'Scam,'" Electrek, May 23, 2016, https://electrek.co/2016/05/23/tesla-founder-marc -tarpenning-hydrogen-fuel-cells-scam/.

58 For yet another view, see Union of Concerned Scientists, "Fulfilling the Potential of Fuel Cell Electric Vehicles," March 26, 2015, http://www.ucsusa.org/clean -vehicles/electric-vehicles/how-hydrogen-is-made.

59 Lambert, "Tesla Co-Founder."

60 Robin Harding, "Toyota Sells Stake in Tesla as Partnership Dies," *Financial Times*, June 4, 2017, https://www.ft.com/content/130a937a-48fd-11e7-919a -1e14ce4af89b.

61 Town of Lexington, Massachusetts, "Fiscal Year 2017 Recommended Budget & Financing Plan," February 29, 2016, http://www.lexingtonma.gov/sites

/lexingtonma/files/uploads/fy2017_recommended_budget_and_financing
_plan_revised_3.14.16_0.pdf.

62 "Sustainable Lexington Committee," n.d., http://www.lexingtonma.gov
/sites/lexingtonma/files/uploads/sustainable_lexington_committee
-2013.pdf, accessed February 26, 2020.

63 Darin Jantzi, "North Dakota Agriculture in One Word—Diverse," U.S.
Department of Agriculture, August 23, 2019, https://www.usda.gov
/media/blog/2019/08/23/north-dakota-agriculture-one-word-diverse.

64 National Weather Service, "North Dakota Severe Weather Events: North Dakota
Tornado Details 1950 On," https://www.weather.gov/bis/ndtorhistory,
accessed March 17, 2020.

65 Bilal Suleiman, "To the Extremes: Flooding and Drought," *Bismark Tribune*,
December 29, 2019, https://bismarcktribune.com/news/state-and-regional
/to-the-extremes-flooding-and-drought-both-highlight-decade-s/article
_c39cfc79-7c97-5f91-89df-f3342924083c.html.

66 Scott L. Montgomery, "The Oil Shock of 2020 Appears to Be Here – And the
Pain Could Be Wide and Deep," The Conversation, March 13, 2020, https://
theconversation.com/the-oil-shock-of-2020-appears-to-be-here-and-the-pain
-could-be-wide-and-deep-133293.

67 U.S. Energy Information Administration, "U.S. States, North Dakota: State
Profile and Energy Estimates," n.d., http://www.eia.gov/state/?sid=ND,
accessed February 24, 2017.

68 Gayathri Vaidyanathan, "How Bad of a Greenhouse Gas Is Methane?," *Scientific
American*, December 2, 2015, https://www.scientificamerican.com/article
/how-bad-of-a-greenhouse-gas-is-methane/.

69 U.S. Energy Information Administration, "U.S. States, North Dakota," accessed
January 10, 2019.

70 U.S. Energy Information Administration, "U.S. States, North Dakota," accessed
January 10, 2019.

71 National Climate Assessment, "Great Plains," in *Climate Change Impacts in the
United States: The Third National Climate Assessment*, 2014, http://nca2014
.globalchange.gov/report/regions/great-plains#narrative-page-16862.

72 Erika Bolstad, "Adaptation: North Dakota Adapts to Climate Change, Without
Saying It's Real," ClimateWire, September 13, 2016, http://www.eenews.net
/stories/1060042691.

73 Jennifer Marlon, Peter Howe, Matto Mildenberger, Anthony Leiserowitz,
and Xinran Wang, "Yale Climate Opinion Maps," August 7, 2018, http://
climatecommunication.yale.edu/visualizations-data/ycom-us-2018/?est=
happening&type=value&geo=county.

74 Bolstad, "Adaptation."

75 Richard Caperton and Rebecca Lefton, "Report: Renewable Standards
    Will Create 2 Million Jobs, Unless Right-Wing Candidates Kill Them,"
    ThinkProgress, October 20, 2012, https://thinkprogress.org/report-renewable
    -standards-will-create-two-million-jobs-unless-right-wing-candidates-kill-them
    -12c05c158e94/.
76 International Renewable Energy Agency, *Renewable Energy and Jobs: Annual Review
    2017* (Dubai: IRENA, 2017), https://www.irena.org/documentdownloads
    /publications/irena_re_jobs_annual_review_2017.pdf.
77 Greg Kats, "How Many Jobs Does Clean Energy Create?," Greenbiz, December 5,
    2016, https://www.greenbiz.com/article/how-many-jobs-does-clean-energy
    -create.
78 Roddy Scheer and Doug Moss, "Finding 'Green Job' Opportunities,"
    Scientific American, July 9, 2011, https://www.scientificamerican.com/article
    /finding-green-job-opportunities/.
79 Justin Gillis and Nadja Popovich, "The U.S. Is the Biggest Carbon Polluter
    in History: It Just Walked Away from the Paris Climate Deal," *New York Times*,
    June 1, 2017, nytimes.com/interactive/2017/06/01/climate/us-biggest-carbon
    -polluter-in-history-will-it-walk-away-from-the-paris-climate-deal.html.
80 Ben Adler, "America Is the Biggest Problem at the Climate Talks," *Mother Jones*,
    December 5, 2015, https://www.motherjones.com/environment/2015/12
    /paris-climate-change-cop21-climate-finance/.
81 Nadja Popovich and Henry Fountain, "What Is the Green Climate Fund and
    How Much Does the U.S. Actually Pay?" *New York Times*, June 2, 2017, https://
    www.nytimes.com/interactive/2017/06/02/climate/trump-paris-green-climate
    -fund.html.
82 Popovich and Fountain, "What Is the Green Climate Fund."
83 Adapted from Bruno Verbeek and Christopher Morris, "Game Theory and
    Ethics," in The Stanford Encyclopedia of Philosophy [online], last revised
    June 8, 2010, https://plato.stanford.edu/entries/game-ethics/; Jean-Jacques
    Rousseau, *Discours sur l'origine et les fondements de l'inégalité parmi les hommes*, ed.
    E.N. Zalta (Paris: Éditions Gallimard, 2010), 166–7.
84 Jared Diamond, *Collapse: How Societies Choose to Fail or Succeed* (New York:
    Penguin, 2004).
85 Carsten K.W. De Dreu, D. Berno Dussel, and Femke S. Ten Velden, "In Intergroup
    Conflict, Self-Sacrifice Is Stronger among the Pro-Social Individuals, and
    Parochial Altruism Emerges Especially among Cognitively Taxed Individuals,"
    Frontiers in Psychology 6 (2015): 572, https://doi.org/10.3389/fpsyg.2015.00572.
86 Peter J. Carnevale and Tahira M. Probst, "Good News about Competitive People,"
    in *Using Conflict in Organizations*, ed. Carsten K.W. De Dreu and Evert Van de Vliert
    (Thousand Oaks, CA: Sage, 1997), 129–46.

87 Esther K. Diekhof, Susanne Wittmer, and Luise Reimers, "Does Competition
    Really Bring Out the Worst? Testosterone, Social Distance and Inter-Male
    Competition Shape Parochial Altruism in Human Males," *PLoS One* 9, no. 7
    (2014): e98977, https://doi.org/10.1371/journal.pone.0098977.
88 See Rae André, *Organizational Behavior: An Introduction to Your Life in
    Organizations* (Upper Saddle River, NJ: Prentice Hall, 2008), 43.
89 Wim B.G. Liebrand, Ronald W.T.L. Jansen, Victor M. Rijken, and Cor
    Suhre, "Might over Morality: The Interaction between Social Values and
    the Interpretation of Decision Making in Experimental Games," *Journal of
    Experimental Social Psychology* 22 (1986): 203–15; Charles G. McClintock and
    Wim B.G. Liebrand, "Role of Interdependence, Individual Orientation, and
    Another's Strategy in Social Decision Making: A Transformational Analysis,"
    Journal of Personality and Social Psychology 55 (1988): 396–409.
90 T. Boone Pickens, "An Open Letter to This Year's Graduating Seniors,"
    LinkedIn, May 16, 2017, https://www.linkedin.com/pulse/open-letter-years
    -graduating-seniors-t-boone-pickens.
91 F. Stephan Mayer and Cynthia McPherson Frantz, "The Connectedness to
    Nature Scale: A Measure of Individuals' Feeling in Community with Nature,"
    Journal of Environmental Psychology 24, no. 4 (2004): 503–15.
92 Adam C. Davis and Mirella L. Stroink, "The Relationship between Systems
    Thinking and the New Ecological Paradigm," *Systems Research and Behavioral
    Science* 33 (2015): 575–86.
93 For more on the view that government can be effective, see https://
    governmentisgood.com.
94 Al Franken, *Giant of the Senate* (New York: Hachette, 2017), 336.
95 Saundra K. Schneider, William G. Jacoby, and Daniel C. Lewis, "Public Opinion
    toward Intergovernmental Policy Responsibilities," *Publius: The Journal of
    Federalism* 41, no. 1 (2010): 1–30.
96 Justin McCarthy, "Americans Still Trust Local Government More Than State,"
    Gallup, September 22, 2014, http://www.gallup.com/poll/176846/americans
    -trust-local-government-state.aspx.
97 Gallup, "Trust in Government," http://www.gallup.com/poll/5392/trust
    -government.aspx, accessed May 25, 2017.

Practice 4 • Define the Business of Business

1 Paraphrasing Milton Friedman, "The Social Responsibility of Business Is to
   Increase Its Profits," *The New York Times Magazine*, September 13, 1970, 126.
2 Lynn A. Stout, *The Shareholder Value Myth: How Putting Shareholders First Harms
   Investors, Corporations, and the Public* (San Francisco: Berrett-Koehler, 2012), 3–4.

3   Steven Munch, "Improving the Benefit Corporation: How Traditional
    Governance Mechanisms Can Enhance the Innovative New Business Form,"
    Northwestern Journal of Law & Social Policy 7, no. 1 (2012): 178.
4   https://www.ceres.org/, accessed March 6, 2017.
5   U.S. Department of Energy, *Buildings Energy Data Book*, prepared by D&R
    International (Youngstown, NY: DOE, 2008).
6   Warren McLaren, "US Buildings Account for 40% of Energy and Materials Use,"
    Treehugger, August 10, 2009, http://www.treehugger.com/sustainable-product
    -design/us-buildings-account-for-40-of-energy-and-materials-use.html.
7   U.S. Green Building Council, "LEED," n.d., http://www.usgbc.org/leed, accessed
    March 6, 2017.
8   See, for example, Anastasia Swearingen, "LEED-Certified Buildings Are Often
    Less Energy Efficient Than Uncertified Ones (Opinion)," *Forbes*, April 30, 2014,
    https://www.forbes.com/sites/realspin/2014/04/30/leed-certified-buildings
    -are-often-less-energy-efficient-than-uncertified-ones; Pete Sepp, "LEED-Ing
    Taxpayers to Waste Money? (Opinion)," *U.S. News and World Report*, May 8, 2014,
    https://www.usnews.com/opinion/economic-intelligence/2014/05/08
    /leed-certification-doesnt-add-value-and-costs-taxpayers.
9   Institute for Supply Management, *Principles of Sustainability and Social Responsibility*
    (Tempe, AZ: ISM, 2015), https://www.instituteforsupplymanagement.org/files
    /SR/PSSRwGuideBook.pdf.
10 Larry Lapide, "Are You Ready for Expensive Oil? Supply Chain Professionals Must
    Recognize That the Era of Cheap Oil Is Long Gone: What's Needed Today Is a
    Supply Chain Strategy Centered on Less Oil Consumption and Greater Energy
    Efficiency (InSIGHTS)," *Supply Chain Management Review*, 16, no. 1 (2012).
11 See Rae André, *Organizational Behavior: An Introduction to Your Life in
    Organizations* (Upper Saddle River, NJ: Pearson, 2008), 126–30.
12 See André, *Organizational Behavior*, 451–2.
13 The information is from this link, which is no longer available: http://www
    .google.com/about/corporate/company/culture.html. See also http://
    sustainability.google; "Green at Google Headquarters," YouTube video, 1:48,
    October 17, 2008, http://www.youtube.com/watch?v=7YGqY5vmEcg.
14 Alison van Diggelen, "How Green Is Google? An Insider's View," *Huffington Post*,
    August 30, 2011, http://www.huffingtonpost.com/alison-van-diggelen/how
    -green-is-google-an-in_b_937028.html.
15 Natasha Lennard, "SF Protesters Block Google Buses: Demonstrators Say
    Private Transport Reflects a 'Two-Tiered' System Produced by Silicon Valley
    Domination," *Salon*, December 9, 2013, http://www.salon.com/2013/12/09
    /sf_protesters_block_google_buses/.
16 Bigad Shaban, Felipe Escamilla, and Kevin Nious, "'Tech Buses' Commit
    Hundreds of Violations on San Francisco Roadways," April 29, 2016, http://

www.nbcbayarea.com/news/local/Tech-Buses-Commit-Hundreds-of-Violations
-on-SF-Roadways-377645131.html.

17 Kiesha Frue, "Who Invented PEST Analysis and Why It Matters," Pestle Analysis,
    May 18, 2017, https://pestleanalysis.com/who-invented-pest-analysis/.

18 Coral Davenport, "Industry Awakens to Threat of Climate Change," *New York
    Times,* January 23, 2014, https://www.nytimes.com/2014/01/24/science/earth
    /threat-to-bottom-line-spurs-action-on-climate.html.

19 References to this literature abound in Rebecca Henderson, Ranjay Gulati, and
    Michael Tushman, eds., *Leading Sustainable Change: An Organizational Perspective*
    (Oxford: Oxford University Press, 2015).

20 John Sterman, "Stumbling toward Sustainability: Why Organizational Learning
    and Radical Innovation Are Necessary to Build a More Sustainable World – But
    Not Sufficient," in Henderson, Gulati, and Tushman, eds., *Leading Sustainable
    Change: An Organizational Perspective,* 52.

21 Sterman, "Stumbling toward Sustainability," 51.

22 Sterman, "Stumbling toward Sustainability," 76.

23 Kathleen Miller Perkins and George Serafeim, "Chief Sustainability Officers:
    Who Are They and What Do They Do?" in Henderson, Gulati, and Tushman,
    eds., *Leading Sustainable Change: An Organizational Perspective,* 196–221.

24 Perkins and Serafeim, "Chief Sustainability Officers."

25 Dina Gerdman, "What Do Chief Sustainability Officers Do?" *Forbes,*
    October 8, 2014, https://www.forbes.com/sites/hbsworkingknowledge
    /2014/10/08/what-do-chief-sustainabilty-officers-do/.

26 Perkins and Serafeim, "Chief Sustainability Officers."

27 https://www.glassdoor.com/Job/chief-sustainability-officer-jobs-SRCH
    _KO0,28.htm, accessed June 26, 2017.

28 Perkins and Serafeim, "Chief Sustainability Officers."

29 Perkins and Serafeim, "Chief Sustainability Officers."

30 Christopher Wright and Daniel Nyberg, *Climate Change, Capitalism, and
    Corporations: Processes of Creative Self-Destruction* (Cambridge: Cambridge
    University Press, 2015), 114.

31 Wright and Nyberg, *Climate Change, Capitalism, and Corporations,* 115.

32 Wright and Nyberg, *Climate Change, Capitalism, and Corporations,* 118.

33 Wright and Nyberg, *Climate Change, Capitalism, and Corporations,* 129.

34 Wright and Nyberg, *Climate Change, Capitalism, and Corporations,* 130.

35 Wright and Nyberg, *Climate Change, Capitalism, and Corporations,* 125–6.

36 Wright and Nyberg, *Climate Change, Capitalism, and Corporations,* 131.

37 Wright and Nyberg, *Climate Change, Capitalism, and Corporations,* 161.

38 See André, *Organizational Behavior,* 46.

39 Rebecca Henderson, "Making the Business Case for Environmental
    Sustainability," in Henderson, Gulati, and Tushman, eds., *Leading Sustainable
    Change: An Organizational Perspective,* 22–49.

40 Henderson, "Making the Business Case for Environmental Sustainability," 36.

41 Henderson, "Making the Business Case for Environmental Sustainability," 37.

42 EPA Center for Corporate Climate Leadership, "2017 Climate Leadership Award Winners," n.d., https://www.epa.gov/climateleadership/2017-climate-leadership -award-winners, accessed March 18, 2020.

43 Ray C. Anderson and Robin White, *Business Lessons from a Radical Industrialist* (New York: St. Martins Griffin, 2009), 9.

44 Ray Anderson, "The Business Logic of Sustainability," TED: Ideas Worth Spreading, February 2009, video, 15:37, https://www.ted.com/talks /ray_anderson_the_business_logic_of_sustainability?language=en.

45 Anderson and White, *Business Lessons*, 44.

46 Anderson and White, *Business Lessons*.

47 Interface, *Lessons for the Future: The Interface Guide to Changing Your Company to Change the World*, 2019, http://interfaceinc.scene7.com/is/content /InterfaceInc/Interface/Americas/WebsiteContentAssets/Documents /Sustainability%2025yr%20Report/25yr%20Report%20Booklet%20Interface _MissionZeroCel.pdf.

48 Alessia D'Amato, Regina Eckert, John Ireland, Laura Quinn, and Ellen Van Velsor, "Leadership Practices for Corporate Global Responsibility," *Journal of Global Responsibility* 1 no. 2 (2010): 225–49, https://doi.org/10.1108 /20412561011079371.

49 Jonathan Watts, "Alternative US Group Honouring Paris Climate Accord Demands 'Seat at the Table,'" *The Guardian*, November 11, 2017, https://www .theguardian.com/environment/2017/nov/11/alternative-us-group -honouring-paris-climate-accord-demands-seat-at-the-table-bonn.

50 "About BICEP," n.d., https://www.ceres.org/bicep, accessed March 7, 2017 (no longer available).

51 "Climate Action 100+," n.d., https://www.ceres.org/initiatives/climate -action-100, accessed February 26, 2020.

52 "Ceres Accelerator of Sustainable Capital Markets," n.d., https://www .ceres.org/accelerator, accessed February 26, 2020.

53 Nancy E. Landrum and Brian Ohsowski, "Content Trends in Sustainable Business Education: An Analysis of Introductory Courses in the USA," *International Journal of Sustainability in Higher Education* 18, no. 3 (2017): 385–414.

54 Landrum and Ohsowski, "Content Trends in Sustainable Business Education."

55 Rieneke Slager, Sareh Pouryousefi, Jeremy Moon, and Ethan D. Schoolman, "Sustainability Centres and Fit: How Centres Work to Integrate Sustainability within Business Schools," *Journal of Business Ethics* 161 (2020): 375, https://doi .org/10.1007/s10551-018-3965-4.

56 Annie Snelson-Powell, Johanne Grosvold, and Andrew Millington, "Business School Legitimacy and the Challenge of Sustainability: A Fuzzy Set Analysis of

Institutional Decoupling," *Academy of Management Learning & Education* 15, no. 4 (2016): 703.

57 Kleio Akrivou and Hilary Bradbury-Huang, "Educating Integrated Catalysts: Transforming Business Schools toward Ethics and Sustainability," *Academy of Management Learning & Education* 14, no. 2 (2015): 222–40.

58 Landrum and Ohsowski, "Content Trends in Sustainable Business Education," 401.

59 Sanjay Sharma and Stuart Hart, "Beyond 'Saddle Bag' Sustainability for Business Education," *Organization & Environment* 27, no. 1 (2014): 10–15.

60 Andreas Rasche and Dirk Ulrich Gilbert, "Decoupling Responsible Management Education: Why Business Schools May Not Walk Their Talk," *Journal of Management Inquiry* 24, no. 3 (2015): 239–52.

61 Schumpeter, "Out with the Old: Management Theory Is Becoming a Compendium of Dead Ideas," *The Economist*, December 17, 2016, https://www.economist.com/business/2016/12/17/management-theory-is-becoming-a-compendium-of-dead-ideas.

62 *The Journal of Management for Global Sustainability*, https://www.ignited.global/publications/journal-management-global-sustainability.

63 Danna N. Greenberg, Stephen Deets, Sinan Erzurumlu, James Hunt, Melissa Manwaring, Vikki Rodgers, and Elizabeth Swanson, "Signing to Living PRME: Learning from a Journey towards Responsible Management Education," *International Journal of Management Education* 15, no. 2 (2017): 205–18.

64 Rae André, "Teaching Strong Sustainability: An Experiential Course on Leadership in the Anthropocene," 2020, under review.

Practice 5 • Engage Global Leadership

1 See Rae André, *Organizational Behavior: An Introduction to Your Life in Organizations* (Upper Saddle River, NJ: Prentice Hall, 2008), 96–106.

2 David J.C. MacKay, "*Sustainable Energy – without the Hot Air*," (Cambridge: UIT, 2008), https://www.withouthotair.com/about.html, 250.

3 See Richard Heinberg, *Powerdown: Options and Actions for a Post-Carbon World* (British Columbia: New Society Publishers, 2004).

4 MacKay, *Sustainable Energy without the Hot Air*, 250.

5 MacKay, *Sustainable Energy without the Hot Air*, 234–5.

6 MacKay, *Sustainable Energy without the Hot Air*, 234–5.

7 David MacKay, "A Reality Check on Renewables," TEDxWarwick, March 2012, https://www.ted.com/talks/david_mackay_a_reality_check_on_renewables.

8 Smarter Business, "UK Renewable Energy Percentage 2018," July 18, 2018, https://smarterbusiness.co.uk/blogs/uk-renewable-energy-percentage-2018/.

9   Committee on Climate Change, *Net Zero: The UK's Contribution to Stopping Global Warming* (London: Committee on Climate Change, 2019), 137.

10 Committee on Climate Change, *Net Zero*, 137.

11 Committee on Climate Change, *Net Zero*, 147.

12 Edward Abbey, *Beyond the Wall: Essays from the Outside* (New York: Henry Holt and Company, 1984).

13 Corinne Le Quéré, Robbie M. Andrew, Pierre Friedlingstein, Stephen Sitch, Judith Hauck, Julia Pongratz, Penelope A. Pickers, et al., "Earth System Science Data," *Carbon Budget and Trends* 10 (2018): 1–54, https://doi.org/10.5194/essd -10-2141-2018; "Global Carbon Budget," n.d., http://www.globalcarbonproject .org/carbonbudget/, accessed January 11, 2020.

14 Robert McSweeny and Rosamund Pearce, "Carbon Countdown: Analysis: Just Four Years Left of the 1.5C Carbon Budget," Carbon Brief, April 5, 2017, https://www.carbonbrief.org/analysis-four-years-left-one-point-five-carbon -budget.

15 Paul Hawken, ed., *Drawdown: The Most Comprehensive Plan Ever Proposed to Reverse Global Warming* (New York: Penguin, 2017).

16 "Table of Solutions," Project Drawdown, n.d., https://drawdown.org /solutions/table-of-solutions, accessed March 19, 2020.

17 MacKay, *Sustainable Energy – without the Hot Air*, 250.

18 Hawken, *Drawdown*, ix.

19 Hawken, *Drawdown*, 217.

20 Hawken, *Drawdown*, 216.

21 Eduardo Porter, "Does a Carbon Tax Work? Ask British Columbia," *New York Times*, March 1, 2016, https://www.nytimes.com/2016/03/02/business/does -a-carbon-tax-work-ask-british-columbia.html.

22 Porter, "Does a Carbon Tax Work?"

23 Marisa Beck, Nicholas Rivers, Randall Wigle, and Hidemichi Yonezawa, "Carbon Tax and Revenue Recycling: Impacts on Households in British Columbia," *Resource and Energy Economics* 41 (2015): 40–69.

24 ClimateXchange, "S1747, 'An Act Combatting Climate Change': Basic Features of Its Carbon Fee-and-Rebate Design," n.d., http://climate-xchange.org/wp -content/uploads/2015/05/S1747-Carbon-Fee-and-Rebate-Basic-Features .pdf, accessed February 26, 2020.

25 World Bank, "Pricing Carbon," n.d., http://www.worldbank.org/en/programs /pricing-carbon, accessed February 26, 2020.

26 Colin A. Young, "Supports Tout Carbon Pricing Plan from Lexington State Senator," *Lexington Minuteman*, June 29, 2017, B5.

27 Porter, "Does a Carbon Tax Work?"

28 Gordon Hoekstra, "Latest Figures Show B.C.'s Carbon Emissions Continue to Increase," *Vancouver Sun*, January 12, 2018, https://vancouversun.com

/business/energy/latest-figures-show-b-c-s-carbon-emissions-continue-to
-increase.

29 Dana Nuccitelli, "Canada Passed a Carbon Tax That Will Give Most Canadians
More Money," *The Guardian*, October 26, 2018, https://www.theguardian.com
/environment/climate-consensus-97-per-cent/2018/oct/26/canada-passed
-a-carbon-tax-that-will-give-most-canadians-more-money.

30 The Economist, "Alberta's Secession Movement Spells Trouble for Justin
Trudeau," *The Economist*, December 7, 2019, https://www.economist.com
/the-americas/2019/12/05/albertas-secession-movement-spells-trouble
-for-justin-trudeau.

31 Ryan Lizza, "As the World Burns: How the Senate and the White House Missed
Their Best Chance to Deal with Climate Change," *New Yorker*, October 11, 2010,
http://www.newyorker.com/magazine/2010/10/11/as-the-world-burns.

32 Climate Xchange, "Regional Cap and Trade Report: Lessons from the Regional
Greenhouse Gas Initiative and the Western Climate Initiative," n.d., https://
climate-xchange.org/wp-content/uploads/2018/08/Regional-Cap-and-Trade
-Report-Fact-Sheet.pdf, accessed February 26, 2020.

33 IPCC, "Question 1," in *Climate Change 2001: Synthesis Report: A Contribution of
Working Groups I, II, and III to the Third Assessment Report of the Intergovernmental
Panel on Climate Change (IPCC)*, ed. R.T. Watson and The Core Writing Team
(Cambridge: Cambridge University Press, 2001), 37–42.

34 Staff and Agencies, "Canada Pulls Out of Kyoto Protocol," *The Guardian*,
December 13, 2011, https://www.theguardian.com/environment/2011
/dec/13/canada-pulls-out-kyoto-protocol.

35 Ed King, "Kyoto Protocol: 10 Years of the World's First Climate Change
Treaty," Climate Home News, February 6, 2015, http://www.climate
changenews.com/2015/02/16/kyoto-protocol-10-years-of-the-worlds
-first-climate-change-treaty/.

36 See Center for Climate and Energy Solutions, "Paris Climate Agreement Q and
A," n.d., https://www.c2es.org/international/2015-agreement/paris-climate
-talks-qa, accessed February 26, 2020.

37 George Orwell, "In Front of Your Nose," in *The Collected Essays, Journalism and
Letters of George Orwell*, vol. 4 (London: Secker and Warburg, 1968), 124.

38 Daniel Kahneman, *Thinking, Fast and Slow* (New York: Farrar, Straus and Giroux,
2011), 305.

39 Cited in Brad Plumer, "The World Just Agreed to a Major Climate Deal in
Paris: Now Comes the Hard Part," *Vox*, December 12, 2015, https://www.vox
.com/2015/12/12/9981020/paris-climate-deal.

40 Plumer, "The World Just Agreed."

41 Cited in Oliver Milman, "James Hansen, Father of Climate Change Awareness,
Calls Paris Talks 'a Fraud,'" *The Guardian*, December 12, 2015, https://www

.theguardian.com/environment/2015/dec/12/james-hansen-climate-change
-paris-talks-fraud.

42 Leon Kaye, "'Father of Climate Change' Sides with GOP on Carbon Tax,"
Triple Pundit, April 18, 2017, http://www.triplepundit.com/story/2017
/father-climate-change-sides-gop-carbon-tax/18051.

43 James H. Williams, Benjamin Haley, Fredrich Kahrl, Jack Moore, Andrew D.
Jones, Margaret S. Torn, and Haewon McJeon, *Pathways to Deep Decarbonization in
the United States* (San Francisco: Energy and Environmental Economics, 2014).

44 David Wallace-Wells, "The Uninhabitable Earth," *New York Magazine,* July 9, 2017,
https://nymag.com/intelligencer/2017/07/climate-change-earth-too-hot-for
-humans.html.

45 John Sterman, Andrew Jones, Ellie Johnston, and Lori Siegel, "Climate
Interactive Ratchet Success Pathway: Assumptions and Results," Climate
Interactive: Tools for a Thriving Future, November 26, 2015, https://www
.climateinteractive.org/wp-content/uploads/2015/11/Ratchet-Success.pdf.

46 International Maritime Organization, "Third IMO GHG Study 2014,"
2015, http://www.imo.org/en/OurWork/Environment/Pollution
Prevention/AirPollution/Pages/Greenhouse-Gas-Studies-2014.aspx.

47 Jad Mouawad and Coral Davenport, "E.P.A. Takes Step to Cut Emissions from
Planes," *New York Times,* June 10, 2015, https://www.nytimes.com/2015/06/11
/business/energy-environment/epa-says-it-will-set-rules-for-airplane-emissions
.html.

48 Intergovernmental Panel on Climate Change, "Global Warming of 5 °C," 2018,
https://www.ipcc.ch/sr15/.

49 Myles R. Allen, Opha Pauline Dube, William Solecki, Fernando Aragon-Durand,
Wolfgang Cramer, Stephen Humphreys, Mikiko Kainuma, et al., "Framing and
Context," in *Global Warming of 1.5°C: An IPCC Special Report on the Impacts of
Global Warming of 1.5°C above Pre-Industrial Levels and Related Global Greenhouse Gas
Emission Pathways, in the Context of Strengthening the Global Response to the Threat of
Climate Change, Sustainable Development, and Efforts to Eradicate Poverty,* ed. Valérie
Masson-Delmotte, Panmao Zhai, Hans-Otto Portner, Debra Roberts, James Skea,
Priyardashi R. Shukla, Anna Pirani, et al. (Geneva: IPCC, 2018), 75.

50 IPCC, "Global Warming of 5 °C"; see also John Sutter, "COP24 Climate Talks
End in Agreement: Barely," *CNN,* December 16, 2018, https://www.cnn
.com/2018/12/15/health/cop24-climate-change-talks-agreement/index.html.

51 Stan Cox, *Any Way You Slice It: The Past, Present, and Future of Rationing* (New York:
The New Press, 2013).

52 Cited in Cox, *Any Way You Slice It,* 65.

53 Kahneman, *Thinking, Fast and Slow,* 304.

54 Kenneth Boulding, "The Economics of the Coming Spaceship Earth," in *Radical
Political Economy,* ed. Victor D. Lippit (Armonk, NY: M.E. Sharpe, 1966), 362.

55 Boulding, "Economics of the Coming Spaceship Earth," 8.
56 The discussion of ecological economics here is based on Herman E. Daly
    and Joshua Farley, *Ecological Economics: Principles and Applications*, 2nd ed.
    (Washington, DC: Island Press, 2011).
57 Daly and Farley, *Ecological Economics*, 165–231.
58 Cited in Cox, *Any Way You Slice It*, 246.
59 Cited in Cox, *Any Way You Slice It*, 9.
60 Joshua Farley, "Ecological Economics," in *The Post Carbon Reader: Managing
    the 21st Century Sustainability Crises*, ed. Richard Heinberg and Daniel Lerch
    (Healdsburg, CA: Watershed Media, 2010), 273–4.
61 David Barstow, "Up Is Down: Trump's Unreality Show Echoes His Business Past,"
    New York Times, January 28, 2017, https://www.nytimes.com/2017/01/28/us
    /politics/donald-trump-truth.html.
62 Schumpeter, "Out with the Old: Management Theory Is Becoming a
    Compendium of Dead Ideas," *The Economist*, December 17, 2016, https://
    www.economist.com/business/2016/12/17/management-theory-is-becoming
    -a-compendium-of-dead-ideas.
63 J. Paul Getty, *How to Be Rich* (New York: Berkley Publishing Group, 1965), 143–5.
64 Farley, "Ecological Economics," 277.
65 K. Girling and K. Gibbs, *Evidence in Action: An Analysis of Information Gathering
    and Use by Canadian Parliamentarians*, Evidence for Democracy, November 2019,
    https://evidencefordemocracy.ca/sites/default/files/reports/evidence
    -in-action-report-final_0.pdf; David Moscrop, "Are Evidence-Based
    Decisions Impossible in Politics?" Global Policy Journal Blog, November
    27, 2019, https://www.globalpolicyjournal.com/blog/27/11/2019
    /are-evidence-based-decisions-impossible-politics.
66 Frankfurt School of Finance & Management and the United Nations
    Environment Programme, *Global Trends in Renewable Energy Investment 2017*,
    https://captive.fs.de/wp-content/uploads/2019/11/Global_Trends
    _Report_2017.pdf.
67 See also Benjamin Hulac, "Strong Future Forecast for Renewable Energy: Wind,
    Solar and Other Forms of Renewable Energy Could Be the Fastest Growing
    Power Sources over the Next Few Decades," *Scientific American*, April 27, 2015,
    ehttps://www.scientificamerican.com/article/strong-future-forecast-for
    -renewable-energy/.
68 U.S. Energy Information Administration, "EIA Projects 48% Increase in World
    Energy Consumption by 2040," Today in Energy, May 12, 2016, https://www.eia
    .gov/todayinenergy/detail.php?id=26212.
69 U.S. Energy Information Administration, "EIA Projects 48% Increase."
70 Frankfurt School of Finance & Management and the United Nations
    Environment Programme, *Global Trends*, 5.

71 Kahneman, *Thinking, Fast and Slow*, see chapter 8, "Bad Events."

72 David J.C. MacKay, Peter Cramton, Axel Ockenfels, and Steven Stoft, "Price Carbon: I Will If You Will," *Nature* 526 (2015): 315–16.

73 Eduardo Porter, "To Curb Global Warming, Science Fiction May Become Fact," *New York Times*, April 4, 2017, https://www.nytimes.com/2017/04/04/business/economy/geoengineering-climate-change.html.

74 Esther K. Diekhof, Susanne Wittmer, and Luise Reimers, "Does Competition Really Bring Out the Worst? Testosterone, Social Distance and Inter-Male Competition Shape Parochial Altruism in Human Males," *PLoS One* 9, no. 7 (2014): e98977, https://doi.org/10.1371/journal.pone.0098977.

75 Peter J. Carnevale and Tahira M. Probst, "Good News about Competitive People," in *Using Conflict in Organizations*, ed. Carsten De Dreu and Evert Van de Vliert (Thousand Oaks, CA: Sage, 1997), 129–46.

76 Diekhof, Wittmer, and Reimers, "Does Competition Really Bring Out the Worst?"

77 Charles Heckscher, *Trust in a Complex World: Enriching Community* (Oxford: Oxford University Press, 2015), 169–70.

78 Rae André, "An Examination of the Competitive Attitudes of Entrepreneurs: Implications for Entrepreneurial Orientation at the Individual Level," *Journal of Developmental Entrepreneurship* 18, no. 2 (2013): 1–22.

79 Matthew Kugler, Joel Cooper, and Brian Nosek, "Group-Based Dominance and Opposition to Equality Correspond to Different Psychological Motives," *Social Justice Research* 23, nos. 2–3 (September 2010): 117–55.

80 Richard M. Ryckman, Max Hammer, Linda M. Kaczor, and Joel A. Gold, "Construction of a Hypercompetitive Attitude Scale," *Journal of Personality Assessment* 55 (1990): 630–9.

81 Thomas D. Fletcher and David N. Nusbaum, "Trait Competitiveness as a Composite Variable: Linkages with Facets of the Big-Five," *Personality and Individual Differences* 45 (2008): 312–17.

82 John M. Keynes, *The General Theory of Employment, Interest and Money* (London: Macmillan, 1936), 161–2.

83 Keynes, *General Theory of Employment*, vii.

84 adriver, "$4 Million in Prizes for Innovation in Renewable Energy," Para el Energia Futuro (blog), May 19, 2016, https://blogs.iadb.org/energia/en/4-million-in-prizes-for-innovation-in-renewable-energy/.

85 See http://cep.mit.edu/impact/, accessed July 11, 2017.

What's the Plan?

1 Margaret A. Brown, "The Power of Generosity to Change Views on Social Power," *Journal of Experimental Social Psychology* 47, no. 6 (November 2011): 1285–90.

2 Attracta Mooney, "Biggest Asset Managers Attacked over Role in Climate
   Change," *The Financial Times*, January 11, 2020, https://www.ft.com/content
   /8aade207-09bc-41a7-9f0a-24417882f1bc.
3 Larissa Z. Tiedens, Miguel M. Unzueta, and Maia J. Young, "An Unconscious
   Desire for Hierarchy? The Motivated Perception of Dominance Complementarity
   in Task Partners," *Journal of Personality and Social Psychology* 93, no. 3 (2007):
   402–14.
4 Ronald Schouten and James Silver, *Almost a Psychopath* (Center City, MN:
   Hazelden, 2012), 58.
5 Sigrid Gustafson and Darren Ritzer, "The Dark Side of Normal: A Psychopathy-
   Linked Pattern Called Aberrant Self-Promotion," *European Journal of Personality*
   9 (1995): 147–83; Tonya Perthman and Soly Erlandsson, "Aberrant Self-
   Promotion or Subclinical Psychopathy in Swedish General Population,"
   Psychological Record 52 (2002): 33–50.
6 BloombergNEF, "Clean Energy Investment Exceeded $300 Billion Once Again
   in 2018," January 16, 2019, https://about.bnef.com/blog/clean-energy
   -investment-exceeded-300-billion-2018/.
7 David Wallace-Wells, "Bill Gates: 'I Don't See Anything Worthy of the Word *Plan*' to
   Fight Climate Change," *New York Magazine*, September 17, 2019, https://nymag
   .com/intelligencer/2019/09/bill-gates-on-addressing-climate-change.html.
8 Jennifer Marlon, Peter Howe, Matto Mildenberger, Anthony Leiserowitz, and
   Xinran Wang, "Yale Climate Opinion Maps," September 17, 2019, https://
   climatecommunication.yale.edu/visualizations-data/ycom-us/.
9 L. Sanna and Russell Geen, "Defensive Pessimism, Optimism, and Simulating
   Alternatives: Some Ups and Downs of Prefactual and Counterfactual Thinking,"
   Journal of Personality and Social Psychology 71, no. 5 (1996): 1021.
10 Greta Thunberg, "Transcript: Speech at the U.N. Climate Action Summit,"
   National Public Radio, September 23, 2019, https://www.npr.org/2019
   /09/23/763452863/transcript-greta-thunbergs-speech-at-the-u-n
   -climate-action-summit.
11 Cited in Michael Slezak, "The Great Barrier Reef: A Catastrophe Laid
   Bare," *The Guardian*, June 6, 2016, https://www.theguardian.com
   /environment/2016/jun/07/the-great-barrier-reef-a-catastrophe
   -laid-bare.
12 Erich Fromm, *The Anatomy of Human Destructiveness* (Greenwich, CT: Fawcett,
   1973), 485.

INDEX

Abbey, Edward, 172
academic publishing, 35–6. *See also*
  scientific research
actions: and anxiety, 16, 47–8; and
  cognitive dissonance, 47–8; and hope,
  221; journalism representations, 39–40;
  local and systemic, 214; motivating
  (*see* motivation); and Paris climate
  meetings, 186; and sentiment, 172;
  single action bias, 49; and systemic
  leadership, 123–4. *See also* plans/
  solutions
adaptation, 71, 72–3
Africa, 79–80
albedo effect, 60–1
altruism, 131, 205–6, 214. *See also*
  parochial altruism
analysis. *See* System 1 analysis; System 2
  analysis
The Anatomy of Human Destructiveness
  (Fromm), 221
Anderson, Ray, 154–7
animal spirits, 208–9
Anthropocene, 60
anxiety, 16, 47–8, 219
Any Way You Slice It: The Past, Present, and
  Future of Rationing (Cox), 188
ARENA Investments, 116–17
Arroyo, Vicki, 73
Atlantic Meridional Overturning
  Circulation (AMOC), 68–9
automobiles, 107–9, 151, 173–4
aviation, 153, 173–4

balanced reporting, 37–8
Barrett, Michael J., 177
Barrett, Scott, 205
Berman, Art, 90–1
BEST (Berkeley Earth Surface
  Temperature) project, 25–7
bias, 41–2, 49
BICEP, 158
binding agreements, 184
bloggers, 42
Blood, David, 55
Bloomberg, Michael R., 72, 80, 198
Boulding, Kenneth E., 191
branding, 137–8
Bretton Woods agreement, 196–7
Brown, Jerry, 73
Brown, Lester, 212
Buffett, Warren, 74
buildings/construction, 111–12, 132–3, 173
bureaucracy, 196
burnout, 6–7, 145–6, 147–8
Bush (George W.) administration,
  34, 106
business schools, 159–63
businesses/organizations: carbon
  surcharges, 175–81; competing with
  government, 125–6; and competition
  as myth, 195; Define the Business
  of Business overview, 9, 129–30;
  environmental scanning systems,
  138–41; global recognition, 199–200;
  lawsuit risks, 74–5; legal requirements,
  130–1; and manageable risks, 80; and

predicting and finding, 22; sectors consuming, 87; semantics of, 40; and supply chains, 133–4; and war, 92–3. *See also* fossil fuels
100-year storm, 72
oligarchy, 194
OPEC (Organization of Petroleum Exporting Countries), 90, 93
open-access journals, 36
optimism, 161, 200–2, 208, 216
organizations. *See* businesses/organizations
Orr, David, 190
Orwell, George, 183–4
overconfidence, 17

Paris climate meetings: and 1.5° Celsius, 117; and binding commitments, 205; and building green energy, 118; core facts of, 182–3; vs. Kyoto climate meetings, 181; limitations in, 211–12; overview, 185–8; and US Climate Action Center, 158
Paris Rulebook, 187
parochial altruism, 121–3, 124, 206
passion, 6
past leaders, 3–4
Paulson, Hank, 81, 198
peak oil, 91–2
peer-review research, 23–5, 35, 63
persistence, 6–7. *See also* resilience
pessimism, 218–20
PESTEL framework, 138–9
Peters, Glen, 28
petrochemicals, 92
PG&E, 74
Pickens, T. Boone, 123, 204
Plan B (Brown), 212
plans/solutions: altruism, 214; business initiatives, 149; competition recognition, 215; computer servers in San Diego scenario, 29–30, 35; and cooperation, 174; for CSO burnout, 148; diversity of, 127; dominance recognition, 216; Farley's suggestions, 196–7; farmer growing forest scenario, 57–8; as figure, 3; Global Carbon Project, 172–3; hope, 216; individualistic, 20; innovations, 215; and leaders, 212; MacKay's calculations,

169–70; as non-existent, 211–12; NY resilience plan, 72; of the past, 212; and rapid changes, 79; System 1/ System 2 analysis, 213; systemic leadership, 214; that add up, 168–70, 172; three challenges for leaders, 200; trust, 216; United Kingdom zero emissions, 171–2; as visions for change, 200, 204; What's the Plan overview, 10. *See also* models
plastics, 134
policy, 172
policymakers, 69–70, 172
politics, 34–5, 36
power: centralization of, 195–6; managing, 4; news ownership, 41–2; and propaganda, 95–6; and resources, 5; and risk analysis, 47; soft, 185
practice, defined, 7
The Prize (Yergin), 41
Procter & Gamble (P&G), 154
production, 192–3
profit, 35, 96–7, 130–1
Project Drawdown, 173–4
propaganda, 95–6
psychological distancing, 49–50
psychology, 3, 46–53, 69, 120, 190, 206
punishment and reward: carbon surcharges, 175–81; and competition, 126; distributing, 124; effective delivery time, 51–2, 175; focus on punishments, 52–3; human tendencies, 217–18; and models, 61; and power, 166–7; stag hunt dilemma, 119–21; tax breaks as rewards, 176–7

radiative forcing, 64–5
Rand, Ayn, 125
rationing, 188–90
RCP (representative concentration pathway), 64–6, 67
refugees, 75, 76
Regional Greenhouse Gas Initiative (RGGI), 180–1
regulatory changes, 75, 98, 99, 142–3
renewable energy: and civilization changes, 86; demand for, 149–50; and fossil fuel sectors, 4, 202; *Global Trends in Renewable Energy Investment* (report),